Speaking for Nature

BY PAUL BROOKS

Roadless Area
The Pursuit of Wilderness
The House of Life: Rachel Carson at Work
The View from Lincoln Hill
Speaking for Nature

PAUL BROOKS

Speaking for Nature

How Literary Naturalists from
Henry Thoreau to Rachel Carson
Have Shaped America

with drawings by the author

HOUGHTON MIFFLIN COMPANY
BOSTON 1980

Library of Congress Cataloging in Publication Data

Brooks, Paul.
    Speaking for nature.

    Bibliography: p.
    Includes index.
    1. Naturalists — United States—Biography.
2. Authors, American — 19th century — Biography.
3. Authors, American — 20th century — Biography.
4. Nature conservation — United States — History.
I. Title.
QH26.B68   333.95'092'2   80-17217
ISBN 0-395-29610-2

Printed in the United States of America

M 10 9 8 7 6 5 4 3 2 1

To S.M.B.
the best of editors

I wish to speak a word for Nature . . .
— Henry David Thoreau

The views of nature held by any people
determine all its institutions.
— Ralph Waldo Emerson

ACKNOWLEDGMENTS

I AM INDEBTED to Richard B. McAdoo of Houghton Mifflin Company for encouraging me to undertake this book. It is an outgrowth of the chapter in *The View from Lincoln Hill* which deals with Emerson, Thoreau, Hawthorne, Alcott, and Margaret Fuller in respect to their attitudes toward nature.

I wish to thank Wayne Hanley and John Hay for reading the manuscript, my wife for invaluable editorial comments, and LaVerne Kehr for typing with a writer's trained eye.

Parts of this book have appeared in *Audubon*, in *The Living Wilderness*, in *Sierra*, and in the introductory essay to *Yosemite and the Range of Light* by Ansel Adams.

Space limitations have precluded printing a complete bibliography. However, a list of the principal writers dealt with here, followed by suggestions for further reading, will be found on p. 289. The standard biographies, to whose authors I am indebted, are included. The final chapter, "A New Direction," is based on my own biography of Rachel Carson, *The House of Life*.

AUTHOR'S NOTE

AMERICA'S interest in nature goes back to the earliest days of the republic. Books like Buffon's *Natural History*, White's *Selborne*, Bartram's *Travels* — and later, for those who could afford it, Audubon's magnificent *Birds* — were to be found in many private libraries. Since that time, owing largely to the work of our popular nature writers, this interest has spread throughout our society to the point where a unique wild area or a rare species of bird or mammal is valued as highly as a man-made work of art. In short, appreciation of nature has become a part of our national culture.

Though many fine works in American natural history were published before his time, Henry David Thoreau is generally considered the father of the nature essay as a literary form. In recent years, his life and his philosophy have been the subject of countless articles and books. Here I am concerned largely with those who came after him — with the men and women who shared his insights and, during the course of a century, shaped not only our attitude toward our natural heritage but in many cases the future of the landscape itself. Some of them were professional writers who found their inspiration in nature. Others were scientists who also knew how to write. A few are famous for their achievements in other fields. Since this is not an anthology, I quote sparingly from authors whose books are well known and easily available. In the case of less familiar figures, or those whose books are hard to come by, I include sample passages to give some idea of the flavor and significance of their work. Suggestions for further reading will be found on page 289.

I have not sought to cover the entire field of American nature writing, but rather have concentrated on certain authors whose work seems particularly original, influential, or just plain engaging. Nor have I more than touched on writers whose careers are still too recent to view in perspective. Among the latter Rachel Carson — with whom this book concludes — is the exception, since the impact of her work is already a matter of historical record.

CONTENTS

INTRODUCTION

A Century of Changing Values

O<small>N A DAY</small> in early May of 1962, Stewart L. Udall, Secretary of the Interior, held an outdoor reception to commemorate the hundredth anniversary of the death of Henry David Thoreau. Here at Washington's Dumbarton Oaks his guests followed a winding path through open woods still bright with spring; at each turn in the path stood a park ranger, since this is the domain of the National Park Service. During an informal ceremony beneath the trees they listened, against a background of birdsong, to addresses by their host, by Robert Frost, and by Justice William O. Douglas. At the same moment, up in Boston, a book entitled *Silent Spring* was being prepared for the press. The two events are not unrelated. No American authors have written more eloquently or profoundly about nature than Henry Thoreau and Rachel Carson. In their very different ways they have had an immeasurable influence on the way we think about the world. Both were at heart poets as well as naturalists. They were unique, but they were not alone. Like all writers, however original or prophetic, they were in some degree representative of their times. Henry Thoreau (in the words of a family friend) "was not begotten by the northwest wind, as many have supposed," nor did Rachel Carson burst forth fully armed, like Athena from the head of Zeus. Both were part of a literary as well as a scientific tradition, influenced by their contemporaries and by the climate of their age.

In Thoreau's case, it was an age of intellectual and moral revolution, centered in the little town of Concord, Massachusetts, where the political revolution had begun in 1775. Under the benign leadership of Ralph Waldo Emerson, the Concord writers would engage in what has often been called a second war of independence: against cultural domination from abroad and against religious bigotry and rampant materialism at home. Emerson's first book, *Nature*, appearing when Thoreau was still in college, was (according to the latter's biographer) "one of the seminal books of his life." By the time Thoreau left Harvard he had already set his course, from which he never deviated. One can only speculate on how many members of the audience at the 1837 commencement exercises realized what they were hearing when he delivered his "part." "This curious world we inhabit," he declaimed, "is more wonderful than convenient; more beautiful than it is useful; it is more to be admired and enjoyed than used." Having rejected the Puritan philosophy that anything not "useful" to man is somehow evil, he went on to suggest that one should work for a living one day a week, leaving the other six "in which to range this widespread garden, and drink in the soft influences and sublime revelations of nature." The following day Emerson delivered before the Phi Beta Kappa Society his celebrated oration, "The American Scholar," in which he declared that "our day of dependence, our long apprenticeship to the learning of other lands, draws to a close." The goal was self-reliance, and to follow this austere path Emerson found unfailing support in the world of nature. "Hail to the quiet fields of my fathers!" he had written in his journal on leaving the city for rural Concord. "Henceforth I design not to utter any speech, poem or book that is not entirely and peculiarly my work."

All this strikes a familiar note today. These young men and women in Concord, who came to be known as "transcendentalists," were defying the establishment. Deeply read in

Eastern philosophy and religion, they believed in intuition as the road to understanding, in a truth that transcends the material world of everyday experience. Then as now, they sought strength in wild nature. They shared — in the words of an Oriental scholar — "the age-old Chinese regard for nature as an escape from the machine of society, an escape . . . into a world of refinement and grace and quiet." They firmly rejected the doctrine that set man apart from the natural world.

Deeply influenced as he was by Emerson, Thoreau would surpass his master as a prophet for our time. In the century between his death and Rachel Carson's *Silent Spring*, his fame would slowly grow. *Walden*, and the great journal from which later books were also quarried, would inspire scores of writers whose names are less familiar but whose work can be read today with fresh appreciation and delight — even with a shock of recognition.

"The question is not what you look at," wrote Thoreau in his journal, "but what you see." Later he commented: "A man has not seen a thing who has not felt it." Natural science, he complained, was studied as a dead language; he was repelled by the collections of lifeless specimens in the museums. "A man's interest in a bluebird," he wrote, "is worth more than a complete but dry list of the fauna and flora of a town." Since his time there has grown up a literature of nature in America that has opened the eyes of millions of readers, leading to a widespread feeling of kinship with the other forms of life with which we share the earth. "The literary naturalists," in the words of one of the finest since Thoreau, Edwin Way Teale, "have been the *appreciators*, and their appreciation of and interest in the life of the out-of-doors have led readers to a similar attitude. They have stressed the fascination of the living creatures, and led more and more people to observe instead of kill."

Their books and articles also reflect a growing appreciation of rural values as America becomes more urbanized. They reveal intuitive understanding of the importance of the natural environment, of the need for conservation, of the principles of ecology, long before any of these words was in common use or the concepts they stand for generally understood. This was the century during which fundamental beliefs about the origin of the earth and of man's place in it were shattered beyond repair; when the approach to nature shifted from the romantic and moral to the scientific; when exploitation gradually began to yield to some thought for the future. The concern of the few grew to be the concern of the many, until no less than the federal government itself became involved in protecting what was now recognized as a national heritage. Ten years after Thoreau's death, the United States Congress created the first of our national parks — a radical concept, unique to America, later imitated all over the world. The national park system was slow in getting under way, but meanwhile national forests were established to halt the squandering of a priceless resource. In 1901, for the first time since Thomas Jefferson, a naturalist became President of the United States. When Theodore Roosevelt entered the White House, our nature writers suddenly gained stature in the public eye. Their work had been quietly preparing America for the bold strokes that the government now took to implement a new policy called "conservation." Great natural history museums were reaching out to enlighten the scientifically illiterate; Audubon societies — conceived by a big-game hunter in the womb of a sportsmen's magazine — were building up a national force for bird protection. About the time of Roosevelt's death another novel concept, that of the "wilderness area," was being developed by two young members of the Forest Service, to reach fruition over three decades later when enough voters had become aware of the value of wilderness to science and to the enrichment of our lives.

By the time Rachel Carson began work on *Silent Spring*, we had entered a new world, a technological society in which man's power over nature was virtually absolute. World War II left us not only the means literally to move mountains or obliterate an island in the sea, but also a wholly new type of synthetic poisons whose long-term effects on the environment and ourselves are yet to be known. As the author of *The Sea Around Us*, one of the best-selling nature books of all time, Miss Carson had a ready-made audience. The response to *Silent Spring* was instantaneous. Eight years after its publication, an editorial writer remarked: "A few thousand words from her, and the world took a new direction." Every year that passes confirms that comment. Yet no one was more aware than she of the many thousands — millions — of words published during the preceding century that had led readers like herself to appreciate "the beauty of the living world I was trying to save." The country was prepared for her message, thanks in large part to the writers who had preceded her.

CHAPTER I

"The Two Johns": Burroughs and Muir

*"There is nothing of age in America but the woods
. . . That is well worth monuments and ancestors."*
— Châteaubriand, VOYAGE EN AMERIQUE, 1836

V ERNAL EQUINOX, 1911. Theodore Roosevelt, two years out of the White House, is in California delivering a lecture under the auspices of a scientific institute. Before reaching his main theme — his recent African adventures — he brings up a subject that has remained close to his heart throughout all the turmoil of politics and the presidency. What the world needs, he says, is more men with scientific imagination — men who can take the facts of science and write of them with fidelity, yet with such an interpretative and poetic spirit as to make them into literature: "I mean such men and such writers as John Muir and John Burroughs."

Both men were in the audience that evening, Burroughs on one of his rare trips away from his beloved Catskills, Muir on his home ground. Aged seventy-four and seventy-three respectively, with temperaments as different as the tame Catskills and the wild Sierra Nevada, they had introduced thousands of Americans to the joys of outdoor nature. They had developed and popularized the "nature essay": a literary form hitherto cultivated only by a few writers of talent and one of genius, Henry David Thoreau. In one way or another, they had been associated with virtually every American nature writer of their time. Looking back, they could see tangible evidence of what they had accomplished. Burroughs could see it in the hordes of children who crowded around the rear platform of his train, singing and throwing flowers, as he left for home; Muir in the silent wilderness of Yosemite, the Grand Canyon, the national parks that he had worked so hard to create. But looking ahead, they could hardly have anticipated the threats that would arise to everything they held sacred. In 1911 they were standing midway in the century between the death of Thoreau in 1862 and the publication of Rachel Carson's *Silent Spring*. The frontier was officially dead, its obsequies performed by historian Frederick Jackson Turner, but the frontier philosophy persisted, growing more lethal with each advance in technology. On a continent of supposedly limitless resources, conservation was still a novel concept,* promoted by naturalists, by fashionable sportsmen who had noted with alarm the dwindling of the wild game, and fortunately by a few men of power in government. It was barely recognized by the public at large. Whatever hope there might be for the future would depend on men and women like themselves, able to build on the foundation they had laid. Specifically it would depend on the efforts of articulate naturalists who, as Theodore Roosevelt had said, could take the facts of science and transmute them into literature. Americans must be made to recognize the natural world as part of their culture. Preaching, however impassioned, would never do it. Poetry would: that is, in the broad sense of any writing that seizes on the reader's imagination and reveals the poetic truth that lies beneath the scientific fact.

೪

Burroughs and Muir had barely set out on their long careers when Thoreau's brief life ended at the age of forty-four. Leaving the crowded church in Concord, Massachusetts, after the funeral, Louisa May Alcott remarked to a friend: "Though he wasn't made much of while living, he was honored at his death." The obituaries were many and impressive, including Emerson's in the *Atlantic Monthly*. *Walden* and *A Week on the Concord and Merrimack Rivers* — the only two of his books published during his lifetime — were immediately brought back into print, and four posthumous volumes were compiled from his journal and other writings during the next four years. But as John Burroughs wrote some quarter-century later, Thoreau's fame "was little more than in the bud at that time, and its full leaf and flowering are not yet, perhaps not in many years yet. He improves with age . . . The generation he

* The importance of conserving wild nature was implicit, however, in the work of such popular writers as Washington Irving and William Cullen Bryant, and quite explicit in James Fenimore Cooper's *Leatherstocking Tales*. The great painter of the American Indian, George Catlin, and later Henry Thoreau, had independently conceived the idea of the national park.

lectured so sharply will not give the same heed to his words as will the next and the next." On first reading, Thoreau could be irritating; time is required "to take off a little of his asperity and fully ripen him . . . The world likes a good hater and refuser almost as well as it likes a good lover and acceptor, only it likes him farther off."

Emerson predicted that Thoreau's massive journal, if it were ever published, would produce "a plentiful crop of naturalists." He was right about that; yet the full impact of Thoreau's life and writing, particularly on young readers, would not be felt for another century. And then it was not so much the naturalist as the philosopher of nature that evoked so deep a response in a generation frustrated by the materialism and synthetic standards of the world it had inherited.

Born in 1837, Burroughs was twenty-five years old when Thoreau died. Nothing in his life so far had foreshadowed the national celebrity to whom singing schoolchildren tossed spring flowers. His forebears were dirt farmers, of no cultural pretensions. His father (Burroughs recalled), though a good husband and a worthy citizen, had "no aesthetic sensibility and no manners. The primrose by the river's brim would not have been seen by him at all." A religious bigot, he read nothing but the weekly newspaper and church publications. "Mother, I think, never read a page of anything." However, in the rare moments of escape from running a household of ten children, she would take her son berrying in the hills surrounding the Burroughs homestead in upstate New York, with their flowering meadows and their view of the long sweep of the western Catskills. It was from her that he first derived his feeling for nature, and it was she who defended his right to more schooling, which his father thought would just spoil him as a farmer.

In reconstructing the life of a famous man, biographers like to find some youthful experience which, however trivial it seemed at the time, became the "turning point" of their subject's career. In her *Life and Letters of John Burroughs*, Clara Barrus, the close companion of his later years, tells of his childhood excitement over the songs and bright colors of birds. "When, at the age of seven or eight, his attention was arrested by a strange bird in the Deacon woods, the experience proved of signal importance: only a small bluish warbler with a white spot on its wing [a black-throated blue warbler], but it challenged him as had no other bird before. Through it he got a glimpse of the world of birds of which he knew nothing; a glimpse which so fired his imagination that he half-resolved to know more about the birds some day." Nor could he ever forget the cloud of passenger pigeons that poured down, one spring morning, into the beechwoods till "the air and woods and earth were blue with them . . . and the whole world seemed turned to pigeons." (They would become extinct during his lifetime.) These childhood enthusiasms were fortified when, as a young man, he chanced upon Audubon's monumental *Birds of America* in — of all places — the library of the Military Academy at West Point.

The charm and beauty of birds have, I suspect, lured more men and women into the field of natural history than any other aspect of nature. For Burroughs they remained an abiding passion. Yet he was a writer before he was a naturalist. Here the part of the black-throated blue warbler was played by Ralph Waldo Emerson. At the age of nineteen, Burroughs was teaching school to earn enough money to continue his own education, and writing essays in ponderous Johnsonian style. Then he discovered Emerson. "I read him in a sort of ecstasy. I got him in my blood, and he colored my whole intellectual outlook. He appealed to my spiritual side; his boldness and unconventionality took a deep hold upon me." (One recalls Thoreau's similar reaction on reading Emerson's *Nature* twenty-two years before.) So great was the impact that Burroughs' first, unsigned article in the *Atlantic Monthly*, published four years later, was attributed by many readers to Emerson — though surely it resembled Emerson at a very low ebb. Clearly the master's hold on him was too strong. He soon realized that he had better find his own style and his own subject matter — less high-flown philosophy, more about country life and the outdoor world that he knew at first hand — in short, the nature essay. "It was mainly to break the spell of Emerson's influence," he wrote many years later, "and to get upon ground of my own that I took to writing upon outdoor themes."

Meanwhile his personal life had taken a turn which boded no good for either his birding or his writing. He married a girl who despised both, but nonetheless wanted John. Ursula North, according to her sister, was "endowed with a strong will power." John, who was not, harbored doubts till the last minute; on the way to the wedding he sat down to think it over and almost turned back. Proud and aggressive, this nineteenth-century Delilah had already asserted herself by making him cut his hair — esthetically an error, to judge from the handsome daguerreotype taken a short time before. Once married, she apparently continued to live with her family until he could make enough money to set up housekeeping. Only a week after the wedding he wrote her: "I sometimes think I will not make the kind of husband that will always suit you. If I live, I shall be an author." Ursula thought otherwise; he should go to New York City and enter the business world. Her replies to his protestations of love and loneliness were "short and businesslike." He attempted again and again to obey her command but always had to fall back on schoolteaching. For a short time he sought to combine writing with the study of medicine, but that failed also. Finally, in 1862, lured by the excitement of the Civil War, he decided to try his luck in Washington. "I believe it is good for us to be apart, don't you?" he wrote to his wife. "I think love increases as does the distance between us."

(This marriage, if such it can be called, somehow endured, perhaps because Burroughs soon began to make money from his writing — enough eventually to satisfy even her. On that happy day in 1911 when — by now a venerable and fabulously successful author — he received the accolade from Theodore Roosevelt and the tribute of flowers from the California schoolchildren, she was properly impressed and thereafter looked upon his work with respect. "My books couldn't do it," he said, "but — well — the fine houses and servants are good for something, after all.")

With the help of Washington friends, Burroughs landed (and then lost) various menial government jobs, till finally he wound up as a clerk in the Currency Bureau of the Treasury Department. For the next ten years he sat at a high desk guarding a steel vault filled with bank notes. "How I reacted against the door of that old safe!" he recalled later. "But the rebound sent me back to the fields and woods of my boyhood." Here in the bowels of the Treasury he wrote the essays that make up the first two of his long series of nature books, *Wake-Robin* and *Winter Sunshine*, and here he wrote his *Notes on Walt Whitman*.

Burroughs' meeting with Whitman was another of those turning points, a sudden source of warmth and companionship for a man who desperately needed both. They met in the fall of 1863, when Whitman was working in the army hospitals. Burroughs had read *Leaves of Grass*, which Emerson had termed "the most extraordinary piece of wit and wisdom that America has yet contributed." He also recalled Emerson's description of the poet as "half song thrush and half alligator," and was astonished to find him "a new type of man, a new type of gentleman, a new type of philosopher . . . the greatest, sweetest soul I have yet met in this world." They took to each other instantly. Thereafter Burroughs regularly accompanied Whitman on his rambles through the streets of Washington and long walks about the surrounding countryside. The observer of nature and the poet complemented each other. "He thinks natural history, to be true to life, must be inspired, as well as poetry," notes Burroughs after one such expedition. "The true poet and the true scientist are close akin. They go forth into nature like friends . . . The interests of the two in nature are widely different, yet in no true sense are they hostile." His association with Whitman undoubtedly broadened and deepened Burroughs' attitude toward nature; in fact, Walt's influence during those formative years can scarcely be exaggerated. "I loved him as I never loved any man," Burroughs recalled much later. ". . . I owe more to him than to any man in the world . . . He was a tremendous force in my life."

Notes on Walt Whitman was both Burroughs' first published book and the first book written about the poet. He saw Whitman as "a return to Nature" and *Leaves of Grass* as "an utterance from Nature, and opposite to modern literature, which is an utterance from Art." Personally, Whitman was not only a source of literary inspiration to the younger man but a balm to his loneliness. "The more I see of Walt, the more I like him," he writes to a friend. He goes on to say — with perhaps a touch of naïveté — "Walt loves everything and everybody . . . He kisses me as if I were a girl." Their warm friendship must have done much to make bearable those long hours outside the cold steel safe. And Whitman, who had collaborated in the little book about himself, also showed a real interest in Burroughs' nature writing. It was he who insisted on naming that first collection of essays *Wake-Robin*. "I took a number of titles to him, and he held me to that one." In doing so, Whitman sowed the seeds of confusion for generations of readers unaware that "wake-robin" does not refer to a bird being roused from sleep but rather to "the white trillium, which blooms in all our woods, and which marks the arrival of all the birds."*

Published in 1871 by the Boston firm of Hurd & Houghton (later Houghton, Mifflin), *Wake-Robin* made an immediate hit. Burroughs' name was already known. Most of these essays had appeared as magazine articles, principally in the *Atlantic Monthly*, which had printed the first chapter, "The Return of the Birds," as a lead article six years earlier. The *Atlantic*'s editor, William Dean Howells, was prepared to like *Wake-Robin* and he did. "The dusk and cool and quiet of the forest seem to wrap the reader of his book, and it is a sort of

---

* Burroughs is referring to the painted trillium, *Trillium undulatum*. Today the name "wakerobin" is generally applied to the red or purple trillium, *T. erectum*.

summer vacation to turn its pages . . . Perhaps it would be difficult not to be natural and simple in writing of such things as our author treats of . . . but Mr. Burroughs adds a strain of genuine poetry, which makes his papers unusually delightful, while he has more humor than generally falls to the ornithological tribe." Other reviewers drew comparisons with Thoreau's essays and with Gilbert White's *Natural History of Selborne.** And though it may be true, as Bliss Perry once remarked, that Burroughs did not find his own voice till some years later, the essential elements were all here, enhanced by the freshness and undercurrent of enthusiasm which so often colors an author's first book.

The opening chapter, "The Return of the Birds," is followed by "In the Hemlocks," which contains the well-known passage on one of America's finest songbirds, beginning: "Ever since I entered the woods, even while listening to the lesser songsters, or contemplating the silent forms about me, a strain has reached my ears from out the depths of the forest that to me is the finest sound in nature — the song of the hermit thrush. I often hear him thus a long way off, sometimes over a quarter of a mile away, when only the stronger and more perfect parts of his music reach me; and through the general chorus of wrens and warblers I detect this sound rising pure and serene, as if a spirit from some remote height were slowly chanting a divine accompaniment. This song appeals to the sentiment of the beautiful in me, and suggests a serene religious beatitude as no other sound in nature does." (No doubt the symbolism of the hermit thrush in Whitman's "When Lilacs Last in the Dooryard Bloom'd" was inspired by his country walks with Burroughs.) This gentle essay was followed by a rather uncharacteristic account of an Adirondack

* Only the London *Athenaeum* sounded a sour note, as Burroughs noted with apparent amusement: "It makes the mistake of reviewing it [*Wake-Robin*] under the head of Science instead of Literature, and says that I tell too much about myself, and not enough about the birds; that I am a master of rounded sentences and faultless periods with nothing in them; that it is a pity when I got lost in the woods, that I had not staid lost, etc."

deer hunt — with a cold-blooded description of revolver practice on a rabbit — and by essays on the spring bird migration in Washington,* on trout fishing in the Catskills, on the bluebird, and on the joys of ornithology. With the exception of his literary and philosophical essays, *Wake-Robin* touches on most of the subjects that, in the next fifty years, would provide material for innumerable magazine pieces and twenty-seven volumes. These would reach a vast audience and make their author one of the best loved of all American writers. More important, they would open a window on the natural world for thousands of young readers who would, when they grew up, have the fate of this world in their hands. (In old age Burroughs remarked: "Whenever I see young men walking through the country like that [i.e., with camping equipment on their backs] I sometimes flatter myself that maybe my books have had a share in sending them forth.") In the words of a friend, he created "an army of nature-students." They and their successors have been fighting our conservation battles ever since.

Not that Burroughs was a born fighter, like John Muir. He was a man of peace who assiduously cultivated the contemplative life. With the publication of *Wake-Robin* he had found his métier. "As a youth I was a philosopher; as a young man I was an Emersonian; as a middle-aged man I am a literary naturalist, but always I have been an essayist." He was only thirty-nine years old when the distinguished editor of *Scribner's Monthly*, Richard Watson Gilder, went out on a critical limb: "John Burroughs is one of the half-dozen or less prose writers who are adding anything vital by means of books to the thought and life of the country."

Burroughs was mildly annoyed with the inevitable comparisons between his writing and Thoreau's. "That Thoreau business, I think, will play out pretty soon," he wrote to his comrade, Myron Benton. "There is really little or no resem-

* *Cf.* Louis J. Halle's *Spring in Washington*, three quarters of a century later.

"The Two Johns" 11

blance between us . . . Thoreau's aim is mainly ethical . . . my own aim, so far as I have any, is entirely artistic . . . I will not preach one word . . . I paint the bird, or the trout, or the scene, for its own sake, truthfully anyhow, and picturesquely if I can." In his essay on Thoreau, whose work he vastly admired, Burroughs remarks that "his mood was subjective rather than objective. He was more intent on the natural history of his own thought than on that of the bird." But, late in life, when his own name was a household word, Burroughs commented with amazing objectivity as well as humility: "I think it probable that my books send people to nature more than Thoreau's do . . . I do not take readers to nature to give them a lesson, but to have a good time . . . I am more than his equal in powers of observation . . . But Thoreau's *morale* is much superior to mine . . . I wish I had a little more of [his] quality — that high moral and stoical tone . . . that makes his books nearer the classical standards." For all his success, Burroughs felt that he had erred in not heeding Thoreau's example: "I try to say things in too pretty a way — aim to have the page too smooth. I am too afraid to give the mind a jolt, which is a mistake." Yet one cannot help feeling that, no matter how hard he might have tried to model himself on Thoreau, it would not have worked. Thoreau was tough-minded and prickly; Burroughs, in his own words, was "a soft man, easily bruised, easily hurt, but getting at Nature through those very qualities of sympathy and tenderness." When, in his seventies, he first visited the Grand Canyon, the scenes that most appealed to him were those that reminded him of places back home. Whereas Thoreau sought wildness in the familiar, Burroughs clung to every touch of the familiar in the wild.

The Boston essayist and nature writer Dallas Lore Sharp made an amusing comparison between Burroughs and Thoreau:

If Mr. Burroughs were to start from my door for a tramp over these small Hingham hills he would cross the trout-brook by my neighbor's stone bridge, and nibbling a spear of peppermint on the way, would follow the lane and the cowpaths across the pasture. Thoreau would pick out the deepest hole in the brook and try to swim across; he would leap the stone walls of the lane, cut a bee-line through the pasture, and drop, for his first look at the landscape, to the bottom of the pit in the seam-face granite quarry. Here he would pull out his notebook and a gnarly wild apple from his pocket, and intensely, critically, chemically, devouring said apple, make note in the book that the apples of Eden were flat, the apples of Sodom bitter, but this wild, tough, wretched, impossible apple of the Hingham hills united all ambrosial essences in its striking odor of squash-bugs.

Mr. Burroughs takes us along with him. Thoreau comes upon us in the woods — jumps out at us from behind some bush, with a *"Scat!"* Burroughs brings us home in time for tea; Thoreau leaves us tangled up in the briars.

It won't hurt us to be jumped at now and then and told to *"scat!"* It won't hurt us to be digged by the briars. It is good for us, otherwise we might forget that *we* are beneath our clothes. It is good for us and highly diverting, but highly irritating too.

For my part, when I take up an outdoor book I am glad if there is quiet in it, and fragrance, and something of the saneness and sweetness of the sky . . .

Thoreau is a succession of showers — "tempests"; his pages are sheet-lightning, electrifying, purifying, illuminating, but not altogether conducive to peace.

In contrast to other "nature writers" — Audubon, Muir, even Thoreau — writing came easily to Burroughs. With each successive volume his reputation mounted, and so did his royalties. "Every new book brought him in more money," wrote a friend rather caustically, "and it was therefore impossible for him to resist publishing everything he wrote." Perhaps he wrote *too* easily, and too much, but his loyal readers could never get enough. For, as Howells had said, he wrapped them in the cool and quiet of the forest, and it was like a summer vacation to turn his pages. For today's readers, particularly the young, this is not enough. Once so popular, Burroughs' books gather dust on the library shelves, while Thoreau gains in stature year by year.

During his long life Burroughs got around a good deal more than did the Concord philosopher. But, on the whole, travel was an interruption, accepted with reluctance. Like the queen bee, he was superlatively productive but very much a homebody. After a decade in Washington, he bade farewell to city life and built himself a gloomy stone house, which he named Riverby, eighty miles north of New York on the Hudson. Here he planted orchards and vineyards, sallying forth regularly during the early years to supplement his writing and fruit-growing income with the incongruous job of part-time bank examiner. Here his wife gave birth to a son, Julian. Apparently she also contributed indirectly to his literary production. "The very conditions of incompatibility which made a happy home life impossible for either, and which sent him persistently out of doors," writes Clara Barrus, "resulted both in his own peace and contentment and in the books born of his intimate and sympathetic intercourse with Nature." The rustic study he added apart from the main house was still, alas, within range of Mrs. Burroughs' dinner bell, summoning him in midpassage to perform some household chore. After twenty-two years of this, he finally built himself a cabin back in the hills, which was called "Slabsides." Here he found "peace and contentment" both indoors and out, living alone at first, later with his brother Hiram. As his fame grew and devotees, including Theodore Roosevelt, made their way to his doorstep, Slabsides became a nationwide symbol of a way of life.

No hermit, Burroughs discovered to his surprise that he enjoyed lecturing, and soon found himself more and more in demand. He was invited to literary clubs in New York; he visited old friends in Washington — where he attended the inauguration of Grover Cleveland and dined with a new friend, Theodore Roosevelt. He went to Cambridge for Harvard commencement and to Concord, where he met Bronson Alcott and visited Thoreau's grave. He even took a trip to the British Isles. But by all odds his most adventurous journey — during which he made an unsuccessful attempt to jump ship — was the Harriman Expedition to Alaska in the summer of 1899, on which he served as historian. He was then sixty-two years old. Included in the large company of explorers, big-game

hunters, botanists, mining experts, artists, and eminent scientists was the man who later thwarted his escape, John Muir.

❦

Muir and Burroughs had long admired each other from a distance. Their first meeting, however, six years earlier in New York City, had not been a notable success. Burroughs had attended a Walt Whitman memorial celebration the night before and was apparently suffering from a hangover. "He had made a speech, eaten a big dinner, and had a headache," Muir recalled. "So he seemed tired, and gave no sign of his fine qualities . . . I tried to make him go to Europe with me . . . but he answered today by letter that circumstances would not allow it. The 'circumstances' are his wife." Burroughs noted briefly in his journal: Muir was "an interesting man with the Western look upon him. Not quite enough penetration in his eyes." (An odd comment, judging from photographs of Muir.) Things went better when Muir visited Slabsides three years later. "He is a poet and almost a Seer," wrote Burroughs. "Something ancient and far-away in the look of his eyes. He could not sit down in the corner of the landscape, as Thoreau did; he must have a continent for his playground . . . Probably the truest lover of Nature . . . we have yet had." But he was "a little prolix . . . Ask him to tell you his famous dog story [this was "Stickeen," to appear shortly in *Century* magazine] and you get the whole theory of glaciation thrown in."

From the moment they set foot on shipboard, the two men naturally gravitated to each other. Yet in many ways it was the attraction of opposite poles. Their temperaments, and the early years that shaped them, could scarcely have been more different — except for their love of the outdoors. In *The Story of My Boyhood and Youth*, Muir recalls the wild Scottish country where he was born, on the shores of the stormy North Sea, and his rough playmates, "wild as myself," who loved to listen to the birds and delve into the rock pools, but "best of all to watch the waves in awful storms thundering on the black headlands and craggy ruins of the old Dunbar Castle . . ." Inside the castle grounds they wrestled with each other, fought with their fists, and "tried to see who could climb highest on the crumbling peaks and crags." When a servant girl warned them of going to hell if they misbehaved, young Muir was unimpressed; he insisted that he could easily find toeholds on the walls and climb out.

He was eleven when his father left Scotland for good and moved the family to the wilderness of Wisconsin, where he had taken up a quarter-section of open woodland to establish a farm. Young John, on whom much of the work fell, later recalled his joy in the wild country, but even more vividly the backbreaking toil (that permanently injured the health of his sisters) and the beatings he took regularly from his father, who sat back reading the Bible while his family slaved. If Burroughs' father was a religious bigot, Muir's was a true fanatic. "Father carefully taught us to consider ourselves very poor worms of the dust, conceived in sin, etc., and devoutly believed that quenching every spark of pride and self-confidence was a sacred duty." One thing about his son, however, he did respect. From boyhood, John had a consuming interest in machinery and a talent for mechanical inventions that almost matched his passion for nature. He used "every spare or stolen moment" for whittling ingenious and practical devices out of wood: water wheels, a self-setting sawmill, thermometers, hygrometers, "an automatic contrivance for feeding horses at any required hour," and a series of complex clocks, one of which was exhibited at the local state fair. By the time he was twenty-one he had reached the point where he thought he could leave home and earn a living as a machinist, and eventually as a professional inventor. But first, with his Scottish passion for learning, he would attend the University of Wisconsin, supporting himself by farm work and schoolteaching. Here his love of nature was rekindled by his first lesson in botany — a lesson that sent him "flying to the woods and meadows in wild enthusiasm." After four years at the university, he worked — most successfully — in a carriage factory, until an accident almost cost him his sight. It was decisive. He left the machine shop for the wilderness, never to return.

Free at last to wander at will, Muir, now thirty years old, set out on the famous journey from Louisville, Kentucky, to Florida, later recorded in *A Thousand-Mile Walk to the Gulf.* "My plan was simply to push on in a general southward direction by the wildest, leafiest, and least trodden way I could find, promising the greatest extent of virgin forest." From the Florida Keys he sailed to Havana, hoping to find a vessel bound for Brazil and to realize his dream of exploring the Amazon (which the great naturalist at Harvard, Louis Agassiz, had ascended two years before). Finding none, he reluctantly stayed with his schooner on its return trip to New York City, where he felt "completely lost in the vast throngs of people, the noise of the streets, and the immense size of the buildings. Often I thought I would like to explore the city if, like a lot of wild hills and valleys, it was clear of inhabitants." The woodsman who found his way easily through trackless wilderness did not dare to go beyond sight of his schooner. As soon as he could book passage, he took ship for California — the land that he would come to know and love as he did no other, and whose mountains and glacial valleys and redwood groves would forever be associated with him as with no other man. By the following spring of 1869, he was herding sheep in the High Sierra; in mid-July, he got his first sight of the summit peaks and Yosemite Valley. "I shouted and gesticulated in a wild burst of ecstasy." Whether he knew it or not, his career as a writer had begun.

Unlike Burroughs, Muir could never be described as a "natural writer" — whatever that term means. He *was* a "noted talker," which may have been part of the trouble. At no loss for words in conversation, in his journals, in private letters, he seems to have frozen up when writing for publication, becoming, he confessed, "slow as a glacier." Happily, a professor at the University of Wisconsin, James Davie Butler, had recognized young Muir's literary gift. Butler not only introduced him to the writings of Emerson and Thoreau but persuaded him to keep a journal, as they did — a source of future books. Like Thoreau, he took notes on the spot, in all weathers, his fingers sometimes numb with the cold. The difference is that Thoreau, a systematic craftsman, would conscientiously shape and polish these notes at day's end for entry in his massive journal, whence they could later be lifted for publication, often word for word. Muir was more haphazard. Over forty years passed before he reworked this early journal to become *My First Summer in the Sierra* — a book that nonetheless retains all the joy and freshness of a first encounter. Though Thoreau made his journal his chief life work, neither he nor Muir was ever in awe of the written word: "Books," wrote Thoreau, "are to be attended to as new sounds merely . . . They are but a new note in the forest." Muir was even more skeptical; he despaired of capturing the glory of the High Sierra in print. "No amount of word-making

will ever make a single soul to *know* these mountains . . .
Books are but piles of stones set up to show coming travelers
where other minds have been, or at least smoke signals to call
attention." Both men preferred the sky to a roof; both liked
their nature untamed. The country around Concord was
Thoreau's garden: superior, he claimed, to any artificial garden he had ever read of. "For a garden I should not have anything less than a piece of pure nature," wrote Muir from Yosemite to his friend Mrs. Carr. He continues: "I was reading
Thoreau's *Maine Woods* a short time ago. As described by
him, these woods are exactly like those of Canada West." Not
only in their philosophy but in their expression of it, the two
men are often strikingly similar. "In wildness," wrote
Thoreau, "is the preservation of the world." Muir added God.
"In God's wildness lies the hope of the world." They both
looked on town life and money-grubbing with disdain.
Thoreau saw his Concord neighbors living lives of quiet desperation; Muir doubted that there was a truly sane man in
San Francisco.

In the beginning at least, he had no intent to write for publication. But friends who received his letters recognized his
literary ability, even if he did not. Chief among these was Mrs.
Jeanne C. Carr, wife of a professor of natural science at the
University of Wisconsin (who later moved to the University of
California). A warm and talented woman, an ardent amateur
botanist, she had helped young John to exhibit his clocks at the
state fair, and had kept a solicitous eye on him during his
college days. When he was twenty-seven years old, lonely and
drifting, unable to decide on a career, she proposed that they
initiate a regular correspondence, since they had so much in
common. The suggestion moved him deeply. "You propose,
Mrs. Carr, an exchange of thoughts for which I thank you very
sincerely. This will be a means of pleasure and improvement
which I could not have hoped ever to have been possessed of."
He protests his own inability to respond in kind: "If, however,
you are willing in this to adopt the plan that our Saviour endeavored to beat into the stingy Israelites, *viz.* to 'give, hoping

for nothing again,' all will be well." It was. The fruit of her solicitude was a spate of long letters over the years that show Muir at his best: spontaneous, self-searching, humorous, fiercely devoted to the view of life that they held in common. These letters led to his first appearance in the public press.

In the fall of 1871 — the year of Burroughs' *Wake-Robin* — Muir published three reports on Yosemite in the New York *Daily Tribune*. The following spring Mrs. Carr arranged for a series of articles in the *Overland Monthly*, which, under the editorship of Bret Harte, had become the leading magazine on the Pacific Coast. Beginning with a dramatic account of a great storm and flood in Yosemite Valley, they impressed and thrilled his readers. Mrs. Carr went on to combine letters written to her and to Professor Le Conte (an authority on glaciers) and sent them to Ralph Waldo Emerson, with a view to publication in the *Atlantic Monthly*. Nor did she stop there. "All this fugitiveness is going to be gathered up," she wrote Muir, "lest you die like Moses in the mountains and God should bury you where 'no man knoweth.' " Two years later, fearing that others might leap in and take credit for his revolutionary studies of glaciers, she persuaded him to publish a further series specifically on this subject. Meanwhile she had shown one of his papers to the other great authority on glacial action, Louis Agassiz, who was then visiting San Francisco. Agassiz told her, she reported, that "Muir is studying to greater purpose and with greater results than anyone else has done."

Ever a reluctant writer — aside from his journals and personal letters — Muir was nonetheless moving inevitably toward his principal life work: the preservation of our wilderness through scientific knowledge and the power of the pen. His purpose was "to entice people to look at Nature's loveliness." It was a formidable assignment. "The love of Nature among Californians," he remarked, "is desperately moderate." He sought to stir them up with a fiery article in the Sacramento paper entitled "God's First Temples: How Shall

We Preserve Our Forests?" In it he attacked the sheepmen who, by overgrazing and burning of the mountain pastures, were destroying both the woods and the watersheds, to the eventual impoverishment of the whole state. Already he was enough of a politician to stress the economic loss, in his plea for legislative action. He was not too hopeful. "Whether our loose-jointed Government is really able or willing to do anything in the matter remains to be seen." The California legislature did not respond but the reading public did. The article focused widespread attention on Muir as the leader of what would become a national conservation movement.*

He began to make plans for several books. "Although I never meant to write the results of my explorations, now I have begun I rather enjoy it," he writes to his sister Sarah from San Francisco. He bemoans his "limited vocabulary" and lack of facility, but goes doggedly ahead. "I always make out to accomplish in some way what I undertake."

Muir could not yet see himself as a professional writer. "After my first article I was greatly surprised to find that everything else I offered was accepted and paid for. That I could earn money simply with written words seemed very strange." It was not, however, his main means of support. In 1880 he had married Louie Wanda Strentzel, daughter of a Polish physician who had become one of the first and most successful horticulturalists in California. For the next ten years he ran a fruit farm acquired from his father-in-law, "until I had more money than I thought I would ever need for my family or for all expenses of travel and study." Now he could leave the farm and, "free from all breadwinning cares," return to his true calling.

He had never really abandoned it. Whenever the orchards and vineyards did not need his personal attention, he had hastened to the mountains, pushing his explorations farther and farther. How different his voice sounds when he is back in his beloved mountains! They are his sure source of inspira-

* The word "conservation," in its present sense, did not come into official use until the Theodore Roosevelt administration.

tion, literally his breath of life. The higher the source, the greater is the power of his prose. After a particularly harassing climb, or perhaps the discovery of a rare flower or the sight of a gorgeous sunset, his words flow and overflow and effervesce in a rushing, aerated stream, until one feels that a trout could live happily in every paragraph. On a mid-December morning he writes from Yosemite Valley to the famous botanist Asa Gray:

I had some measurements to make about the throat of the South Dome, so yesterday I climbed there, and then ran up to Cloud's Rest for your Primulas ... I witnessed one of the most glorious of our mountain sunsets; not one of the assembled mountains seemed remote — all had ceased their labor of beauty and gathered around their parent sun to receive the evening blessing ... I ran home in the moonlight with your sack of roses slung on my shoulder by a buckskin string — down through the junipers, down through the firs, now in black shadow, now in white light, past great South Dome white as the moon, past spirit-like Nevada, past Pywiack, through the groves of Illilouette and spiry pines of the open valley, star crystals sparkling above, frost crystals beneath, and rays of spirit beaming everywhere.

Toward the end of the decade, an event occurred that was not only a lucky break for Muir but for America and the world. In the summer of 1889 he revisited his old haunts in Yosemite. "I was accompanied," he wrote, "by one of the editors of the *Century*, and had a delightful time. When we were passing the head of the Vernal Falls I told our thin, subtle, spiritual story to the editor." His companion was Robert Underwood Johnson, himself an ardent conservationist and a vivid writer. "In the wilderness," he later recalled, "Muir looked like John the Baptist, as portrayed in bronze by Donatello."

Muir had previously contributed to the magazine (then known as *Scribner's Monthly*). Now Johnson suggested that he write two articles describing the glories of these mountains as only he could do, and recommending the establishment of a national park. The valley itself had already been set aside "for public use, resort and recreation" through an unprecedented Act of Congress twenty-five years before.* Johnson's and Muir's purpose was to enlarge the protected area to include the surrounding high country, making altogether a vast reserve of some 1500 square miles. Muir wrote the articles and supplied Johnson with detailed letters and maps to serve as ammunition in hearings before the congressional committees when the park bill was introduced. On October 1, 1890, largely through the efforts of these two men, Yosemite National Park was born.

It existed, on paper, but could it be protected in fact? Aware of the power of commercial interests, Johnson promptly made another suggestion: that California mountaineers and outdoorsmen who enjoyed the wilderness unite to form a Yosemite Defense Association. "Count me in," replied Muir. Informal meetings were held in the winter and spring of 1892, organized by Warren Olney, a San Francisco lawyer, and Professor Henry Senger of Stanford University. Muir promised to do all in his power to abet the project. On June 4 the new association was legally incorporated under the name of the Sierra Club, with twenty-seven members and Muir as president. "He came back jubilant from that meeting," reported a young friend. "In the Sierra Club he saw the crystallization of the dreams and labor of a life-time." His joy was justified; in due course the club would grow to become the most powerful conservation organization in the western hemisphere.

By now Muir's magazine articles and conservation efforts had won him a national reputation. On a visit to New York City — which included that first disappointing call on John Burroughs — he was entertained in grand style by the staff of the *Century* magazine. He met men like Gifford Pinchot, who would become Theodore Roosevelt's choice to save the American forests, and Henry Fairfield Osborn, a future founder and president of the American Museum of Natural History. "Almost every day in town here," he wrote to his wife, "I have

* See p. 42.

been called out to lunch and dinner at the clubs and soon have a crowd of notables about me. I had no idea I was so well known, considering how little I have written."

There is nothing like appreciation to prime an author's pen. The next year we find Muir laboring over the manuscript of his first book, *The Mountains of California*, which grew out of his contributions to the *Century*. "I have worked hard," he writes to Johnson, "adding lots of new stuff, and killing adjectives and adverbs of redundant growth — the *verys, intenses, gloriouses, ands,* and *buts,* by the score." Published in the fall of 1894, the book was acclaimed by reviewers and the first printing was quickly sold out. Probably more important to Muir was the warm response from authorities like his friend Charles S. Sargent, then at work on his classic *Silva of North America,* and J. D. Hooker, the great English botanist. "I have never read descriptions of trees that so picture them to the mind as you do," wrote Sargent. "Your book is one of the great productions of its kind." (Years later Osborn commented: "Muir wrote about trees as no one else in the whole history of trees, chiefly because he loved them as he loved men and women.") Hooker was impressed and delighted: "I do not know when I have read anything that I enjoyed more . . . It has recalled half-forgotten scientific facts, geology, geography, and vegetation that I used to see when in California and which I have often tried to formulate in vain." Invariably readers were taken with the evocative quality of Muir's prose, the poetic imagination that turns facts into literature. The reception of *The Mountains of California* apparently reconciled him to the literary labor pains that he was never to outgrow. He was soon considering a similar volume devoted specifically to Yosemite Valley, and he revisited his favorite spots with that in mind: "I can still climb as well as ever. I am trying to write another book, but it is harder than mountaineering."

In the years immediately preceding the Harriman Alaska Expedition, he undertook a series of articles on the national parks for the *Atlantic Monthly*. So began a close and fruitful friendship with the *Atlantic*'s editor, Walter Hines Page, and a permanent publishing connection with the magazine's owner, Houghton, Mifflin & Company, who would bring out *Our National Parks* and all his subsequent books. Page was the sort of editor that every writer yearns for. When Muir apologized for his slowness, Page replied: "I thank God that you do not write in glib, acrobatic fashion: anybody can do that. Half the people in the world are doing it all the time, to my infinite regret and confusion . . . The two books on the Parks and on Alaska will not need any special season's sales, nor other accidental circumstances: they'll be Literature!" John Burroughs, Page reminded him, keeps insisting that Muir's bags of notes be written up in book form, otherwise the loss would be inestimable. (Burroughs was clearly the least jealous of writers.) Though Muir was new to the *Atlantic*, his subject was not. The editors had recently printed an article on "The Next Stage in the Development of Public Parks" and another entitled "White Mountain Forests in Peril." Back in the eighteen-sixties, the *Atlantic* had given Burroughs his start, and for almost a century thereafter it remained a principal outlet for the type of writing in which he and Muir excelled.

Nature's violence appealed to Muir as much as its calm. In *The Mountains of California* he describes a gale in the Sierra, in the midst of which he climbed to the very top of a Douglas fir: "The slender tops fairly flapped and swished in the passionate torrent, bending and swirling backward and forward, round and round, tracing indescribable combinations of vertical and horizontal curves, while I clung with muscles firm braced, like a bobolink on a reed." He even gloried in a violent earthquake that occurred while he was living in Yosemite Valley. Long aware of the "life and gentle tenderness of the rocks," he suddenly felt them heave and shake, and heard them speak with an audible voice. "Though I had never enjoyed a storm of this sort the thrilling motion could not be mistaken, and I ran out of my cabin, both glad and frightened, shouting, 'A noble earthquake!' feeling sure I was going to learn something. The shocks were so violent and varied, and succeeded one another so closely, that I had to balance myself carefully in walking as if on the deck of a ship among waves, and it seemed impossible that the high cliffs of the valley could escape being shattered." Nor did they. Presently Eagle Rock on the south wall collapsed with a deafening roar. "I saw it falling in thousands of the great boulders I had so long been studying, pouring to the Valley floor in a free curve luminous with friction, making a terribly sublime spectacle — an arc of glowing passionate fire, fifteen hundred feet span, as true in form and as serene in beauty as a rainbow in the midst of the stupendous roaring rock-storm."

In Muir's experience, only one other place on the continent could match the sublime grandeur of the Sierra, and that was Alaska. When in the spring of 1899 he was invited to join the Harriman Alaska Expedition, he hesitated — or at any rate, so he told his editor, Walter Hines Page. He said — somewhat unconvincingly — that he was deep in the national parks book and hated to leave it. "I would not have gone, however tempting, were it not to visit the only part of the coast I have not seen and one of the scenes I would have to visit sometime

anyhow." To Page, as to editors since his time, the words must have had a familiar ring.

Burroughs had hesitated for different reasons. He was content at Slabsides. Why should he leave its serenity and peace just as the sun was gathering warmth and his vineyards bursting with new green? "Have I made a mistake," he wonders, "in joining this crowd for so long a trip? Can I see Nature under such conditions? But I am in for it."

Now for the first time, "the two Johns," as they came to be known, would be together day after day. The two-months voyage would at once nourish their friendship and point up the contrast between them. As they steamed up the Inside Passage, Burroughs was overawed by the spectacular scenery; when they reached what is now Muir Glacier at the head of Glacier Bay, his companion gave him a nonstop lecture on glaciers that fired his imagination. Yet what apparently moved him most among all this grandeur were the songs of birds like the golden-crowned sparrow and the Lapland longspur, the memory of which inspired some of his best-known poems. "The strange and grand scenery warms my spirit," he wrote to a young friend at Vassar, "but the air is the air of March . . . At last we have a touch of summer; flowers everywhere . . . This little forget-me-not covers the hillsides — it is bluer than your eyes." When they stopped at the Aleutian Islands, before crossing the rough Bering Sea to Siberia, Burroughs planned to quietly disembark and await the ship's return, meanwhile studying and enjoying these new surroundings on his own. But Muir caught him at the gangplank and shamed him into staying aboard.

Ten years after the Harriman Expedition, when both men were past seventy, the two Johns visited the Grand Canyon and Yosemite Valley. Again Burroughs was the greenhorn, Muir the guide. Too much of this could be irksome. Clara Barrus, who accompanied Burroughs on this trip, recalled remarking to a companion: "To think of our having the Grand Canyon, and John Burroughs and John Muir thrown in!" Burroughs overheard her. "I wish Muir *was* thrown in sometimes," he muttered, "when he gets between me and the Canyon." Muir was forever bantering, and sometimes scolding: "I puttered around here for ten years," he complained on the visit to Yosemite, "but you expect to see and do everything in four days! You come in here, then excuse yourself to God, who has kept these glories waiting for you, by saying, 'I've got to get back to Slabsides' or 'We want to go to Honolulu.' " Conversation with Muir, Burroughs later wrote in his journal, was not an exchange of ideas but "a sparring match with gads. He likes to get in the first cut and follow it up. It delights him to see you wince . . . See how tender Muir assumes to be toward the animals! Yet he likes to walk over the flesh of his fellow men with spurs in his soles . . . Muir had too much of the rough, bruising experience in his life, and I had too little. It made him callous, and it made me a tenderfoot."

But they maintained a warm friendship for the remainder of their lives. The summer following the Grand Canyon trip, Burroughs invited Muir to Slabsides. "It would all be pure pleasure, my dear Johnnie," Muir replied, "but work seems to be piling on thicker than ever." He was completing *My First Summer in the Sierra* from those notes written in his youth. (When Ellery Sedgwick, the new editor of the *Atlantic*, read the manuscript, he was ecstatic: "I felt almost as if I had found religion!") In the same letter to Burroughs Muir goes on to compliment him on a recent *Atlantic* article in terms which, unconsciously perhaps, seem a trifle patronizing: "It was splendidly written, and no doubt will be enjoyed by a wide circle of readers who are compelled to take their geology at second or third hand." Muir urges his friend — fruitlessly as it turned out — to join him on a trip to the Amazon. A year later, he writes Burroughs again: "I have never worked harder in my life, although I have not very much to show for it. I have got a volume of my autobiography finished* . . . I have been working for the last month or more on the Yosem-

---

The Story of My Boyhood and Youth. His friend E. H. Harriman had gotten him started by providing a stenographer to follow him around during a visit to Harriman Lodge, taking down his every word.

ite book, trying to finish it before leaving for the Amazon . . . I do not know what has got into me, making so many books all at once. It is not natural."

One detects a note of desperation. Muir, so indifferent to publication in his youth, now in his seventies puts on a final burst of speed, driven by awareness of his power to change public opinion before it is too late. Ellery Sedgwick was right; Muir's love of nature had the force of a religion. In contrast to the early settlers who saw themselves doing God's work in subduing the wilderness and converting the heathen, Muir was a missionary *from* the wilderness, bringing light to the benighted victims of civilization. The natural world he saw as an expression of God's power "inseparably companioned by love. Civilized man chokes his soul as the heathen Chinese their feet." During his last years he carried a double burden. Work on his books was interrupted by political battles — above all by the prolonged and bitter fight to save Hetch Hetchy. This was the beautiful valley adjacent to Yosemite which obviously belonged in the Park but which San Francisco politicians wanted to dam up, as the cheapest site for a new reservoir. "Dam Hetch Hetchy!" cried Muir. "As well dam for waterworks the people's cathedrals and churches, for no holier temple has ever been consecrated by the heart of man." But this time the people lost. "Anyhow I've done my best," he wrote to his daughter at the end of a twelve-year fight, "and am now free to go on with my pen work. The book now in hand is Alaska."

Travels in Alaska would be published posthumously. The manuscript, on which he was still working, was at his bedside when he died — on Christmas Eve, 1914. As a penniless young man he had once camped in a graveyard in Savannah, Georgia, on his thousand-mile walk to the Gulf. Gazing at the venerable live oaks, watching the flocks of butterflies, listening to the songs of hidden warblers, he felt that "on no subject are our ideas more warped and pitiable than on death. Instead of the sympathy, the friendly union of life and death so apparent in Nature, we are taught that death is an accident, a deplorable punishment for the oldest sin, the arch-enemy of life . . . But let children walk with Nature, let them see the beautiful blendings and communions of life and death, their joyous inseparable unity, as taught in woods and meadows, plains and mountains and streams of our blessed star, and they will learn that death is stingless indeed, and as beautiful as life, and that the grave has no victory, for it never fights. All is divine harmony."

Burroughs was stricken by the news. "An event that I have been expecting and dreading for more than a year," he wrote in his journal. There follows a comment that shows what an overwhelming impression Muir must have made on those who met him face to face — enough, in this case, to obscure the power of his writing. "A unique character — greater as a talker than as a writer — he loved personal combat and shone in it. He hated writing and composed with difficulty, though his books have charm of style; but his talk came easily and showed him at his best. I shall greatly miss him . . ." Blessed himself with a facile pen, Burroughs seemed momentarily unaware that writing which comes hard may be most likely to endure.

Burroughs outlived Muir by more than six years. Toward the end of his life, he made some new — and unlikely — friends. He was seventy-five years old when, to his surprise, he received a letter from Henry Ford, expressing gratitude for his books and offering to give him a Ford car as a token of esteem. The gift was not a complete success. "In driving the car in the old barn," Burroughs notes in his journal, "I get rattled and let it run wild; it bursts through the side of the barn like an explosion." However, it initiated a warm relationship which would include Ford's friends, Thomas A. Edison and Harvey Firestone. They went on luxurious auto-camping trips together, to Florida, to the Great Smoky Mountains, during the course of which Burroughs gave these industrial tycoons a personal introduction to the delights of nature, and so instilled in them some sympathy for the growing conservation movement. Ford even invited Burroughs to join the "peace ship," whose impossible mission was to stop World War I. He had the sense to refuse: "Mr. Ford's heart is bigger than his head."

Meanwhile he kept on writing for the magazines, which would take anything he submitted, be it science or philosophy or literary criticism, the song of birds or the soul of man. He had already become a "contemporary classic." Schoolbooks included his essays, and his publishers brought out a limited autographed edition of his works, in which he kept company with James Russell Lowell, Bret Harte, and Sarah Orne Jewett. He continued to produce a new book every year or two: *Time and Change*, 1912; *The Summit of the Years*, 1913; *The Breath of Life*, 1915; *Under the Apple Trees*, 1916; *Field and Study*, 1919; *Accepting the Universe*, 1920; *Under the Maples*, 1921 (the year of his death). There had even been a book *about* him, by his companion and authorized biographer, Clara Barrus, entitled *Our Friend John Burroughs*. He and his wife were on a trip with the Edisons and the Fords when he received an advance copy. He was pleased, in a quiet way, but Mrs. Burroughs reacted true to form. "She said your book made her nervous," he reports to Dr. Barrus. "It irritates her to hear me praised or made much of. She said last night: 'Do you think you deserve all that praise? If people only knew you as well as I do . . .' " Perhaps they knew him better. They had read his books, which had given them a new awareness of the world around them. In his gentle way he had enriched their lives, and they loved him for it.

Not that Burroughs was always gentle when his convictions were at stake. In attacking the "nature-fakers"* during the early years of the century, he wielded almost as heavy a club as Theodore Roosevelt. And Henry Fairfield Osborn, a close friend of Muir, described Burroughs as "an ardent and sometimes violent prophet of conservation." Burroughs himself felt somewhat guilty about not having played a more militant role in preserving the world he loved. But as Peter Wild

* See Chapter IX.

has written: * "The early activists [in the conservation movement] succeeded only because of widespread sympathy and political support from a public made aware of nature's fragility by such writers as Burroughs. That has been one of the most essential, if uncelebrated, roles in the story of protecting the environment."

Burroughs was always slightly embarrassed when his admirers referred to him as a "great naturalist." In the preface to his first book of nature essays, *Wake-Robin*, he explained that, while he had taken no liberty with the facts, he had written "less in the spirit of exact science than with the freedom of love and old acquaintance." Osborn, in summing up Burroughs' career fifty-odd years later, agreed: he was a "natural philosopher — a nature-lover more than a naturalist."

In his later years, when he was a national celebrity, Burroughs displayed an almost excessive humility about his stature as a literary figure. "I always feel a little sheepish," he wrote to a friend, "when I am much praised. I know how poor the books are." He resented being compared favorably to Henry Thoreau: "I am not worthy to tie Thoreau's shoes . . . It is more painful to me to be unjustly praised than unjustly blamed." He suffered from an almost Puritanical sense of guilt, as if success had come with too little pain. "Mine has been a selfish life — mainly because it has been hard for me to do things I do not enjoy doing." Theodore Roosevelt, however, had the last word. Dedicating one of his own outdoor books to John Burroughs, he wrote: "It is a good thing for our people that you have lived."

* In an excellent series on pioneers of American conservation, published by *High Country News*.

CHAPTER II

East Meets West:
The Yosemite Story

*"The good of going into the mountains is that life is
reconsidered."*
— Ralph Waldo Emerson, JOURNAL

Enchanted Valley
Olympic Na Park
P.B. '56

HENRY THOREAU once remarked that, when he set out on his daily walk around Concord, he naturally turned toward the west. "Eastward I go only by force; but westward I go free." For literary Easterners the vast expanses of a still unknown continent had a compelling appeal. In 1849, Francis Parkman published his famous *Oregon Trail.* Horace Greeley advised rootless young men to go west to seek their fortunes. Even that archetype of the urban bluestocking, Margaret Fuller, had ventured into the wilds of Wisconsin, alone with the Indians, and wrote enthusiastically of her adventures.

Thoreau, of course, never saw the Sierra, the "range of light," as John Muir called it. Yet he wrote in his journal: "every sunset which I witness inspires me with the desire to go to a West as distant and as fair as that into which the sun goes down." To most Americans of the mid-nineteenth century, the land beyond the Mississippi was still *terra incognita.* Exploitation of its resources had begun with the defeat of Mexico and the gold rush that followed, but esthetic appreciation of its natural wonders was still confined to a few explorers and the artists who accompanied them into the heart of the continent. For the average frontiersman, wilderness was an enemy to be conquered. The long range of the Sierra, with its precipitous eastern escarpment, was seen principally as a barrier to the riches that lay beyond.

Today, when we treasure these mountains for their own sake, we look back with gratitude to those who first took joy in them, and whose eloquent words did so much to save them for the future. To put their achievements in perspective we must recall how relatively recent, in the long history of Western civilization, is the concept that wild mountain scenery can be a source of beauty and inspiration to mankind.

From earliest times, untamed wilderness had been considered wasteland, if not positively hostile. The Greeks, with their pantheon of nature gods, nevertheless found their chief delight in the gentle face of nature, in the pastoral scene. "Every Homeric landscape intended to be beautiful," wrote

John Ruskin, "is composed of a fountain, a meadow, and a shady grove . . . Homer, living in mountainous and rocky countries, dwells delightedly on all the flat bits." So with the Romans. Horace sings the praises of his Sabine farm, but not of the mountains or the forest, which — in the succeeding centuries — became for the Christian world symbols of the sinful and the unholy. With the coming of the Renaissance these attitudes began to change; there was a new concern for the beauties of this world as well as those of the next. In the words of Havelock Ellis, "it embraced elements of the love of the wild, and these were notably shown in a new and actively adventurous love of mountains." The great change, however, was brought about by the so-called Romantic Movement of the late eighteenth century, heralded in France by Jean Jacques Rousseau and in England by the "Lake Poets." No longer was beauty to be found only in a tamed and ordered landscape; no longer could a poet like Andrew Marvell call mountains "ill-designed excrescences" or a famous writer like Madame de Staël feel obliged to draw the curtains of her carriage when she passed through the Alps. By the end of the century, Wordsworth was celebrating the rugged beauty of the English Lake Country. Shelley gazed with awe, not with repulsion, at the serene grandeur of Mont Blanc: " — I look on high;/Has some unknown omnipotence unfurled/The veil of life and death?" So might he have written of the Sierra: "Its subject mountains their unearthly forms/Pile around it, ice and rock; broad vales between/Of frozen floods, unfathomable deeps,/Blue as the overhanging heaven . . ."

In America, Ralph Waldo Emerson's first book, *Nature*, opened the way to an esthetic and even a religious delight in natural scenery. In contrast to the early churchmen, who castigated themselves for enjoying the fleeting beauties of a sinful world, ministers were not ashamed to seek inspiration in the hills. Emerson himself, as a young man, had sought the solitude of the White Mountains as he wrestled with his religious convictions; here, he knew, "the pinions of thought should be strong." These same mountains would be linked, through a unique chain of circumstances, with the literary career of a young friend of his, a Universalist minister in Boston named Thomas Starr King, author of the first book fully to appreciate the White Mountains, and of a series of articles that for most Easterners first put Yosemite Valley on the map, nine years before John Muir laid eyes on it.

"Boston is in full bloom intellectually," wrote King to a friend in 1857. "Whipple is lecturing twice a week on the literary men of Shakespeare's time . . . Emerson also lectures on Wednesday evenings . . . Beecher is to be here . . . And we have been enjoying great music. Moreover, I am working hard on my White Mountain book." Starr King — as he is generally known — was himself one of the sturdiest and most fascinating flowers in this garden of intellectual delights: a charismatic figure who in his short, intense life introduced thousands of Americans still oriented toward Europe to the beauties of their own land, East and West.

Born in 1824, the son of a Universalist clergyman, King became the sole support of his family at the age of fifteen. Harvard College, seedbed of Boston intellectuals, was not for him.* Schoolteaching and a variety of jobs kept him going while he applied his brilliant mind to educating himself, with a view to the ministry. By the age of twenty, through the efforts of the famous radical preacher Theodore Parker, he had his first parish. Soon Parker was referring to him as the best preacher in Boston. Lyceum audiences loved him. Described as "a diminutive, unhandsome young man with long, lank hair and the luminous eyes of a spaniel," blessed with a "manly and sonorous voice," he charmed everyone — including Emerson and the literary establishment — with his humor, his happy disposition, and the sheer force of his personality. He took no one too seriously, including himself. "Alcott comes to see me often, and we have gloriously muddy talks. He thinks I am a splendid fellow, and the way I pour mysticism into him is a caution."

* Harvard later awarded him an honorary A.M.

Along with these transcendental pursuits went a passion for natural scenery, dating perhaps from his first experience of New Hampshire's White Mountains, at the age of thirteen. For King, as for Emerson and Thoreau, nature was a continual revelation of God. In the summer of 1854, on the way to Dixville Notch with the publisher James T. Fields, he read an advance copy of *Walden*. He was disappointed in the opening chapters, "but the latter half is wonderful . . . the 'Conclusion' being more weird and winding farther into the awful vitalities of nature than any writing I have yet seen . . ."

As he continued to explore the White Mountains, King began a series of articles for the Boston *Evening Transcript*, which became the basis of his only book, *The White Hills*, published in 1859.* His purpose was a good deal less ambitious than Thoreau's. "The object of this volume," he writes in the preface, "is to direct attention to the noble landscapes that lie along the routes by which the White Mountains are now approached by tourists . . . to help persons appreciate landscape more adequately; and to associate with the principal scenes poetic passages which illustrate, either the permanent character of the view, or some peculiar aspects in which the author of the books has seen them." His aim was to do for mountain tourists what Thomas Wentworth Higginson, in an anthology entitled *Thalatta*, had done for visitors to the seashore.

King grew up in the romantic period of the "Hudson River School." It was an age when the beauties of nature were appreciated in terms of the "picturesque"; then, following Ruskin, natural scenery was judged according to the rules of art. God's work sometimes lacked perfection. "If we had full power over the scenery near the highest range to alter or amend it," writes King of a choice White Mountain view, "we should order a lake to appear forthwith in 'The Glen.' " King was quite frankly — in the term Emerson applied scornfully

---

* In 1962 John A. Hussey edited a collection of King's letters from Yosemite, entitled *A Vacation among the Sierras*.

to Wordsworth — a "view-hunter." And his urge to share with others his own joy in the mountains could make him didactic, as when he instructs visitors in "all the emotions they ought to feel and all the imaginations they ought to shape, in viewing magnificent scenery." But in fact he imposes himself very little on his reader. *The White Hills* is the most charming of guidebooks, full of information, bursting with enthusiasm. The first of its kind, it established its young author as a leading authority on appreciation of wild nature.

No sooner had *The White Hills* been published than King decided, to the despair of his friends and devoted parishioners, to accept a call to the new and struggling Unitarian Church in San Francisco. "I do think," he wrote to a friend, "we are unfaithful in huddling so closely around the cosy stove of civilization in this blessed Boston, and I, for one, am ready to go out into the cold and see if I am good for anything." He intended to stay for two years at the most, but he remained in the West for the rest of his brief life.

So began a new career in public affairs which would make Starr King, by the time he died at the age of forty, a hero in his adopted state of California. An ardent abolitionist, he did not hesitate to use his gifts as preacher and orator to help save the state for the Union. Fortunately he still found time for the mountains. He had already heard of the glories of the Sierra, which he yearned to compare with his beloved White Hills. His opportunity came when some of his new San Francisco friends told him of the wonders said to exist in the valley of the Merced River, called "Yo Semite" (the Indian name for grizzly bear, applied to the local tribe because of its ferocity). In mid-July of 1860 he and four companions set out on a ten-day journey through rugged country best known to the gold miners of the Sierra foothills and volunteer troops engaged in subduing the Indians. Yosemite Valley itself — where ten thousand visitors now camp on a summer's day — had been discovered by a military battalion in 1851. Four years later the first sightseers had entered the valley and their leader, James Mason Hutchings, had publicized it in his *California* magazine. A primitive hotel had been erected shortly before King arrived. Horace Greeley had paused briefly in Yosemite Valley on his way west and had described its wonders in articles for the New York *Tribune*, later published as *An Overland Journey*. King himself had in mind something different: a series of long letters to the *Transcript*, similar to those he had written on the White Mountains, but devoted solely to the Yosemite trip. His already established reputation as an authority on mountain scenery assured him of a wide readership in the East, and he gave his readers full measure — by modern standards a bit too full and overflowing, perhaps, but intoxicating in its superlatives, in its evocation of scenes scarcely imaginable to eastern eyes.

King's narrative starts out at a leisurely pace, informal and chatty, but when he gets among the towering sugar pines and the gigantic redwoods, as he looks up at Yosemite Falls and El Capitan, he is overwhelmed. Scraps of poetry and classical allusions mingle with awesome statistics. Remembering his Boston readers, he describes trees "in whose trunk Bunker Hill monument could have been inserted and hidden, while the stem would still spring more than two hundred feet above its apex-stone." After giving us guidebook measurements of Yosemite Falls, he paints a word picture as best he can, aware that "there has been a deal of mighty rhetoric born in California from the Yo-Semite and its wonders. The cataracts are responsible for much more spouting than is seen":

It is the upper and highest cataract that is most wonderful to the eye, as well as most musical. The cliff is so sheer that there is no break in the body of the water during the whole of its descent of more than a quarter of a mile. It pours in a curve from the summit, fifteen hundred feet, (the height of six Park street spires, remember,) to the basin that hoards it but a moment for the cascades that follow. And what endless complexities and opulence of beauty in the forms and motions of the cataract! It is comparatively narrow at the top of the precipice, although as we said, the tide that pours over is thirty-five feet broad. But it widens as it descends, and curves a little on one side as it widens, so that it shapes itself, before it reaches its first bowl of granite, into the figure of the comet that glowed on our sky two years ago.

Back in New England the *Transcript* articles, published in late 1860 and early 1861, brought letters of congratulation from both Oliver Wendell Holmes and John Greenleaf Whittier. King hoped someday to write a book on the Sierras, a companion volume to *The White Hills* (he said he was glad he had used the word "hills"). Meanwhile, on summer holidays and lecture tours, he and his wife traveled to "all sorts of places where hardship is to be experienced and good scenery to be found": to northern California, to the Columbia River, to the Cascade Mountains, and Vancouver Island, providing more material for the ever-eager *Transcript*.

King had been overworked almost from the day he reached San Francisco — as indeed he had been in Boston. Early in 1864 he died of a sudden illness, brought on by exhaustion. The California legislature declared a statewide period of mourning. Appropriately, a statue by Boston's Daniel Chester French was erected in San Francisco's Golden Gate Park. Peaks were named for him in the White Mountains and the

Sierra Nevada. King was no great writer, and it is not principally for his writings that Californians remember him. But, as John A. Hussey remarks in his introduction to a volume of the *Transcript* letters, "his narrative marked a milestone in Yosemite literature because of his ability to make others visualize the scenes described and because of his already established reputation as a nature writer. If the naturalists who interpret our nation's great scenic parks have learned anything from years of dealing with the public, it is that there are many persons who must be told that a view is beautiful before they will be impressed." Starr King, wrote the editor of the San Francisco *Evening Bulletin*, "had made the White Mountains classical." So when he described the beauties of the western ranges, New Englanders listened. "No one had really seen the Sierra Nevada, Mt. Shasta, the Yo Semite Valley, or the coast of Oregon and the region of Mt. Hood," wrote his friend Henry W. Bellows, "until his fine eye saw and his cunning brain and hand depicted them."

On June 25, 1864, only a few months after Starr King's death, Yosemite Valley and Mariposa Grove were set aside by an Act of Congress for "public use, resort and recreation . . . inalienable for all time." It was the first such act in our history.

😇

For at least three reasons, the name of King will always be associated with the Sierra Nevada. Starr King is one. Another is the King's River, from the Spanish *el Rio de los Santos Reyes*, the River of the Holy Kings. (King's Canyon is now a national park.) But for historians of the West, the magic name is that of a geologist, mountaineer, and writer whom Henry Adams considered to be "the most remarkable man of our time": Clarence King.

Born in Newport, Rhode Island, in 1842, eighteen years after his Boston namesake (they were not related), Clarence King came of a distinguished family which had won and lost a fortune in the China trade. As a young man he was aware that he was growing up in a period of transition, of revolutionary ideas about man's place in the cosmos: "We stand on the greatest dividing line since the birth of the Christian era." Rejecting the archaic classical education offered by Yale College — which he later described as a calamity for "a young man born with a talent for literature" — he took a two-year course at Yale's newly founded Scientific School. Here, as at Harvard before the advent of Louis Agassiz, science was yet to be considered a part of a college education. But King himself saw no conflict between what, in our time, has been called "the two cultures." As a schoolboy he had acquired a passionate interest in nature and the out-of-doors, in plants and rocks and fossils. At Yale he studied under James Dwight Dana, whose classic *Manual of Geology* was about to appear; he read John Tyndall's great work on the Alpine glaciers and went up to Cambridge to hear Louis Agassiz lecture. In the midst of this torrent of new scientific thought he discovered, with a joyful sense of recognition, the writings of an English esthete with a romantic feeling for nature, John Ruskin.

"Ruskin alone," King wrote later, "among prose writers on the Alps, re-echoes the dim past in ever-recurring myth-making, over cloud and peak and glacier . . . To follow a chapter of Ruskin's by one of Tyndall's is to bridge forty centuries and realize the full contrast of archaic and modern thought." King had the rare gift of uniting the two. Scientifically trained, he would become a superb field geologist, an expert in mapping the mountains, a wizard in interpreting the story of the rocks. Yet at the same time he saw nature, as Ruskin did, with a poet's and painter's eye; he "fitted into the ways of thinking of artists," as John LaFarge would later put it.

Clarence King's initial acquaintance with the mountains had been largely through books. He had done some local geologizing, such as field trips in the Hudson River Valley, but the more he read, the more his thoughts turned to the West. Unlike Henry Thoreau, he was in a position to give substance to his dreams. During his last year at Yale, he had read with intense excitement a letter from Professor William H. Brewer of the California Geological Survey describing an ascent of Mount Shasta. This was enough to set him off. In the spring of 1863, a few months after his twenty-first birthday, King and two young companions started out on an adventurous journey by rail and mule train and horseback to California, armed with letters of introduction to the men in the field. In San Francisco they met Brewer, as well as Josiah Dwight Whitney, head of the Survey, who impressed them as being of even "heavier calibre than Agassiz" — and for whom they would one day name the highest mountain south of Alaska. With Brewer, King climbed Lassen's Peak in northern California. His biographer, Thurman Wilkins, describes the scene. "A raw wind howled across the mountain during their first ascent, on September 26th. King reached the topmost shaft, only to be blown back by the gale. Clouds obscured the landscape below, defeating the purpose of the climb. But Mount Shasta, seventy-five miles away, loomed from the mists, sharp and majestic — the peak which had drawn King like a magnet. He shouted to Brewer above the wailing of the wind: 'What would Ruskin have said if he had seen *this!*' "

If Clarence King had any doubts about his calling, that day dispelled them. The following spring found him again with Brewer, engaged in the first of a series of expeditions charged with the Herculean task of surveying the High Sierra and so filling in a vast blank area on the map of California. King had already seen and wondered at these mountains from a distance: "Of their great height I was fully persuaded; and Professor Whitney, on the strength of these few observations, commissioned us to explore and survey the new Alps." * From these youthful adventures he drew the material for *Mountaineering in the Sierra Nevada*, which remains a classic account of man's reaction to nature.

In 1869 James T. Fields, editor of the *Atlantic Monthly*, heard King describe his adventures at a social gathering and

* The term "American Alps" is now generally applied to the North Cascades.

was so impressed that he promptly commissioned a series of articles for the magazine, to be published later as a book. *Mountaineering*, dedicated to Professor Whitney and the Geological Survey, appeared in 1872, the same year as Mark Twain's *Roughing It*. The publication of these two books, in the words of Wallace Stegner, "represents the high-water mark of frontier literature that belongs properly to belles-lettres." (John Muir also began that year to publish his Sierra experiences in Bret Harte's *Overland Magazine;* but his first book, *The Mountains of California*, was still more than two decades away.)

King once referred to *Mountaineering* as "a slight book of travel," but this was doubtless a graceful show of modesty. It is more than an account of high adventure. It is a work of literature, written with grace and humor, full of glowing descriptions of wild nature and mountain scenery that have been matched only by John Muir. In retrospect, William Dean Howells thought King worthy to be compared with John Burroughs for "the charm of his science." (An odd equation of opposites.) Reviewing *Mountaineering*, he wrote: "The light, the

color, the vastness of that sky and earth, which seem another sky and earth from ours, have transferred themselves to Mr. King's page with a freshness and force that give us a new sense of the value of descriptive writing." Critics generally agreed that Clarence King, a hitherto unknown geologist, had produced "the first real literature of the Sierra."

Mountaineering is the work of a romantic, courageous, and self-confident young man for whom the apparently impossible was merely a welcome challenge. Granted that he was given to exaggeration, and willing to embroider a bit to make a good story, the account of his daredevil climbs, such as the ascent of the peak he christened Mount Tyndall, are vivid enough to give the reader vertigo, and bearable only because one knows the writer lived to describe them.* Yet beyond the thrill of the adventure itself one senses an almost mystical exaltation. As he struggles along the ridge below Mount Tyndall he gazes up at "cliff above cliff, precipice piled upon precipice . . . culminating in a noble pile of Gothic-finished granite and enamel-like snow. How grand and inviting looked its white form, its untrodden, unknown crest, so high and pure in the clear strong blue! I looked at it as one contemplating the purpose of his life; and for just one moment I would have rather liked to dodge that purpose, or to have waited, or have found some excellent reason why I might not go; but all this quickly vanished, leaving a cheerful resolve to go ahead." At the end of a long day's climb, he and his companion made camp by a mountain tarn amid "fields of alpine grass, pale yet sunny, soft under our feet, fragrantly jewelled with flowers of fairy delicacy, holding up amid thickly clustered blades chalices of turquoise and amythyst, white stars, and fiery little globes of red . . . After the stern grandeur of granite and ice, and with the peaks and walls still in view, it was a relief to find our-

---

* John Muir, however, was not impressed: "He must have given himself a lot of trouble. When I climbed Tyndall, I ran up and back before breakfast." But even granting Muir some poetic license, it seems clear that he was mistaken about the identity of Mt. Tyndall, as Francis P. Farquhar points out (*History of the Sierra Nevada*, p. 172).

selves again in the region of life. I never felt for trees and flowers such a sense of intimate relationship and sympathy."

When at last they reached the summit, King, for all his joy in wild nature, was overwhelmed by the stark, cold grandeur of a world where there seems no place for man:

There is no sentiment of beauty in the whole scene; no suggestion, however far remote, of sheltered landscape; not even the air of virgin hospitality that greets us explorers in so many uninhabited spots which by their fertility and loveliness of grove or meadow seem to offer man a home, or us nomads a pleasant camp-ground. Silence and desolation are the themes which nature has wrought out under this eternally serious sky . . . I have never seen Nature when she seemed so little "Mother Nature" as in this place of rocks and snow, echoes and emptiness.

Like other mountaineers before him, he found contact with the human world in the natural architecture of the rocks:

As I sat on Mount Tyndall, the whole mountains shaped themselves like the ruins of cathedrals, — sharp roof-ridges, pinnacled and statued; buttresses more spired and ornamented than Milan's; receding doorways with pointed arches carved into blank facades of granite, doors never to be opened, innumerable jutting points with here and there a single cruciform peak, its frozen roof and granite spires so strikingly Gothic I cannot doubt that the Alps furnished the models for early cathedrals of that order.

In page after page of *Mountaineering* one senses the contrast — if not the actual conflict — between the scientist's and the artist's view of the universe, between Tyndall and Ruskin. Of a later expedition King wrote:

I was delighted to ride thus alone, and expose myself, as one uncovers a sensitized photographic plate, to be influenced; for this is a respite from scientific work, when through months you hold yourself accountable for seeing everything, for analyzing, for instituting perpetual comparison, and as it were sharing in the administering of the physical world. No tongue can tell the relief to simply withdraw scientific observation, and let Nature impress you in the dear old way with all her mystery and glory, with those vague indescribable emotions which tremble between wonder and sympathy.

Yet the scientist was always present. On a mission to Yosemite in the autumn of 1864 (four years after Starr King's visit) to survey the boundaries of the newly created park, he watched the falls in spate during a violent storm, when gusts of wind would swing "the whole mighty cataract like a pendulum . . . would gather up the whole fall in mid-air, whirl it in a festoon, and carry it back over the very summit of the walls." In the midst of all this, he "got out the theodolite to measure the angle of its deflection."

Clarence King's adventures in the High Sierra were but the prelude to a precocious scientific and administrative career. When only twenty-five he persuaded the federal government to launch the most important scientific expedition of his generation: a survey of the so-called Great American Desert along the fortieth parallel between the Rockies and the Sierra — with himself, naturally, in charge. His technical study, entitled *Systematic Geology*, marked a high point in government scientific publications.* But alas he never wrote a popular account of this pioneering expedition along the future route of the transcontinental railroad. *Mountaineering* remains his only book for the general reader, for the growing number of nature lovers who were responding to the gentle essays of Burroughs and who would soon be reading Muir. Like other brilliant persons before and since, King apparently

---

* In the words of Henry Adams, King "was creating one of the classic scientific works of the century." The two young men first met in the summer of 1871 when Adams, then editor of the *North American Review*, joined a field trip to the Rocky Mountains as a guest of the Fortieth Parallel Survey. They fell into each other's arms. "King had everything to interest and delight Adams. He knew more than Adams did of art and poetry; he knew America, especially west of the hundredth meridian, better than any one . . . He knew even women; even the American woman; even the New York woman, which is saying much" (*The Education of Henry Adams*). Soon thereafter, in Washington, D.C., King became an intimate friend of the Adamses and the John Hays, the fifth member of a brilliant group of conversationalists that called itself "The Five of Hearts."

spoke even better than he wrote; those who heard him in New York's Century Club — which published a memorial volume after his death in 1901 — considered him one of the great raconteurs of his time. But unlike Burroughs, who wrote almost too easily, or Muir, who drove himself with a missionary's zeal to get his message on paper, King talked away the books he might have written. With his wit, his charm, his zest for life, he became a sort of romantic hero to Henry Adams and the intellectuals of the Adams circle. Eventually, however, the Panic of 1893 and the subsequent collapse of his financial enterprises led to a nervous breakdown and the untimely end of a spectacular career. For Adams, he was always "young and bloomful . . . He remained the best companion in the world to the end."

ಔ

When Clarence King, in the autumn of 1864, undertook to survey the boundaries of the newborn Yosemite Park, he did not know that the man who gave him the assignment would have a unique influence in shaping the American landscape. Frederick Law Olmsted, an ardent advocate of both city parks and wilderness preservation, was chairman of the first board of Yosemite Valley Commissioners. A forty-two-year-old New Englander, he was a pioneer in the — for America — new profession of "landscape architecture." The previous year, owing to a disagreement with the city authorities, he had interrupted the monumental task of creating Central Park in New York to take over the management of the Mariposa Estate, General Frémont's huge gold-mining property that King had been studying for the Geological Survey, and from which he had had his first close view of the peaks he was soon to climb. Thus, through a happy accident of geography, Olmsted had come to know the Yosemite country at the precise moment in history when his leadership was most needed to ensure its preservation.

Olmsted was a complex character: a man with the imagination and sensitivity of an artist and the iron will of an executive; an idealist, a perfectionist with a driving social conscience who nevertheless remained uncertain for many years about the choice of a career. Born in Hartford in 1822, he came of Puritan stock, dating back to the early days of the Bay Colony and the founding of Connecticut; his forebears were simple people, seafarers, farmers. Fortunately his father had an innate love of nature, which expressed itself in family excursions through the Connecticut River Valley, the White Mountains, and along the coast of Maine; to Lake George and the Hudson; to Quebec and Niagara Falls. These vacation trips sharpened young Olmsted's powers of observation. They gave him a feeling for rural scenery and a firsthand acquaintance with agricultural practices, which he put to good use when, at the age of twenty-six, he took up scientific farming on Staten Island. And out of this experience grew his second career, that of writer. He began with a series of articles on American farming and later, after a summer's study abroad, he wrote *Walks and Talks of an American Farmer in England*. This, his first book, reflects his almost passionate response to the English countryside — "green, dripping, glistening, gorgeous." It also recognizes the close bond between landscape design and the other arts and foreshadows his own life work: "Probably there is no object of art that Americans of cultivated taste generally more long to see in Europe, than an English park. What artist, so noble, has often been my thought, as he, who with far-reaching conception of beauty and designing power, sketches the outline, writes the colours, and directs the shadows of a picture so great that Nature shall be employed upon it for generations, before the work he has arranged for her shall realize his intentions." In another passage Olmsted makes the distinction between two equally valid approaches to the appreciation of nature: the joy in pure wildness on the one hand and, on the other, the age-old love of the pastoral scene. "The sublime or the picturesque in nature is much more rare in England, except on the sea-coast, than in America; but there is everywhere a great deal of quiet, peaceful, graceful beauty which the works of man have generally added to, and which I remember but little like at home." In other words, wild scenery such as Yosemite and, in contrast, the sort of thing that he would seek to create in Central Park.

For a time it seemed as if he would become a professional writer. Shortly after *Walks and Talks* was published, he was commissioned by the *New York Times* to produce a series of articles on conditions in the slave states. These essays (in the words of Arthur M. Schlesinger) "present a uniquely candid and realistic picture of the pre–Civil War South." They became the basis for *The Cotton Kingdom*, published in 1861. By now he was "a recognized litterateur" both at home and abroad. Ironically, this distinction all but lost him the great chance of his life, which led to his final decision on a career. When the New York State legislature — prodded by William Cullen Bryant and the famous landscape gardener, Andrew Jackson Downing — authorized the establishment of Central Park, Olmsted, with his experience in land use and his familiarity with the parks of Europe, was the obvious choice for superintendent. The commissioners, however, questioned whether a literary man could also be "practical." Despite this, he got the job, thanks to the backing of Bryant and of a number of prominent citizens, including Washington Irving, Asa Gray, Horace Greeley, Bayard Taylor, and the artist Albert Bierstadt. Today when we look back on his amazing accomplishments in shaping and refining not only the land itself, but also the American public's attitude toward it, we realize that his gift for words was one of his greatest assets.

Shortly after the outbreak of war, Olmsted was appointed director of the United States Sanitary Commission, predecessor of the American Red Cross, an appallingly difficult job that he handled with distinction, and that all but ruined his health. In 1863, when he resigned and went west to take over Mariposa, he met Starr King, head of the California Commission (who doubtless told him something of the glories of Yosemite). At about this time, Charles Eliot Norton described his appearance in a letter to a friend: "All the lines of his face imply refinement and sensibility to such a degree that it is not till one has looked through them to what is beneath, that the force of his will and the reserved power of his character become evident." He had already shown these qualities in his government service and in cutting his way through the political thickets that had blocked the establishment of Central Park (a struggle to which he would presently return). He would show them again as he planned the future of Yosemite.

In the summer of 1864, accompanied by his family and a group of friends, Olmsted got his first view of the Valley. En route the party explored the Mariposa Big Trees and enjoyed a visit from Clarence King, just back from the high country, who "spent several days in camp squiring the ladies on rides and entertaining them with stories of his adventures."* When at length they reached the Valley itself, the impact was overwhelming:

There are falls of water elsewhere finer, there are more stupendous rocks, more beetling cliffs, there are deeper and more awful chasms, there may be as beautiful streams, as lovely meadows, there are larger trees. It is in no scene or scenes the charm consists, but in the miles of scenery where cliffs of awful height and rocks of vast magnitude and of varied and exquisite coloring, are banked and fringed and draped and shadowed by the tender foliage of noble and lovely trees and bushes, reflected from the most placid pools, and associated with the most tranquil meadows, the most playful streams, and every variety of soft and peaceful pastoral beauty.

The union of the deepest sublimity with the deepest beauty of nature, not in one feature or another, not in one part or one scene or another, not in any landscape that can be framed by itself, but all around and wherever the visitor goes, constitutes the Yo Semite, the greatest glory of nature.

After leaving the Valley, Olmsted joined Professor William

* Laura Wood Roper, *FLO: A Biography of Frederick Law Olmsted* (1963). Another distinguished visitor that summer was Olmsted's friend and enthusiastic supporter, Henry Whitney Bellows, who wrote an article for the *Atlantic Monthly* on the progress of Central Park. A popular Unitarian minister, he was temporarily filling the pulpit left open by the tragic death of Starr King. (See p. 42.)

H. Brewer, recently returned from leading the Geological Survey expedition that Clarence King describes so dramatically in *Mountaineering in the High Sierra*. Together they climbed among the high peaks, which impressed Olmsted as they had King with their variety of form: "some being of grand simplicity, while others are pinnacled, columnar, castellated and fantastic." In all his travels, this was the most awesome scenery he had ever encountered.

Olmsted's concern with the influence of the natural scene on the mind of man went very deep. He had always been aware of the limited power of words to convey the total impact of a beautiful landscape. On his walking trip in England, he had made precisely the same observation that he would reiterate twelve years later in his report on Yosemite. "Beauty, grandeur, impressiveness in any way, from scenery," he had written in *An American Farmer*, "is not often to be found in a few prominent, distinguishable features, but in the manner and the unobserved materials with which these are connected and combined. Clouds, lights, states of the atmosphere, and circumstances that we cannot always detect, affect all landscapes . . ." This last comment is particularly true, perhaps, of mountain scenery such as he encountered in the Sierras, where the timeless and the ephemeral are so closely wedded.*

His approach to landscape, however, was not purely esthetic. Everything he had set his hand to — scientific farming, the study of the South under slavery, the Sanitary Commission — was directly concerned with human welfare. So in his official report on the preservation of Yosemite for public purposes he writes: "If we analyze the operation of scenes of beauty upon the mind, and consider the intimate relation of the mind upon the nervous system and the whole physical economy, the action and reaction which constantly occur between bodily and mental conditions, the reinvigoration which results from such scenes is readily comprehended."

* Olmsted's comment is beautifully illustrated in the great photographs of Yosemite and the Sierra by Ansel Adams.

The great virtue of natural scenery, the secret of its restorative powers, lies in the fact that it is divorced from any utilitarian purpose, from any future goal:

> It is for itself and at the moment it is enjoyed. The attention is aroused and the mind occupied without purpose, without a continuation of the common process of relating the present act or thought or perception to some future end. There is nothing else that has this quality so purely. There are few entertainments with which regard for something outside and beyond the enjoyment of the moment can ordinarily be little mixed . . . In all social pleasures and all pleasures which are usually enjoyed in association with the social pleasures, the care for the opinion of others, or the ideas of others largely mingles. In the pleasures of literature the laying up of ideas and self-improvement are purposes which cannot be kept out of view.
> This, however, is in very slight degree, if at all, the case with the enjoyment of the emotions caused by natural scenery. It therefore results that the enjoyment of scenery employs the mind without fatigue and yet exercises it; tranquillizes it and yet enlivens it; and thus, through the influence of the mind over the body, gives the effect of refreshing rest and reinvigoration to the whole system.

Olmsted also looked upon the Yosemite reserve as "a museum of natural science" in which, for example, rare species of plants endangered by the invasion of exotics would be protected — thus anticipating the current view of our parks and wilderness areas as "living museums." The point is worth stressing, since it is often said that the first two parks, Yosemite and Yellowstone, were established for the sake of their "natural curiosities" rather than to save wilderness as such. True, this was the main motivation, but in the case of Yosemite it was by no means the only one.

As a young man, Olmsted's pleasure in the splendid private parks of England had been tempered by the realization that they could be enjoyed only by the rich and powerful, a minute proportion of the population. The great mass of society, including those who would most benefit from them, were excluded. He was determined that this should not happen in America. In granting Yosemite Valley and the Mariposa Big

Trees to the state of California, the United States Congress had stipulated that "the premises shall be held for public use, resort, and recreation, and shall be inalienable for all time." Thus a precedent was set for the founding of the first national park, Yellowstone, eight years later, and eventually for the whole national park system.

Olmsted was ahead of his time in recognizing man's joy in nature as an integral part of his culture, comparable to his appreciation of art or literature or music. "The power of scenery to affect men is, in a large way, proportionate to their civilization and the degree to which their taste has been cultivated." This does not mean, however, that such an esthetic experience need be confined to the privileged few. On the contrary, he shares the prediction of the great authority on landscape gardening, "the revered [Andrew Jackson] Downing" that the day would come when those who "have no faith in the refinement of a republic will stand abashed before a whole people whose system of voluntary education embraces . . . common enjoyments for all classes in the higher realms of art, letters, science, social recreation and enjoyments." Downing was employing the word "recreation" in its root sense of "re-creation," as was Olmsted later when he sought to save islands of tranquillity in urban areas for what he called "passive recreation" — a term widely used today in land-use planning.

Olmsted was an idealist who dreamed of a harmonious relation between man and nature that has yet to be realized. "The essence of Olmsted's theory of environmental planning," writes Albert Fein, "was a reverence for the fundamental characteristics of all living matter . . . If ecological laws were violated, there was little hope for social planning based on a belief in a rational relationship between human beings and the physical environment." It is not surprising that Olmsted should have been an ardent admirer of Charles Darwin — who, incidentally, had praised his writings on the prewar South, and who later became a personal friend. In establishing the importance of the environment in the development of all living creatures, *The Origin of Species* gave scientific support to Olmsted's own philosophy of life. Unfortunately Darwin's theories were soon to be perverted by Herbert Spencer, who coined the term "survival of the fittest" and became the father of "social Darwinism" — a devil-take-the-hindmost theory completely at variance with Olmsted's concern for the common man which he had expressed so eloquently in the report on Yosemite, and which remained his guiding principle throughout his life.

Olmsted was not primarily a writer; his extraordinary accomplishments are to be read in the landscape itself, in the parks he designed from coast to coast, rather than on the printed page. Yet few writers have had a more sensitive response to nature, or held to their beliefs with a fiercer conviction. In 1890, when Yosemite Valley and the surrounding high country finally were made a national park after years of mismanagement and neglect by the state of California,* he wrote a pamphlet on *Governmental Preservation of Natural Scenery*, in which he looked back across a quarter of a century to an experience that the hurried tourist could never know. There is an almost religious quality in his growing love for the Valley, his discovery of new levels of beauty and meaning on each visit, his sadness at departing with so much still beyond his grasp. For Olmsted, landscape — be it the Sierra or Niagara Falls or Yellowstone or any "natural wonder" — was no mere spectacle, to be gaped at and checked off in the guidebook:

The distinctive charm of the scenery of the Yosemite does not depend, as it is a vulgar blunder to suppose, on the greatness of its walls and the length of its little early summer cascades; the height of certain of its trees, the reflections in its pools, and such other matters as can be entered in statistical tables, pointed out by guides and represented within picture frames. So far, perhaps, as it can be told in a few words, it lies in the rare association with the grandeur of its rocky elements, of brooks flowing quietly through the ferny and bosky glades of very beautifully disposed great bodies, groups, and

* See p. 23.

clusters of trees . . . I felt the charm of the Yosemite much more at the end of a week than at the end of a day, much more after six weeks when the cascades were nearly dry, than after one week, and when, after having been in it, off and on, several months, I was going out, I said, "I have not yet half taken it in."

In the decade following the cession of Yosemite Valley to the state of California, its fame spread rapidly throughout the country. In 1866 there appeared a charming travel book by Samuel Bowles of the Springfield (Massachusetts) *Republican*, who had visited the Valley with Olmsted and a large party the previous summer, and who subsequently became one of his warmest friends and supporters. Bowles' reaction to such scenery was one of inexpressible awe: "The Yosemite!" he begins. "As well interpret God in thirty-nine articles as portray it to you by word of mouth or pen." But he goes on to do his best, with considerable success, and moreover has the foresight to recognize in the saving of Yosemite a precedent for similar action elsewhere: Niagara Falls, the Adirondacks, the Maine Woods.

The main event of this period, in the light of Yosemite's future, occurred with no fanfare whatever. This was the meeting — described earlier — between John Muir and Robert Underwood Johnson, *Century* magazine's crusading conservationist, which led to the founding of Yosemite National Park (and indirectly to Sequoia and General Grant national parks as well). There have been few clearer illustrations of the power of the printed word.

However, the last word had yet to be spoken. The national park, created by Congress in 1890, did not include the Valley itself, which still belonged to the state of California. In the early nineteen-hundreds the Sierra Club, led by Muir and its dynamic secretary, William E. Colby, launched an all-out drive on the state legislature to re-cede Yosemite Valley to the federal government. The timing was good. Muir's book, *Our National Parks*, had engendered widespread support for the national park movement. And in the spring of 1903 President Roosevelt invited Muir to guide him through the Valley. The result was the famous trip when the two of them escaped all the elaborate ceremonies planned in the President's honor and went off to camp by themselves, spending one night tentless in a snowstorm, and another beneath the great rock face of El Capitan. "Just what I wanted!" cried Roosevelt. "This has been the grandest day in my life!" From then on, there was no doubt in the President's mind that Yosemite Valley should belong to the nation.

Thanks to Muir's friendship with E. H. Harriman, president of the Southern Pacific Railroad (and leader of the 1899 Harriman Expedition), the powerful railroad lobby went into action, and the California legislature passed the bill for re-cession by a single vote. "I am now an experienced lobbyist," wrote Muir to Johnson. "My political education is complete." Finally, with the backing of Theodore Roosevelt, the Valley was incorporated into the park by Act of Congress, and Yosemite National Park as we know it today was complete.

CHAPTER III

The Gentle Art of Seeing

"Sight is a faculty; seeing, an art."
— George Perkins Marsh, MAN AND NATURE

"**N**O BOOKS are less dazzling or more immortal than those whose theme is external Nature. Nothing wears so well." Thomas Wentworth Higginson, in 1864, was writing in the *Atlantic Monthly* about his late friend, Henry Thoreau. The same might be said, to a lesser degree, of his own nature essays. Or, for that matter, of two other authors of the Civil War period whose nature writing, though no longer well known, has worn very well indeed: Wilson Flagg — another early contributor to the *Atlantic* — and, far away in the South, a passionate young poet and musician named Sidney Lanier. Obviously none of them ranks with Thoreau, and in the case of Higginson and Lanier — even to some extent of Flagg — nature writing was only one aspect of a varied literary career. This, in a way, was probably a good thing. They were widely read because they knew how to write; thanks to their established literary reputations, they reached many readers hitherto indifferent to the world of nature. A reader of Flagg's books (in the words of a contemporary naturalist) "begins to discover, if he has not before known it, how large a world lies about him, through which he passes almost with closed eyes."

These early writers deserve more credit than they generally get. "As a genre, the nature essay has been surprisingly undeveloped," one reads in a standard literary history of the United States. Burroughs and Muir are cited, together with a handful of later writers. True, "the two Johns" gave a new stature to this literary form. But they did not invent it. Nature essays had been appearing regularly in American periodicals during the early years of the century, and collections of them had been published in book form. They had been a feature of the *Atlantic* since its founding in 1857. Its editor, James Russell Lowell, had written about nature himself and he welcomed contributions in this field. Thanks to Emerson, he got Thoreau's essay on the Maine woods to lead off the June 1858 issue.* Later in the same year, he printed Flagg's "The Sing-

---

* Unfortunately Lowell deleted a sentence from this article, against the au-

ing Birds and Their Songs" and Higginson's "Water Lilies." Thereafter for many decades not only the *Atlantic* but other periodicals, ranging from *Putnam's Monthly Magazine of Literature, Science and Art* to the down-to-earth *New England Farmer*, regularly published articles on the joys of nature, many of them overly literary and mannered by today's standards but nonetheless packed with sound information.

༜

"Imagine an amiable Thoreau, if you can," wrote Thomas Bailey Aldrich, reviewing Wilson Flagg's *The Woods and By-Ways of New England.* Born in Beverly, Massachusetts, in 1805 — two years after Emerson — descendant of an old colonial family, Flagg must have been a singularly appealing character. "His interest in natural history," writes Van Wyck Brooks, "was awakened at the age of eight, on driving from Beverly to lower New Hampshire, through the 'Dark Plains,' a tract of sandy country that was covered with a primitive growth of pines and hemlocks, such as later existed only in northern Maine. The music of these woods, their darkness and silence, their echoes and their solitude and vastness caused in the boy what he called a religious conversion." As a young man, he seems to have had a hard time choosing a career. After studying at the Harvard Medical School (he never practiced), he worked as an insurance agent and as a clerk in the Boston customshouse. He wrote a number of books, including *Analysis of Female Beauty,* and a political satire reminiscent of Alexander Pope. But his true love was nature writing, and his wilderness travels would take him as far south as the great hardwood forests of Virginia and Tennessee.

Flagg's nature essays had appeared in the *Boston Weekly*

---

thor's expressed wishes. Thoreau was furious, and refused to submit anything else to the *Atlantic* during his lifetime. Lowell published some other articles posthumously, but the incident is doubtless responsible, in part at least, for Lowell's surprising denigration of Thoreau's work after the latter's death.

Magazine as early as 1839, and when he began writing for the *Atlantic*, he had already published *Studies in Field and Forest* — one of those innumerable nature books that lead the reader gently by the hand through the changing seasons. "The object of this work," he tells us, "is to foster in the public mind a taste for the observation of natural objects and to cultivate that sentiment which is usually designated as the love of nature . . . No man, like the brute, can be happy from the mere gratification of animal want . . . The ox that grazes in the pasture undoubtedly receives gratification from the sight of green fields and the smell of fresh meadows: but he has no *ideality*."

Flagg's book had been brought to the attention of Henry Thoreau by the latter's naturalist friend Daniel Ricketson. Thoreau was of two minds about it. "Your Wilson Flagg seems a serious person, and it is encouraging to hear of a contemporary [this was three years after the publication of *Walden*] who recognizes Nature so squarely . . . But he is not alert enough. He wants stirring up with a pole. He should practice turning a series of somersets rapidly or jump up and see how many times he can strike his feet together before coming down."

If Thoreau hoped to transform Wilson Flagg into a Mississippi riverboatman, half man and half alligator, he was doomed to disappointment. Nature study, for Flagg, was a genteel and elevating pastime, which put no undue strain on either the muscles or the intellect. The chief value of such rural pleasures was in "their favorable moral influences, which improve the heart, while they lead the mind to observations that pleasantly exercise and develop, without tasking its powers." Harkening to bird songs, we are made happy without resort to expensive and vulgar recreations. But the study of flowers, particularly "that part of botany which belongs to poetry and romance," was more suitable for the female sex, who "cannot without some eccentricity of conduct follow birds and quadrupeds to the woods."

The quaintness — from our point of view — of Flagg's nature writing is deceptive. Despite his concern about putting a strain on his readers, he was himself no dilettante. In a moral age, such as his, the justification of nature study is that it improves us morally; in a scientific age, such as we are now in, that it improves us scientifically. Thoreau himself was forever drawing morals from nature, though he recognized this as a weakness in his writing. Flagg, who was a contemporary of Tennyson, wrote in the manner of his time. Obviously well read in English neoclassical poetry, an heir to the pastoral tradition, he enjoyed nature in terms of symbols — the "noble oak" stands for fortitude, the month of May is "a beautiful virgin, in the early ripeness of her charms," etc., etc. His symbol for happiness was "the husbandman engaged in his rustic toils." But when he gets around to discussing practical husbandry, a very different writer emerges. An ardent birdlover, Flagg explains why, as insect-eaters, songbirds are the farmer's best friends. He knows their feeding habits and he tells us how to attract them. In the manner of his time, he assumes that birds, like all living creatures, were "created for the particular benefit of mankind." But he has a clear concept of the balance of nature, and what happens when man upsets it without being aware of what he is doing. Had he lived in our time, he would have been an archenemy of the Army Engineers: "Man alone can seriously disturb the operations of nature. It is he who turns the rivers from their courses, and makes the little gurgling streams tributary to the sluggish canal."

For all his courtly manner, his cultivation of the poetic and the picturesque, Flagg was a keen observer, with a strong sense of the interrelationships of the natural world. "Mr. Flagg's observations are acute," wrote a fellow naturalist, "and, like those of all patient naturalists, set down with reserve. He seems always to be waiting for some later news from the forest." For Flagg, as for Thoreau and Burroughs and Muir, trees were more than lumber. They sheltered wildflowers, which in turn attracted "insect hosts that charm the student with their beauty and excite his wonder by their mysterious instincts." Flagg grasped the general principles of what we now call ecology, aware that "each species performs certain services in the economy of nature which cannot be so well accomplished by any other species," and he understood the importance — which is so obvious today — of preserving a variety of habitats as well as individual species. No forest clear-cutting for him: "Not without reason did the ancients place the Naiad and her fountain in the shady arbor of trees ... From their dripping shade she distributes the waters, which she has garnered from the skies, over the plain and the valley ... and from her sanctuary in the groves showers them upon the avid glebe and adds new verdure to the plain."

Naiads notwithstanding, Flagg was a serious nature writer whose popular publications, spread over some forty years, must have instructed and influenced many thousands of readers. Though much of his early writing is in a romantic vein, he went on to produce detailed studies of such specialized subjects as "The Colors and Fragrance of Flowers" and the songs of birds, meticulously comparing the principal songsters of America and Europe. In 1875 — four years after Burroughs' *Wake-Robin* — he published *The Birds and Seasons of New England*, the fruit of a lifetime of loving and intelligent observation. In retrospect, his greatest contribution was his rare ability to evoke in others his own joy in nature, to which his quiet but happy life bears eloquent witness. He writes:

Though I have probably passed more time in the woods than any man who is not a woodcutter by trade, I have not been a collector of specimens, nor a dissector of birds and flowers ... I know the value of this kind of research, but my observations are of a different character ... My book differs from learned works ... as a lover's description of a lover's hand would differ from [an] anatomical description of it ... I have pursued my tasks alone, except as I have read and conversed with my wife and children. She and they have been the only companions of my studies and recreations during all the prime of my life. But, perhaps from this cause alone, I have been very happy. The study of nature and my domestic avocations have yielded me a full harvest of pleasures, though it was barren of honors.

Thomas Wentworth Higginson's first contribution to the *Atlantic Monthly*, which followed a month after Flagg's, was entitled "Water Lilies." This article, writes his biographer, Anna Mary Wells, "set a pattern which Higginson was to follow for some years. His nature essays have survived the century since they were written with more vigor, perhaps, than anything else he wrote ... [They] were widely popular in their own day and are still eminently readable. Henry Thoreau and Emily Dickinson were among those who expressed their admiration, and of Thoreau's praise Higginson noted: 'He is the only critic I should regard as really formidable on such a subject.' "

Born a Proper Bostonian — or, more accurately, Cantabridgian — Higginson was connected, by birth and later by marriage, with virtually all of the "right" families. More to the point in shaping his career, he was in contact from his early youth with that unique collection of literary figures who brought about the so-called American Renaissance in the mid-years of the nineteenth century. His dearest ambition was to be a great poet; what he became was an eminent critic, biographer, and general man of letters, one of the most influential writers of his day.

Not yet fourteen when he entered Harvard — by far the youngest member of his class — Higginson was a tall, gangling, shy boy who took little part in the social life of his classmates. Though he had a driving ambition to win high marks as a scholar, he preferred nature study to the classics; he attended private classes in botany and entomology, and became secretary of the college Natural History Society. Unlike the young gentlemen "sportsmen" of his day, he was less interested in hunting than in botanizing and collecting butterflies. His marriage to Mary Channing, sister of Henry Thoreau's poetical friend Ellery Channing, led to his meeting with Henry in Concord. Unlike the public at large, he was delighted with Thoreau's *Week on the Concord and Merrimack Rivers*. "He knows more of nature," wrote Higginson, "than any man in America." Himself a rebel against convention,

Higginson several times considered the idea of retreating from society to the country, but his need for people was too strong. Instead he put his radical views into action: as a minister in the Unitarian church, as an abolitionist, and as a champion of women's rights. When he was ousted from the pulpit for his inflammatory sermons, he consoled himself by taking a year off to enjoy nature. Later on, when he was deep in the abolitionist movement, he still found time to climb Mount Katahdin with a party that included five bold young ladies clad in bloomers, and to write a story about the experience for *Putnam's Monthly Magazine*, which continued to publish his outdoor sketches and nature poems for decades thereafter. Some months later he had a welcome opportunity, while visiting the Azores for Mary's health, to collect marine specimens for Louis Agassiz's museum at Harvard.

Higginson is remembered today chiefly as Emily Dickinson's "dear preceptor." His essays in the *Atlantic* combined precise observation with a romantic charm that appealed to Emily. During 1861 and 1862 she read with admiration his "April Days," "My Out-Door Study," "The Life of Birds," and "The Procession of Flowers"; and when he printed an invitation to potential young contributors, she summoned up the courage to reply, feeling that she was writing to a friend. Later she wrote to him: "I read your chapters in the *Atlantic* and experienced honor for you. I was sure you would not reject a confiding question." So began a correspondence which, as she put it, "saved my Life," and which continued thereafter to be her principal link with the literary world.*

One can see how Emily, whose daily round was limited to the confines of the family garden in Amherst, might well have responded to Higginson's sensitive descriptions of a landscape as full of light and serenity as a Constable painting:

* Though Higginson immediately recognized Emily's genius, his failure to recommend her work for publication is not surprising. He found it barely comprehensible. In the words of Thomas H. Johnson, editor of her *Complete Poems*, "A representative mid-century traditionalist was being asked to judge the work of a 'wholly new' order of craftsman . . . He was trying to measure a cube by the rules of plane geometry."

The noontide of the summer-day is past, when all Nature slumbers, and when the ancients feared to sing, lest the great god Pan should be awakened . . . The floating-bridge is trembling and resounding beneath the pressure of one heavy wagon, and the quiet fishermen change their places to avoid the tiny ripple that glides stealthily to their feet above the half-submerged planks. Down the glimmering lake there are miles of silence and still waters and green shores, overhung with a multitudinous and scattered fleet of purple and golden clouds, now furling their idle sails and drifting away into the vast harbor of the South . . .

The woods are hazy, as if the warm sunbeams had melted in among the interstices of the foliage and spread a soft film throughout the whole. The sky seems to reflect the water, and the water the sky; both are roseate with color, both are darkened with clouds, and between them both, as the boat recedes, the floating-bridge hangs suspended, with its motionless fishermen and its moving team . . .

Higginson's writing could be informative as well as evocative; witness his calendar of wildflowers blooming in Mount Auburn Cemetery, or his comparison of the advent of spring in Cambridge, Massachusetts, and in Chaucer's England. Writing more than a century ago, he was already concerned with the disappearance of some of our delicate native plants, as the coarser "aliens" from abroad took over. Unlike Wilson Flagg, he does not court nature for its moral lessons. "Probably the direct ethical influence of natural objects may be overrated. Nature is not didactic, but simply healthy." He deplored the tendency of young people of his time to turn to nature simply as a retreat from the real world. "In the last twenty years, the love of Nature has at times assumed an exaggerated and even a pathetic aspect, in the morbid attempts of youths and maidens to make it a substitute for vigorous thought and action . . . But this, after all, was exceptional and transitory, and our American life still needs, beyond all things else, the more habitual cultivation of outdoor habits."

For two and a half years, Higginson himself had plenty of outdoor life, as a colonel in the Union Army, in command of the first black regiment. Not, one would think, the ideal situation for tasting the serene delights of nature. But when he was posted to a training camp on the South Carolina coast, he made the most of what chances he had to enjoy, in the midst of war, a natural scene so different from his native New England. "The river-banks were soft and graceful, though low, as we steamed up to Beaufort on the flood-tide," he writes on his arrival in late November 1862. "The air was as cool as at home, yet the foliage seemed green, glimpses of stiff tropical vegetation appeared along the banks, with great clumps of shrubs whose pale seed-vessels looked like tardy blossoms." By January the ground was white with frost and water froze in his tent; the butterflies (also one of his special interests) had vanished, but "we still have mocking-birds and crickets and rosebuds." Two weeks later he writes: "This morning is like May. Yesterday I saw bluebirds and a butterfly; so this winter of a fortnight is over." The following January, while preparing to launch a dangerous raiding party into Confederate territory, he heard "a low continuous noise from the distance, more wild and desolate" than any he could remember. "It came from within the vast girdle of mist, and seemed like the cry of a myriad of lost souls upon the horizon's verge; it was Dante become audible: and yet it was but the accumulated cries of innumerable sea-fowl at the entrance of the outer bay."

Danger sharpens the senses, as Higginson found when he was ordered to ascend the St. John's River in Florida and capture Jacksonville before the Rebels burned it down. Waiting for his gunboat to arrive, scanning the sky anxiously for signs of smoke on the horizon, he climbed the bluffs and watched the pelicans at the mouth of the river. When their vessel finally got under way, in the small hours of the morning, he was enchanted with the scene:

Again there was the dreamy delight of ascending an unknown stream, beneath a sinking moon, into a region where peril made fascination. Since the time of the first explorers, I suppose that those Southern waters have known no sensations so dreamy and so bewitching as those which this war has brought forth. I recall, in this case, the faintest sensations of our voyage, as Ponce de Leon may

have recalled those of his wandering search, in the same soft zone, for the secret of the mystic fountain. I remember how, during that night, I looked for the first time through a powerful night-glass. It had always seemed a thing wholly inconceivable, that a mere lens could change darkness into light; and as I turned the instrument on the preceding gunboat, and actually discerned the man at the wheel and the officers standing about him, — all relapsing into vague gloom again at the withdrawal of the glass, — it gave a feeling of childish delight. Yet it seemed only in keeping with the whole enchantment of the scene; and had I been some Aladdin, convoyed by genii or giants, I could hardly have felt more wholly a denizen of some world of romance.

When the war ended, Higginson, already on leave to recuperate from a minor wound, resumed his literary career. A volume entitled *Outdoor Papers*, consisting of his nature essays in the *Atlantic*, had been published while he was still on duty in the South; *Army Life in a Black Regiment*, one of his most enduring books, would appear a few years later. Now he resumed his warm relationship with Emily Dickinson, the preservation of whose poetry in the years to come would be his greatest contribution to American literature. He himself wrote innumerable biographies, essays, book reviews. Long after Thoreau's death, Higginson was still struggling to arrange publication of the journal. "The impression that Thoreau was but a minor Emerson," he wrote, "will in time pass away . . . It is common to speak of his life as a failure; but to me it seems, with all its drawbacks, to have a great and eminent success."

Higginson's own career refutes the comment that Thoreau made in his journal, in a moment of gloomy introspection: "It appears to be a law that you cannot have a deep sympathy with both man and nature. Those qualities that bring you near to the one estrange you from the other." For Thoreau this may have had some validity, but for Higginson the very opposite was true. His sensitive response to nature was part and parcel of his response to his fellow man: to his countless literary friends, to the illiterate ex-slaves under his command, to the reformers and suffragettes, to the shy recluse in Amherst. It was his response to life.

☙

While Colonel Higginson was commanding his black troops on raids up the southern rivers, a young Confederate officer, destined to be the South's leading man of letters, was joyously defending his homeland farther up the coast. Sidney Lanier reveled in his assignment as a scout along the James River: "Our life was as full of romance as heart could desire. We had a flute and a guitar, good horses, a beautiful country . . . inhabited by friends who loved us, and plenty of hair-breadth 'scapes from the roving bands of Federals who were continually visiting that Debatable Land." When off duty, he read and wrote poetry. But the idyll was not to last. Transferred to a blockade-runner, he was captured and thrown into a sordid military prison, from which he emerged all but dead.

Lanier's life span was less than half of Higginson's, but he burned with a hotter flame. He is the archetype of the romantic Southern poet. Music and poetry were his twin passions. As a child, he could play several musical instruments before he learned to write; later he became a professional musician. And though he never aspired to be a naturalist, he found in nature his surest source of inspiration. In the words of Frank Norris, the novelist, Lanier was "an artist to whom life means beauty. He revivifies nature — is almost pagan in his adoration of the beauty of the sun and water. A half-personification of the sun-myth. He is essentially religious. To Longfellow and Tennyson nature is pretty embroidery; to Emerson it is a dwelling-place of the oversoul, to Lanier it is an object of adoration."

Lanier was born in Macon, Georgia, in 1842, the son of a lawyer and "a woman of much thrift and piety." Both parents were of old southern stock, but what interested their son was his remote ancestors, a family of aristocratic French musicians who, after moving to England, were patronized by Queen Elizabeth and succeeding monarchs down to the Restoration. Their blood, he liked to think, still ran in his veins. A friend described him thus: "His eye, of bluish gray, was more spiritual than dreamy — except when he was suddenly aroused, and then it assumed a hawk-like fierceness . . . His fine-textured hair, which was soft and almost straight and of a light-brown color, was combed behind the ear in Southern style . . . His nose was aquiline, his bearing was distinguished, and his manners were stamped with a high breeding that befitted the 'Cavalier' lineage."

Sidney Lanier was only nineteen when war broke out, but he promptly enlisted in the Confederate Army, his flute tucked in the sleeve of his uniform. He had dreamed of a cultural renaissance when the South should be free. Instead, after Appomattox, he found his dream shattered and himself stricken with tuberculosis, and penniless. Like John Burroughs, he sought government work; but, as a Southerner without influence, he got nowhere. "I have allowed a friend to make application to every department in Washington for even the humblest position . . . but without success." During those "dark raven days," as he termed them, of Reconstruction, he could barely support his wife and young children — by helping in his father's law office, by teaching, by literary hackwork. Weakened from repeated bouts of illness, aware that time was running out, he finally quit the law — to write, to compose, to play the flute; to create some beauty that would outlive him.

"How *can* I settle myself down to be a third-rate struggling lawyer for the balance of my little life, as long as there is a certainty almost absolute that I can do some other thing so much better?" He was writing to his father from Baltimore, where his musical talent had already been recognized by the patrons of the newly formed symphony orchestra. Literary recognition, alas, came more slowly. Unlike Higginson, Lanier had not been born among books or fledged among poets and scholars at the hub of the solar system. The wartorn South was remote from the cozy world of the *Atlantic* or the lively literary marketplace of New York. But a breakthrough came at last with the publication of his poem "Corn" in *Lippincott's Magazine*. Though the impact was not world-shattering, Lanier's sensitive evocation of the southern landscape struck a spark with some persons of influence: Gibson Peacock, editor of the Philadelphia *Evening Bulletin*, who gave it a warm review; the famous actress, Charlotte Cushman; and Bayard Taylor, one of the most distinguished men of letters of his time. Miss Cushman — a fellow-sufferer from consumption — soon found herself the willing target for a barrage of chivalrous and adoring epistles from her passionate young admirer. To her Lanier dedicated his first volume of poetry, and shortly before her death he visited her in

Boston, where he also spent two "delightful afternoons" with Lowell and Longfellow.

But by far the most fruitful of his new friendships was that with Bayard Taylor who (in the words of Lanier's biographer, Edwin Mims) "was the means of bringing the poet into the world of letters, and became one of the most inspiring influences in his life." A journalist, poet, traveler, diplomat, Taylor is probably best known for his famous translation of Goethe's *Faust*. To Lanier he was a godsend. "Perhaps you know," Lanier wrote to him, "that with us of the younger generation in the South since the war, pretty much the whole of life has been simply not dying." Taylor became his good angel, criticizing his poems, helping him to get them published, introducing him to the literary world — much as Mrs. Carr had recently done for John Muir. The young man blossomed in the warmth of this new friendship. "If only you had there the sweetness of spring which is now in full leaf and overflowing song all about us here!" he writes from Georgia to Taylor in New York City. "I have at command a springy mare, with ankles like a Spanish girl's, upon whose back I go darting through the green overgrown woodpaths like a thrasher about his thicket. The whole air seems full of fecundity; as I ride, I'm like one of those insects that are fertilized on the wing, — every leaf that I brush against breeds a poem." For all his exuberance, Lanier liked to keep his natural history straight. After sending Taylor a poem entitled "The Bee" for criticism, he writes: "It occurs to me that I have carelessly used the pronoun 'him' referring to the bee, — forgetting that, although the worker bees were formerly thought to be sexless, they have recently been found to be imperfectly developed females."

To Lanier, as to Thoreau and Emerson and their followers, cities were anathema — particularly the industrial towns poisoned by "the hell-colored smoke of the factories." By contrast, he cherished every natural scene, from the broad, fecund marshes of the Georgia coast to the Allegheny Mountains: "How necessary it is," he writes to his wife, "that one

should occasionally place oneself in the midst of those more striking forms of nature in which God has indulged His fantasy! . . . Thou canst imagine what ethereal and yet indestructible essences of new dignity, of new strength, of new patience, of new serenity, of new hope, new faith, and new love, do continually flash out of the gorges, the mountains, and the streams, into the heart, and charge it, as the lightnings charge the earth, with subtle and heavenly fires . . ."

Music and nature were closely wedded. He shared Thoreau's special fondness for the flute. Playing the flute, he wrote, "is like walking in the woods, amongst wild flowers, just before you go into some vast cathedral. For the flute seems to me to be particularly the woods-instrument: it speaks the gloss of green leaves or the pathos of bare branches; it calls up the strange mosses that are under dead leaves; it breathes of wild plants that hide and oak fragrances that vanish."

There was also a practical side to this ecstatic nature-worship. Lanier loved the southern countryside for its fruitfulness as well as for its wild beauty, and he was heartbroken to see the land being ruined by the cotton planters, who simply wore out the soil and moved on. His first major poem, "Corn," dealt with this tragic situation. "I have endeavored to carry some very prosaic matters up to a loftier plane," he explains to a friendly critic. "I have been struck with alarm in seeing the number of old, deserted homesteads and gullied hills in the older counties of Georgia; and though they are dreadfully commonplace, I have thought they are surely mournful enough to be poetic."

Unlike some of his contemporaries, Lanier saw no conflict between poetry and science. At Oglethorpe University, he had been lucky enough to study under a brilliant former pupil of Louis Agassiz, named James Woodrow (grandfather of Woodrow Wilson), who taught him the value of natural science and its relation to poetry and religion. He read and admired Charles Darwin, carefully annotating his copy of *The Origin of Species* — at a time when the subversive ideas of Darwin and Huxley were being bitterly opposed throughout the fundamentalist South, and had been attacked at Harvard by none other than Louis Agassiz himself. He borrowed a microscope from a friend who recalled: "It was curious and interesting to see how Mr. Lanier kindled to the subject, so foreign to his ordinary literary interests . . . He plunged in with all the ardor of a naturalist, not using the microscope as a mere toy, but doing good hard work with it." And only three months before his death, we find him writing to President Gilman of Johns Hopkins University, requesting the loan of some scientific instruments to make meteorological studies of Tryon Mountain in North Carolina. Early in his career he had stated his belief, which endured throughout his life: "Poetry will never fail, nor science, nor the poetry of science."

As professional flautist with symphony orchestras, Lanier traveled all over the South, reveling in every variety of wild landscape. But what moved him most were the vast marshlands of his native Georgia coast, a sea of grass blending with the Atlantic tides, loud with the haunting cries of countless shorebirds and teeming with life where rivers and ocean meet:

Ye marshes, how candid and simple and nothing-withholding and free
Ye publish yourselves to the sky and offer yourselves to the sea!
Tolerant plains, that suffer the sea and the rains and the sun,
Ye spread and span like the catholic man who hath mightily won
God out of knowledge and good out of infinite pain
And sight out of blindness and purity out of a stain.

. . . .

       Farewell, my lord Sun!
The creeks overflow: a thousand rivulets run
'Twixt the roots of the sod; the blades of the marsh-grass stir;
Passeth a hurrying sound of wings that westward whirr;
Passeth, and all is still; and the currents cease to run;
And the sea and the marsh are one.
How still the plains of the waters be!
The tide in his ecstasy.
The tide is at his highest height:
      And it is night.

And now from the Vast of the Lord will the waters of sleep
Roll in on the souls of men,
But who will reveal to our waking ken
The forms that swim and the shapes that creep
      Under the waters of sleep?
And I would I could know what swimmeth below when the tide
   comes in
On the length and breadth of the marvelous marshes of Glynn.*

Lanier saw himself as a poet; much of his prose writing, done for money, he considered hack work. But we can be grateful for one such chore that he reluctantly undertook in the summer of 1875. He had made several trips to Florida, hoping in the mild climate to find a cure for his consumption, and his publisher suggested that he write a guidebook to the state. The title, *Florida: Its Scenery, Climate and History*, was prosaic enough. But Lanier was incapable of being dull. In his own words, "The thing immediately began to ramify and ex-

---

* "The far-reaching marshes described by Sidney Lanier in his poem *The Marshes of Glynn* constitute one of the most productive coastal areas of the world. They are viewed by thousands of visitors who cross them to visit Georgia's sea islands" (John and Mildred Teal, *Life and Death of a Salt Marsh*, 1969).

pand"; he referred to it as "a sort of spiritualized guidebook." Whatever it was, it contains one of the most beguiling nature essays ever written about that part of the world: a description of a trip by paddle-wheel steamer up the St. John's River (a decade after Higginson's wartime adventure on the same waters) and its enchanting tributary, the Oklawaha:

Presently we abandoned the broad and garish highway of the St. Johns, and turned off to the right into the narrow lane of the Ockla-waha, the sweetest water-lane in the world, a lane which runs for more than a hundred and fifty miles of pure delight betwixt hedgerows of oaks and cypresses and palms and bays and magnolias and mosses and manifold vine-growths, a lane clean to travel along for there is never a speck of dust in it save the blue dust and gold dust which the wind blows out of the flags and lilies, a lane which is as if a typical woods-stroll had taken shape and as if God had turned into water and trees the recollection of some meditative ramble through the lonely seclusions of His own soul . . .

As one steams up the lush, exotic Oklawaha with Sidney Lanier, one is suddenly reminded of young Nathaniel Hawthorne, paddling on the Concord River in the boat he bought from his friend Henry Thoreau. Both writers had a deep emotional — almost religious — response to wild nature, where they found a purity, an ideal beauty which was lacking in the world of man. "Oh that I could run wild! — that is, that I could put myself into a true relation with nature, and be on friendly terms with all congenial elements." The words are Hawthorne's; they could as well have been Lanier's. Both liked to write about their fellow creatures in a playful, affectionate vein — whether it be the crows in Walden woods, who had "no real pretentions to religion, in spite of their gravity of mien and black attire," or Florida's lordly alligators:

Some twenty miles from the mouth of the Ocklawaha, at the right-hand edge of the stream, is the handsomest residence in America. It belongs to a certain alligator of my acquaintance, a very honest and worthy saurian, of good repute. A little cove of water, dark green under the overhanging leaves, placid, pellucid, curves round at the river-edge into the flags and lilies, with a curve just heart-breaking for the pure beauty of the flexure of it. This house of my saurian is divided into apartments — little subsidiary bays which are scalloped out by the lily-pads according to the sinuous fantasies of their growth. My saurian, when he desires to sleep, has but to lie down anywhere: he will find marvelous mosses for his mattress beneath him; his sheets will be white lily-petals; and the green disks of the lily-pads will straightway embroider themselves together above him for his coverlet ... Upon my saurian's house the winds have no power, the rains are only a new delight to him, and the snows he will never see ... Lastly, my saurian has unnumbered mansions, and can change his dwelling as no human householder may; it is but a fillip of his tail, and lo! he is established in another place as good as the last, ready furnished to his liking ...

The romance of the river, the mystery and the enchantment, deepened with the setting of the sun:

— And then, after this day of glory, came a night of glory. Down in these deep-shaded lanes it was dark indeed as the night drew on. The stream which had been all day a baldrick of beauty, sometimes blue and sometimes green, now became a black band of mystery. But presently a brilliant flame flares out overhead: they have lighted the pine-knots on top of the pilot-house. The fire advances up these dark sinuosities like a brilliant god that for his mere whimsical pleasure calls the black impenetrable chaos ahead into instantaneous definite forms as he floats along the river-curves. The white columns of the cypress-trunks, the silver-embroidered crowns of the maples, the green-and-white of the lilies along the edges of the stream, — these all come in a continuous apparition out of the bosom of the darkness and retire again: it is endless creation succeeded by endless oblivion. Startled birds suddenly flutter into the light, and after an instant of illuminated flight melt into the darkness. From the perfect silence of these short flights one derives a certain sense of awe. Mystery appears to be about to utter herself in these suddenly-illuminated forms, and then to change her mind and die back into mystery.

More than a century after its publication, Lanier's glowing "guidebook" still provides inspiration to those who seek to save some remnants of the land he loved.*

---

* In recent years, the very existence of the Oklawaha River has been threat-

Twelve years after Lanier's death, the popular Southern novelist George W. Cable wrote to John Muir:

I wanted to have sent to you long ago the book I mail now and which you kindly consented to accept from me — Lanier's poems. There are in Lanier such wonderful odors of pine, and hay, and salt sands and cedar, and corn, and such whisperings of Eolian strains and every outdoor sound — I think you would have had great joy in one another's personal acquaintance.

Indeed he would.

---

ened by a project of the Army Engineers for a trans-Florida "barge canal." As of this writing, the multimillion-dollar boondoggle has been halted, one hopes forever.

CHAPTER IV

The Forces of Nature and Man

"The very fact that the word 'desecration' is commonly used to lament the damage men are causing to the environment indicates that many of us have a feeling that the earth has sanctity, that man's relation to it has a sacred quality."

— René Dubos, A GOD WITHIN

THE EIGHTEEN-FIFTIES AND -SIXTIES were a time of ferment and discovery. These were the years when Easterners came to appreciate the beauties of their native landscape; when the more venturesome went forth to report on the still grander spectacle of the virgin West. They were years of scientific popularization, of lectures and lyceums, of books and articles that captured the imagination of the public at large. Shocking new theories of man's origin cracked the very foundations of Christian society; bitter controversies arose not even hinted at in the gentle nature essays of writers like Higginson and Flagg. As science emerged from the laboratory into the field, there was a growing concern about man's role in the natural world. No longer could one complain, as Thoreau had once done, that science was studied as a dead language. Rather it was becoming a major concern in daily life.

In the autumn of 1852, Ralph Waldo Emerson noted in his journal:

I saw in the cars a broad-featured, unctuous man, fat and plenteous as some successful politician, and pretty soon divined it must be the foreign professor who has had so marked a success in all our scientific and social circles, having established unquestionable leadership in them all; and it was Agassiz.

Six years earlier there had arrived in Boston one of Europe's most celebrated scientists — a forty-year-old Swiss biologist, geologist, authority on fossils, mountaineer, inventor of the theory of glaciation, with the impressive name Jean Louis Rodolphe Agassiz. His timing was perfect. New England's "flowering" was reaching its peak. Intellectual curiosity had never been more widespread; learning more revered. "A Boston man had to be learned in something," writes Van Wyck Brooks, "and the passion for learning on the upper levels soon spread through all the other strata." Great books were in the making; Emerson had recently published his first two volumes of essays; Thoreau was living in his cabin on Walden Pond. Even small towns had their lyceums; and the public lecture had become a popular form of entertainment.

Shortly after Agassiz's arrival the eminent geologist Sir Charles Lyell arranged for him to give a course of lectures at the Lowell Institute. His hearers, cultured though they might be in other fields, were on the whole scientifically illiterate. But no matter. "His own enthusiasm," wrote Edward Emerson, "and charming taking for granted the interest in a remote subject of an audience all but absolutely ignorant of advancing modern science, — his genial face, his interesting foreign accent, and his facile blackboard drawing — won the game completely . . . It was the same with the country lyceum audiences . . . Harvard College capitulated the next year. Agassiz was appointed Professor."

This was a time when the Scientific School was still considered by the college administration to be something of an impertinence. But he would change all that. Soon he was launching a ten-volume natural history of the United States and laying plans for Harvard's Museum of Comparative Zoology, which would later become the prototype for the American Museum of Natural History in New York. Here in Cambridge he would nurture a generation of scientists and teachers including Sidney Lanier's mentor, James Woodrow; John Muir's teacher at Wisconsin, Ezra Carr; and the popular geologist Nathaniel Shaler, who became an inspiration to Theodore Roosevelt. Henry Adams, who took a low view of Harvard College, would later write in the *Education:* "The only teaching that appealed to his imagination was a course of lectures by Louis Agassiz on the Glacial Period and Paleontology, which had more influence on his curiosity than the rest of the college instruction altogether."

Nor was Agassiz's influence confined to the world of science. At meetings of the famous Saturday Club, he exchanged ideas about philosophy and the laws of nature with Emerson, and he dined at Emerson's home with Henry Thoreau, who had been sending new species of fish to his laboratory from the Concord River.* He struck up a warm

* "Thoreau also sent a live young fox, which Agassiz promptly caged in his back yard, and offered to put hunters and trappers of Concord to work col-

friendship with Longfellow, who liked to look through the microscope in Agassiz's laboratory as much as Agassiz enjoyed literary talk in the poet's study. He was an impressive figure on the lecture platform: "Strikingly handsome [in the words of a visiting professor] with domelike head under flowing black locks, large, dark, mobile eyes set in features strong and comely, and with a well-proportioned stalwart frame." When he lectured on his special subject of marine biology, his enthusiasm and boundless knowledge captivated thousands of men and women who could scarcely tell a starfish from a horseshoe crab. His female students adored him. "He was so poetical, so grand, so reverent." As for taking science out of the museum, a friend recalls: "We eyed him gingerly, for who could tell what he might have in his pockets? . . . He was on friendliest terms with things ill-reputed, even abhorrent, and could not understand the qualms of the delicate. He was said to have held up once, in all innocence, before a class of schoolgirls a wriggling snake. The shrieks and confusion brought him to a sense of what he had done. He apologized elaborately, the foreign peculiarity he never lost running through his confusion. 'Poor girls, I vill not do it again. Next time I vill bring in a nice, clean leetle feesh.' "*

Agassiz's genius as a popularizer shone most brightly when he stood before an audience; his writings are more scientific than literary. Yet such was his reputation that the *Atlantic* ran a series of nine long, rather technical articles on "Methods of Study in Natural History." The occasion for the series, and doubtless a chief cause of its popularity, was the sudden appearing from England of a book that challenged Agassiz's deepest convictions, and those of the vast majority of his readers. By coincidence, the cornerstone for Harvard's

---

lecting snapping turtles if Agassiz would pay seventy-five cents to a dollar apiece for them. But that offer was not accepted" (Walter Harding, *The Days of Henry Thoreau*).

See also the famous essay by Dallas Lore Sharp, "Turtle Eggs for Agassiz" (*Atlantic Monthly*, February 1910. Reprinted in *The Face of the Fields*, 1911).

*Professor James Kendall Hosmer of Washington University, St. Louis, a classmate of Alexander Agassiz (*The Early Years of the Saturday Club*, p. 31).

Museum of Comparative Zoology (the "Agassiz Museum") was laid the same summer (1859) that Darwin published his *Origin of Species.* Evolution by natural selection denied God's "great plan of creation," and Agassiz would have none of it. A disciple of the great French naturalist Baron Cuvier — the founder of comparative anatomy and the science of paleontology — he held firmly to Cuvier's belief in the immutability of species. He accepted Cuvier's theory of geological catastrophe or world cataclysms to explain the fossil record; after each such cataclysm God created species anew, culminating in the creation of man. Agassiz begins the *Atlantic* series with apologies for the sometimes dry details necessary in expounding a technical subject, and continues: "Yet believing, as I do, that classification, rightly understood, means simply the creative plans of God as expressed in organic forms, I feel the importance of attempting at least to present it in popular guise." Published in book form, the collection of essays ran to nineteen editions, incidentally delighting readers who could not bear the idea that "men are descended from monkeys." Yet Agassiz's complete rejection of Darwin, however popular in many quarters, led to a bitter controversy within the profession: a controversy that estranged him from many of his colleagues, including the great botanist Asa Gray, and that would darken the later years of his life.*

Fortunately, in his next *Atlantic* series Agassiz turned back to the subject that had so fascinated him as a young man in the Swiss Alps: the geological record of our planet and the life upon it. Here he was at his best and his most eloquent:

With what interest do we look upon any relic of early human history! The monument that tells of a civilization whose hieroglyphic records we cannot even decipher, the slightest trace of a nation that vanished and left no sign of its life except the rough tools and utensils buried in the old site of its towns or villages, arouses our imagi-

---

* Even more unfortunate from the social point of view was Agassiz's conclusion, based on his theory of special creation, that the Negro constituted a separate and inferior species. Defenders of slavery welcomed such statements as justifying their position.

nation and excites our curiosity. Men gaze with awe at the inscription on an ancient Egyptian or Assyrian stone; they hold with reverential touch the yellow parchment-roll whose dim, defaced characters record the meagre learning of a buried nationality; and the announcement, that for centuries the tropical forests of Central America have hidden within their tangled growth the ruined homes and temples of a past race, stirs the civilized world with a strange, deep wonder.

To me it seems that to look on the first land that was ever lifted above the waste of waters, to follow the shore where the earliest animals and plants were created when the thought of God first expressed itself in organic forms, to hold in one's hand a bit of stone from an old sea-beach, hardened into rock thousands of centuries ago, and studded with the beings that once crept upon its surface or were stranded there by some retreating wave, is even of deeper interest to men than the relics of their own race, for these things tell more directly of the thoughts and creative acts of God . . .

Indeed, the fossil remains of all times tell us almost as much of the physical condition of the world at different epochs as they do of its animal and vegetable population. When Robinson Crusoe first caught sight of the footprint on the sand, he saw in it more than the mere footprint, for it spoke to him of the presence of men on his desert island. We walk on the old geological shores, like Crusoe along his beach, and the footprints we find there tell us, too, more than we actually see in them. The crust of our earth is a great cemetery where the rocks are tombstones on which the buried dead have written their own epitaphs.

By his lectures, his writing, his founding of a great museum, above all by the force of his personality, Agassiz broke through the barriers between the scientist and the layman, between the professor and the public. In so doing, he disseminated a general understanding and love of nature without which conservation is a lost cause. Although his field trips with his students had extended only as far as the Lake Superior region, his influence penetrated to the farthest reaches of the West. Before taking up his post at the University of Wisconsin, Dr. Carr had become imbued with the Swiss professor's glacial theories. Inspired by Carr's enthusiasm, young Muir read Agassiz's famous Alpine studies in the original French, and later applied their findings to the High Sierra.

Another of Agassiz's former pupils, Joseph LeConte, professor of geology at the University of California, invited Muir — then thirty-two — on a geological field trip through Yosemite, and later suggested to his old teacher that Muir probably knew "more about the glaciation of the Sierra than anyone else." "He knows all about it!" replied Agassiz.

It is a pity that the two men never met. When Agassiz stopped in San Francisco in 1872, on the way home from a trip up the Amazon, he was too ill to go into the mountains, and Muir could not leave his glacier studies to come to town. Scarcely over a year later, Agassiz was dead. But his influence as a teacher would endure. "He revolutionized the teaching of biology in America, and the effect of this was felt all over the world," wrote Dr. Thomas Barbour, who became director of the Agassiz Museum many years later. "His marvelous ability as a lecturer made him one of the most revered and popular geniuses in America. No other naturalist was ever known to so many people. None was ever so universally beloved."

❦

In his teaching Agassiz had sought, above all else, to train his pupils in the art of observation. "Look! look! look!" he would exclaim as he made them spend days studying a single pickled fish. Meanwhile, far from Harvard in rural Vermont, a self-made scholar named George Perkins Marsh was promulgating precisely the same doctrine. "To the natural philosopher, the descriptive poet, the painter, and the sculptor, as well as to the common observer," he wrote, "the power most important to cultivate and, at the same time, hardest to acquire, is that of seeing what is before him. Sight is a faculty; seeing, an art." This challenging statement appears in the introduction to a formidable volume, bristling with learned footnotes, which has become a classic in the history of conservation. Entitled *Man and Nature*, it was published in 1864, the same year that Frederick Law Olmsted was in Yosemite Valley formulating his profound theories of natural beauty. Marsh's highly original study provided both a contrast and a valuable complement to a literature of nature that was based largely on romantic response and esthetic appreciation. The fruit of years of intense research, going back to the time of the Greeks and the Romans, it was the first book to consider man as a geological force, a force upsetting what we know today as the "balance of nature." Marsh's concern was less with nature's impact on man than with man's impact on nature, and he took not only America, but the whole civilized world as his province. His aim was to show that "whereas others think that the earth made man, man in fact made the earth."

For Americans, this disturbing book could not have appeared at a more appropriate moment. The period of exploration of the continent was coming to an end, the period of massive exploitation was beginning. In five years the golden spike would be driven at Promontory, Utah, joining East and West by rail. Gold miners had already stripped river valleys and fed whole hillsides to their rock-crushers. Massive land grabs were preparing the way for the logging of the virgin forest; and the vast herds of buffalo that for centuries had supported a native culture were being slaughtered all across the plains. Yet at the same time, there had appeared a glimmering of respect for the land itself, a sense that it had a value beyond that of immediate consumption. The esthetic response to the Sierra Nevada, which Starr King and Clarence King and Olmsted portrayed so vividly, was officially recognized in the setting aside of Yosemite Valley, and later the Yellowstone country, for public enjoyment. Both of these dramatic landscapes were treasured as examples of the picturesque, of the sublime grandeur of God's creation. Yet decades would pass before wild nature, with its complex web of life, would be saved for its own sake.

Marsh was already in his sixties when *Man and Nature* appeared. At one time or another he had been a lawyer, a politician, a diplomat, a teacher of the classics, a student of world history at home in twenty languages. Though from childhood he had the closest ties with the outdoors ("the bubbling brook, the trees, the flowers, the wild animals were to me persons, not things"), and though he had personal experience in forest management, he was not, like Agassiz, a professionally trained scientist. Widely traveled, incredibly widely read, he nevertheless lacked Agassiz's charisma on the lecture platform. Nor was he a particularly beguiling writer. *"Man and Nature* is a stylistic melange," writes David Lowenthal in his introduction to the centenary edition, "at once pedantic and lively, solemn and witty, turgid and incisive, objective and impassioned." Yet it caught on almost immediately. It would "have the young to observe and take delight in Nature, and the mature to respect her rights as essential to their own well-being," wrote James Russell Lowell. Looking back many years later, Theodore Roosevelt's Chief Forester, Gifford Pinchot, called the book "epoch-making"; in fact, it led directly to the creation of a national forest commission and government forest reserves.

No one could ever say of *Man and Nature,* as Howells did of Burroughs' *Wake-Robin,* that it is a sort of summer vacation to turn its pages. Marsh is not concerned about straining the reader's intellect. "My aim," he states at the outset, "is to stimulate, not to satisfy, curiosity, and it is no part of my object to save my readers the labor of observation or of thought."

Marsh's diplomatic career had given him plenty of opportunities for both observation and thought. While Minister to Turkey, he had found time to travel through the eroded countryside of Greece, through Palestine and the Nile Valley; he later became intimate with the Italian landscape, journeyed through southern France, and climbed in the Alps. What he saw as he surveyed man's history on earth roused him to an angry eloquence not unlike that of John Muir (who would later own and annotate a copy of *Man and Nature*):

Man has too long forgotten that the earth was given to him for usufruct alone, not for consumption, still less for profligate waste. Nature has provided against the absolute destruction of any of her elementary matter, the raw material of her works; the thunderbolt and the tornado, the most convulsive throes of even the volcano and the earthquake, being only phenomena of decomposition and recomposition. But she has left it within the power of man irreparably to derange the combinations of inorganic matter and of organic life, which through the night of aeons she had been proportioning and balancing, to prepare the earth for his habitation, when, in the fullness of time, his Creator should call him forth to enter into its possession.

Apart from the hostile influence of man, the organic and the inorganic world are, as I have remarked, bound together by such mutual relations and adaptations as secure, if not the absolute permanence and equilibrium of both, a long continuance of the established conditions of each at any given time and place, or at least, a very slow and gradual succession of changes in those conditions. But man is everywhere a disturbing agent. Wherever he plants his foot, the harmonies of nature are turned to discords.

Marsh clearly understood the principles of what we now call ecology, the interdependence of all forms of life on each other and on their environment. But in contrast to natural philosophers like Thoreau and Muir, he held firmly to the belief that God made the world for the use of man; that the human race is not only above, but apart from, the rest of nature. He uses a curious argument to demonstrate man's position as a superior being:

The fact that, of all organic beings, man alone is to be regarded as essentially a destructive power, and that he wields energies to resist which, nature — that nature whom all material life and all inorganic substance obey — is wholly impotent, tends to prove that, though living in physical nature, he is not of her, that he is of more exalted parentage, and belongs to a higher order of existences than those born of her womb and submissive to her dictates.

In our atomic age such an argument would place the human species in a very high order indeed. But while Marsh cites man's power of destruction as elevating him above the beasts, his whole book is a denial that it has brought him any closer to the angels. No sooner does man progress beyond the savage state than he "at once commences an almost indiscriminate warfare upon all the forms of animal and vegetable existence around him, and as he advances in civilization, he gradually eradicates or transforms every spontaneous product of the soil he occupies." In consequence, Marsh points out, "the earth is fast becoming an unfit home for its noblest inhabitant," thereby echoing Thoreau's comment: "What is the use of a house if you haven't a tolerable planet to put it on?"

Yet Marsh did more than just cry havoc. Man's dominion, wisely exerted, could be a constructive force. Forests could be replanted, man-made deserts returned to fertility, eroded hillsides redeemed. A self-styled mechanic — along with countless other pursuits — he was fascinated by the possibilities of new technologies. He considered it "rash and unphilosophical to attempt to set limits to the ultimate power of man over inorganic nature." Looking ahead, he saw a time when man might harness the power of the waves beating against the breakwater at Cherbourg or the tides at the head of the Bay of Fundy. Among the innumerable fascinating footnotes to *Man and Nature* — frequently more diverting than the main text — is a suggestion a century ahead of its time: the use of solar heating. "Some well known experiments show that it is quite possible to accumulate solar heat by a simple apparatus, and thus to obtain a temperature which might be economically important even in the climate of Switzerland . . . Why should not so easy a method of economizing fuel be resorted to in Italy, and even in more northerly climates?"

Man and Nature, wrote a reviewer for the *Nation*, came "with the force of a revelation." Other critics ranked it among the foremost literary productions of America. It went into three editions during Marsh's lifetime, was translated into Italian, and had wide recognition abroad. The philosophy on which it is based has since been accepted to the point of seeming commonplace. Its practical results, which were always the author's chief concern, have been immense. In the second edition * Marsh followed the lead of Thoreau in recommend-

* Published under the title *The Earth as Modified by Human Action* (1874).

ing the establishment of what we now call "wilderness areas." "It is desirable," he wrote, "that some large and easily accessible region of American soil should remain as far as possible in its primitive condition, at once a museum for the instruction of the students, a garden for the recreation of the lovers of nature, and an asylum where indigenous trees . . . plants . . . beasts may dwell and perpetuate their kind."

In the words of Lewis Mumford, *Man and Nature* was "the fountainhead of the conservation movement."

❦

"The pursuit of physical geography," wrote Marsh in the introduction to *Man and Nature*, "embracing actual observation of terrestrial surface, affords to the eye the best general training that is accessible to all." He comments on the new school of geographers in Europe who concerned themselves with the influence of external physical conditions — especially the configuration of the earth's surface — on the social life and progress of mankind. At the time he wrote, a young man named John Wesley Powell was training his eye to undertake just such studies of the vast arid regions of the American West. Powell is a charismatic figure: the daring one-armed veteran of the Civil War who first ran the rapids of the Grand Canyon. But until Wallace Stegner wrote *Beyond the Hundredth Meridian*, his significance in our history — including the history of conservation — was not widely recognized beyond professional circles.

Powell was born in New York State in 1834, the son of a Methodist preacher. Like John Muir, four years his junior, he grew up in the Midwest, including brief periods in Ohio and Wisconsin, before his family finally settled in Wheaton, Illinois. Both boys had a keen interest in nature and in books, yet neither could escape more than momentarily from the backbreaking dawn-to-dusk work on a frontier farm. "The parallel is exact even to the religious opposition of the father," writes Stegner. "For Joseph Powell objected to his son's museum, his natural history, his scientific interests, in the same way

that Muir's father protested against reading and invention . . .
Both boys broke away for long rambling excursions justified
by scientific collections." And both boys eventually left home
for good to get an education on their own.

Young Powell found that most midwestern colleges — like
Harvard before Agassiz — gave little attention to the teaching of science. Whereas Muir was lucky enough to encounter
some brilliant teachers at the University of Wisconsin, Powell
apparently found no such inspiration at Wheaton or Oberlin,
where he studied intermittently without taking any degree.
Instead, he joined the Illinois Society of Natural History, of
which he eventually became secretary. He roamed the fields
and woods collecting for the Society's museum, and made
long solitary boat trips on the Ohio and the Mississippi. When
the Civil War broke out, he raised a company of artillery for
the Union Army, and after losing his right arm at the battle of
Shiloh, returned to active service and rose to the rank of
major. Already he had shown the courage and drive, and
above all the staying power, which enabled him to head the
first expeditions through the Grand Canyon of the Colorado,
to explore the incredibly rugged, starkly beautiful country
known to geographers as the Plateau Province, and finally to
take charge of the newborn United States Survey and to develop, during our greatest period of national corruption and
exploitation, an intelligent plan for the future of the public
domain.

Like Clarence King, who first saw the Sierra Nevada
through the eyes of Ruskin, Powell was about to combine esthetic appreciation with scientific study. Before setting out on
the first Colorado River trip, he had made arrangements with
the Chicago *Tribune* for a series of letters describing his adventures, as Starr King had done with the Boston *Evening
Transcript* before entering Yosemite Valley. Later he would
publish a full account in his official *Report of the Exploration
of the Colorado River of the West and Its Tributaries* — a handsome illustrated volume published in 1875 by the United
States government.

On May 24, 1869, Powell and nine companions set out from the town of Green River, Utah, in four heavily built boats specially designed for the wild water and boiling rapids they knew must lie ahead, since the river bed dropped more than a mile from the upper waters of the Green to the foot of the Grand Canyon some nine hundred miles away. "These cañon gorges, obstructing cliffs and desert wastes," writes Powell in his *Report*, "have prevented the traveller from penetrating the country, so that, until the Colorado River Exploring Expedition was organized, it was almost unknown . . . Stories were related of parties entering the gorge in boats, and being carried down with fearful velocity into whirlpools, where all were overwhelmed in the abyss of waters; others, of underground passages for the great river into which boats had passed never to be seen again. It was currently believed that the river was lost under the rocks for several hundred miles. There were other accounts of great falls, whose roaring music could be heard on the distant mountain-summits. There were many stories current of parties wandering on the brink of the cañon, vainly endeavoring to reach the waters below, and perishing with thirst at last in sight of the river which was roaring its mockery into dying ears."

Almost three months after entering the river, after running countless rapids and portaging their heavy craft around the worst of the cataracts, the party at last reached the entrance to the Grand Canyon. Powell notes in his journal:

August 13. — We are now ready to start on our way down the Great Unknown. Our boats, tied to a common stake, are chafing each other, as they are tossed by the fretful river. They ride high and buoyant, for their loads are lighter than we could desire. We have but a month's rations remaining. The flour has been resifted through the mosquito net sieve; the spoiled bacon has been dried, and the worst of it boiled; the few pounds of dried apples have been spread in the sun, and reshrunken to their normal bulk; the sugar has all melted, and gone on its way down the river; but we have a large sack of coffee. The lighting of the boats has this advantage: they will ride the waves better, and we shall have but little to carry when we make a portage.

We are three quarters of a mile in the depths of the earth, and the great river shrinks into insignificance, as it dashes its angry waves against the walls and cliffs, that rise to the world above; they are but puny ripples, and we but pigmies, running up and down the sands, or lost among the boulders.

We have an unknown distance yet to run; an unknown river yet to explore. What falls there are, we know not; what rocks beset the channel, we know not; what walls rise over the river, we know not. Ah, well! we may conjecture many things. The men talk as cheerfully as ever; jests are bandied about freely this morning; but to me the cheer is somber and the jests are ghastly.

Next morning, as the granite walls rise higher and higher above them, they appear to be on the brink of disaster:

About eleven o'clock we hear a great roar ahead, and approach it very cautiously. The sound grows louder and louder as we run, and at last we find ourselves above a long broken fall, with ledges and pinnacles of rock obstructing the river. There is a descent of, perhaps, seventy five or eighty feet in a third of a mile, and the rushing waters break into great waves on the rocks, and lash themselves into a mad, white foam. We can land just above, but there is no foot-hold on either side by which we can make a portage. It is nearly a thousand feet to the top of the granite, so it will be impossible to carry our boats around, though we can climb to the summit up a side gulch; and, passing along a mile or two, can descend to the river. This we find on examination; but such a portage would be impracticable for us, and we must run the rapid, or abandon the river. There is no hesitation. We step into our boats, push off and away we go, first on smooth but swift water, then we strike a glassy wave, and ride to its top, down again into the trough, up again on a higher wave, and down and up on waves higher and still higher, until we strike one just as it curls back, and a breaker rolls over our little boat. Still, on we speed, shooting past projecting rocks, till the little boat is caught in a whirlpool, and spun around several times. At last we pull out again into the stream, and now the other boats have passed us. The open compartment of the "Emma Dean" is filled with water, and every breaker rolls over us. Hurled back from a rock, now on this side, now on that, we are carried into an eddy, in which we struggle for a few minutes, and are then out again, the breakers still rolling over us. Our boat is unmanageable, but she cannot sink, and we drift down another hundred yards, through breakers; how, we scarcely know. We find the other boats have turned into an eddy at the foot of the fall, and are waiting to catch us as we come, for the men have seen that our boat is swamped. They push out as we come near, and pull us in against the wall. We bail our boat, and on we go again.

Like Starr King striving to convey the dimensions of Yosemite Valley to his Boston readers, Powell seeks familiar comparisons, but on a far grander scale, as he looks up from the depths of canyons that could swallow hundreds of Park Street churches and Bunker Hill monuments:

The walls, now, are more than a mile in height — a vertical distance difficult to appreciate. Stand on the south steps of the Treasury building in Washington, and look down Pennsylvania Avenue to the Capitol Park, and measure this distance overhead, and imagine cliffs to extend to that altitude, and you will understand what I mean; or, stand at Canal street, in New York, and look up Broadway to Grace Church, and you have about the distance; or, stand at Lake street bridge, in Chicago, and look down to the Central Depot, and you have it again.

Though danger sharpens the senses, the awful responsibilities that the leader must bear temper his enjoyment of the scene, as he climbs the granite cliffs to survey the river far below:

All about me are interesting geological records. The book is open, and I can read as I run. All about me are grand views, for the clouds are playing again in the gorges. But somehow I think of the nine days' rations, and the bad river, and the lesson of the rocks, and the glory of the scene is but half seen.

Ten days later three members of the expedition, convinced that sure destruction lies ahead on the river, decide to climb out of the abyss.* The others go on, through chutes and eddies and whirlpools, to emerge at long last into the calm waters at the foot of the Grand Canyon, sun-baked, battered and hungry, but their mission accomplished. As for their leader, he

* Long afterward, it was learned that they had almost reached the safety of a Mormon settlement, only to be murdered by a band of Indians who mistakenly believed that they had killed a squaw from the tribe.

became an instant celebrity when the story of his incredible journey spread across the land.

One thinks of Powell as a man of action, not of words. No more than Clarence King or Olmsted or Marsh can he be considered a "nature writer" in the usual sense of that term. Yet he had a strong literary bent. "His young taste ran to the romantic poets," writes Stegner; "on the second river expedition he brought along volumes of Scott, Tennyson, and Longfellow, and through Brown's Hole and on other calm stretches he read them aloud to the crews of the lashed boats floating together. In the *Exploration* his writing is marked by effusiveness, poetic inversions and contractions, sweeping and panoramic effects, the exploitation of every chance for dramatics, but also by precision of line and considerable associative imagination. And he had justification for a high tone. He was in truth engaged in a hazardous and exciting voyage, and the country through which he passed was calculated to stir the superlatives out of almost anyone. Heightened or not, the *Exploration* is an extraordinarily thrilling story, good enough to have been reprinted twice from its official format and to have had several magazine versions."

Powell's trip down the Colorado River was only the prelude to a career of extraordinary accomplishment. In the preface to his Colorado River report he had written: "Begun originally as an exploration, the work has finally developed into a survey embracing the geography, geology, ethnography, and natural history of the country." Thanks to his sudden popularity, a hitherto indifferent Congress appropriated funds for what became the Powell Survey, to explore the canyon region of Colorado, Utah, Arizona, and New Mexico — which encompassed a second Colorado River expedition including an artist and a photographer. Out of the Survey grew a number of accounts and monographs, such as the classic report on *The Lands of the Arid Region*, which gave their readers a whole new idea of the American West, substituting for romantic myth equally romantic fact. Here in the canyon country, land-use policies that had been applied to the Midwest frontier were wholly irrelevant. Water was the key factor, and vast areas were obviously unsuitable for human settlement. Indeed to this day the dry Plateau Province remains largely a wilderness area — a harsh land of great beauty, encompassing some of the most dramatic scenery in North America, and appearing much as it did in Powell's lifetime.

Powell was not only physically courageous; he was a tough-minded and determined administrator. As his reputation and political power continued to grow, he was able to bring about a consolidation of rival surveys into the U.S. Geological Survey, with Clarence King in charge — to be succeeded, after only two years, by Powell himself. Nor did he stop there. All his life he had been as much concerned about the native peoples as with the physical geography of the continent. The Survey produced pioneering studies of the American Indians, their language and culture, in part written by Powell; and from his initiative arose the Bureau of American Ethnology, with Powell at its head.

But it is as an explorer, as an observer of the natural scene, that Powell — like John Muir and Clarence King — made his greatest literary contribution. "In Powell's accounts of his explorations," wrote a friend at the time of his death, "one catches the exalted moods of the poet. He keenly appreciated the wonders and beauties of the region through which he travelled, and his descriptions often become prose poetry."

᭛

With characteristic acerbity, Bernard DeVoto, the great historian of the American West, inveighs against a literary tradition which ranks second-rate novelists and "sixth-rate essayists" above writers and men of action like Powell and King. "Clarence King survives as a name to be mentioned in appraisals of our civilization through his friendship with a literary person of considerably inferior intelligence, Henry Adams . . . but what he added to our civilization is not mentioned." As for Powell, "a few critics understand that he showed a kind of courage in navigating the Colorado River [but] they do not know what he did for our culture . . ." Still less appreciated, DeVoto continues, is a close friend and colleague of Powell, Clarence Edward Dutton. "Dutton laid the basis of what is known about a large American area and, while doing so, incidentally taught some literary persons how to look at the Grand Canyon. Some of them — Charles Dudley Warner, John Muir, John Burroughs — copied a number of Dutton's pages verbatim but were too absorbed to enclose them in quotation marks."

Wallace Stegner has described Clarence Dutton as "a somewhat less sybaritic and less spectacular Clarence King." Born within a year of each other, both went to Yale, where Dutton won literary distinction and began training for the ministry. But volunteer service in the Civil War led to a different career; by war's end he was a captain in the regular army. During the postwar years, being of a curious turn of mind and not overburdened with peacetime military duties, he acquired a consuming interest in geology. Recognizing his talents, influential friends in Washington got him detached from regular army service to join the Powell Survey. In so doing, they made possible some of the most brilliant interpretation and sensitive writing to come from the Plateau Province and the canyons of the Colorado.

In those days, scientific monographs could also be literature. Powell's official account of his Grand Canyon voyage is also a great adventure story. Dutton's *Geology of the High Plains of Utah* and his *Physical Geography of the Grand Cañon District* contain, along with masses of technical material, nature writing of a very high order. Like Frederick Law Olmsted, Dutton was fascinated by the impact of natural scenery on the human mind, and by the difficulties involved in comprehending nature on such a colossal scale. One's first impression of the Grand Canyon, for example, can be confusing:

The observer who, unfamiliar with plateau scenery, stands for the first time upon the brink of the inner gorge, is almost sure to view his surroundings with commingled feelings of disappointment and perplexity. The fame of the chasm of the Colorado is great, but so indefinite and meager have been the descriptions of it that the imagination is left to its own devices in framing a mental conception of it. And such subjective pictures are of course wide of the truth. When he first visits it the preconceived notion is at once dissipated and the mind is slow to receive a new one. The creations of his own fancy no doubt are clothed with a vague grandeur and beauty, but not with the grandeur and beauty of nature. When the reality is before him the impression bears some analogy to that produced upon the visitor who for the first time enters St. Peter's Church at Rome. He expected to be profoundly awe-struck by the unexampled dimensions, and to feel exalted by the beauty of its proportions and decoration. He forgets that the human mind itself is of small capacity and receives its impressions slowly, by labored processes of comparison. So, too, at the brink of the chasm, there comes at first a feeling of disappointment; it does not seem so grand as we expected. At length we strive to make comparisons. The river is clearly defined below, but it looks about large enough to turn a village grist-mill; yet we know it is a stream three or four hundred feet wide. Its surface looks as motionless as a lake seen from a distant mountaintop. We know it is a rushing torrent. The ear is strained to hear the roar of its waters and catches it faintly at intervals as the eddying breezes waft it upwards; but the sound seems exhausted by the distance. We perceive dimly a mottling of light and shadow upon the surface of the stream, and the flecks move with a barely perceptible cloud-like motion. They are the fields of white foam lashed up at the foot of some cataract and sailing swiftly onward.

Perhaps the first notion of the reality is gained when we look across the abyss to the opposite crest-line. It seems as if a strong, nervous arm could hurl a stone against the opposing wall-face; but in a moment we catch sight of vegetation growing upon the very brink. There are trees in scattered groves which we might at first have mistaken for sage or desert furze. Here at length we have a stadium or standard of comparison which serves for the mind much the same purpose as a man standing at the base of one of the sequoias of the Mariposa grove. And now the real magnitudes begin to unfold themselves, and as the attention is held firmly the mind grows restive under the increasing burden. Every time the eye ranges up or down its face it seems more distant and more vast. At length we recoil, overburdened with the perceptions already attained and yet half vexed at the inadequacy of our faculties to comprehend more.

The magnitude of the chasm, however, is by no means the most impressive element of its character; nor is the inner gorge the most impressive of its constituent parts. The thoughtful mind is far more deeply moved by the splendor and grace of Nature's architecture. Forms so new to the culture of civilized races and so strongly contrasted with those which have been the ideals of thirty generations of white men cannot indeed be appreciated after the study of a single hour or day. The first conception of them may not be a pleasing one. They may seem merely abnormal, curious, and even grotesque. But he who fancies that Nature has exhausted her wealth of beauty in other lands strangely underestimates her versatility and power. In this far-off desert are forms which surprise us by their unaccustomed character. We find at first no place for them in the range of our conventional notions. But as they become familiar we find them appealing to the aesthetic sense as powerfully as any scenery that ever invited the pencil of Claude or of Turner.

Dutton was not such a dashing, dramatic figure as either King or Powell, under whom he served faithfully for so many years. But his contribution to our understanding and appreciation of the canyon country of the West, and hence to the future of the conservation and the national park movements, was great and lasting. In a sense we still contemplate the wonders of the Grand Canyon, the incredible pinnacles of Bryce and Canyonlands, the flower-studded trails and awesome peaks of Zion through his eyes. And as secretary of the Commission to Codify Land Laws, he made a lasting impact on government policy. He was also a gifted raconteur and a popular lecturer, not without a sense of humor. Returning from a trip to the Hawaiian Islands, where he had been studying earthquakes and volcanoes, he indulged in his lifelong love of alliteration, as he contrasted the sturdy native women to their "pale and pulmonary sisters of the effete east."

Considering his personal charm, his impressive intellect, and the reverence for the natural world so evident in his writings, Dutton would doubtless have made an excellent minister, had he continued on that path. But we can be happy — as he clearly was — with his final choice of a life work. All but forgotten today, he deserves a firm place alongside such familiar figures as Agassiz and Marsh and Powell in the literary interpretation of our continent.

CHAPTER V

A Naturalist in the White House

"This we know. The earth does not belong to man; man belongs to the earth. This we know. All things are connected like the blood which unites one family. All things are connected. Whatever befalls the earth befalls the sons of the earth. Man did not weave the web of life, he is merely a strand in it. Whatever he does to the web, he does to himself."

— CHIEF SEATTLE

THE 1872 ANNUAL REPORT of the American Museum of Natural History notes that during the previous year — the year, incidentally, of Burroughs' first nature book and Muir's first articles — the Museum's collection had been enriched by "1 Bat, 12 Mice, 1 Turtle, 1 skull: Red Squirrel, and 4 Birds' Eggs." The donor, aged fourteen, was "Mr. Theodore Roosevelt, Jr.," whose father was a founder of the Museum. From early boyhood, Roosevelt had every intention of becoming a professional scientist; a future director of the Museum remembered him as a teenager, "one of a youthful band of bird-lovers, observers and collectors — who came together in the seventies." Considering his keen intelligence and fabulous energy, there is little doubt that he could have achieved his ambition. "If his major interests had not been diverted into the time-consuming field of politics," wrote C. Hart Merriam, head of the U.S. Biological Survey, "he would have been one of America's foremost naturalists." (One is reminded of the Harvard professor's comment that Thoreau would have made a fine entomologist if only he had not come under the influence of Emerson.) The fact that Roosevelt *was* diverted, all the way to the White House, would be of immeasurable importance in the history of America's changing attitude toward nature. The personal interest of a President of the United States would give new weight and dignity, new public recognition, to nature study and nature writing. It would color an entire era.

Despite the enormous responsibilities of his political career, Roosevelt remained all his life on intimate terms with biologists, sportsmen, ornithologists, artists and outdoor photographers, and nature writers of every description. He camped out with John Muir in Yosemite Valley and with John Burroughs in Yellowstone Park. Among his host of friends were Clarence King; George Bird Grinnell, editor of *Forest and Stream* and a co-founder with Roosevelt of the Boone and Crockett Club; Henry Fairfield Osborn, director of the American Museum; Frank M. Chapman, its famous curator of birds; William T. Hornaday, authority on American mammals; Frederic Remington, the great artist of the West; and George Shiras, pioneer in the new art of wildlife photography. Roosevelt, an ardent and rapid reader, was familiar with the nature essays of Ernest Ingersoll, Witmer Stone, and William Cram; and he gave friendly advice to Ernest Thompson Seton, the principal founder of a new school of creative writing about animals.

The professional careers and personal interests of these men, and of countless others who shared their concerns, were woven together in a complex pattern. Sportsmen collected for the museums; museum curators and university professors provided the scientific base for conservation organizations like the newborn Audubon societies; amateur naturalists supplemented the studies of the professionals; and the writers in both their ranks brought the fruits of their labors before the public. To follow a single thread or an individual career in isolation would be to ignore the cross-fertilization that was constantly going on. Such, for example, as the symbiotic relationship between Theodore Roosevelt and the museum that came into being during his lifetime.

Obviously, the richest city in America would sooner or later have a great natural history museum. Philadelphia had its Academy of Natural Sciences, Boston had its Society of Natural History, and Harvard its Museum of Comparative Zoology, still dominated by the monolithic Louis Agassiz. In Washington a national museum, the Smithsonian, was taking shape. New York, with its abundance of wealthy and public-spirited citizens, could not for long allow itself to be left behind. But the timing and the circumstances of the happy event were, as it happens, determined in Cambridge, Massachusetts, an outgrowth of both the strength and the weakness of Louis Agassiz.

The great professor had created a museum that was the envy of the scientific world, at home and abroad. But by the early eighteen-sixties, he had become virtually a dictator of the organization he had created. Through control of faculty appointments, he sometimes blocked the advancement of his students; he forbade them to publish scientific papers without his approval. Finally they had had enough. Many left the museum for other jobs. Among these was an enterprising young man, son of a prosperous Maine sea captain, named Albert S. Bickmore. Bickmore went a step further. He would found a brand-new museum, to be run on "democratic principles" in the hitherto scientific desert of New York City. The time was ripe. Theodore Roosevelt, Sr., and other prominent citizens — including bankers like J. P. Morgan, Sr., and Morris K. Jessup, business magnates, millionaires — seized upon the idea. A valuable natural history collection which had recently come on the market in Paris would form the nucleus of the new enterprise. To get an act of incorporation from the state legislature, Bickmore turned to the man who had both the legislature and the governor under his thumb, the redoubtable Boss Tweed. A specialist in human rather than wild nature, who had probably never heard of the museum in Cambridge, Tweed was nevertheless happy to do a favor for the influential gentlemen who wanted such a museum for New York. On April 9, 1869, Bickmore's dream became a reality.

When the collection arrived from Paris, Mr. Roosevelt brought his fourteen-year-old son to watch it being unpacked. Theodore, Jr., was no mere onlooker. He had already established the "Roosevelt Museum of Natural History" in his home. Books on animals were his favorite reading, and his greatest pleasure was in the outdoors: on family trips to the Adirondacks, on Long Island, and later in the Maine wilderness. He had taken lessons in taxidermy from none other than John G. Bell, a former companion of Audubon; and as his collection grew he began to specialize in birds, in which he would remain passionately interested throughout his life. By the time he was ready for college, young Roosevelt had (as Paul R. Cutright states in *Theodore Roosevelt the Naturalist*) "a collection of birdskins which for size, variety, and skill of preparation was doubtless unequalled by any boy his age in the United States."

At Harvard, where he took several courses in natural history, Roosevelt arrived just too late to study under Louis Agassiz or Asa Gray. He did however have classes with Agassiz's brilliant and popular pupil, Nathaniel Southgate Shaler, who taught him among other things the rudiments of paleontology. Like Thomas Wentworth Higginson a generation earlier, he joined the Harvard Natural History Society; more significantly, he was elected a member of America's first bird club, the Nuttall Ornithological Club of Cambridge, founded by the eminent naturalist William Brewster.

Why did Roosevelt abandon a scientific career? Over a decade after graduation, with Brewster's concurrence, he submitted a report to the Harvard Board of Overseers sharply criticizing the department of zoology for overemphasizing microscopic work in the laboratory at the expense of observing and collecting in the field, for ignoring the importance of the "old school naturalist" — a view doubtless strengthened by the fact that his poor eyesight made use of the microscope difficult.*

"I have been told," wrote John Burroughs, "that his ambition up to the time he went to Harvard had been to be a naturalist, but that there they seem to have convinced him that all the out-of-door worlds of natural history had been conquered, and that the only worlds remaining were in the laboratory, and to be won with the microscope and the scalpel. But Roosevelt was a man made for action in a wide field, and laboratory conquests could not satisfy him."

Roosevelt would later blame his Harvard experience for dampening his enthusiasm for natural history. There is no evidence, however, that he raised these objections when he was an undergraduate. (Nor was this enthusiasm ever really dampened.) Other factors apparently influenced his choice of a career. Early in 1880 he wrote to a friend on the letter paper of Harvard's socially prestigious Porcellian Club: "I write you to

---

* A parallel conflict of emphasis, with the molecular biologists in one court and the ecologists and animal behaviorists in the other, exists to this day.

announce my engagement to Miss Alice Lee . . . I have been in love with her for nearly two years now; and have made everything subordinate to winning her; so you can perhaps understand a change in my ideas as regards science, etc." (Miss Lee's knowledge of the animal world was rudimentary. Cutright refers to an incident during their honeymoon in Europe, which occurred at the Paris Zoo. Roosevelt "momentarily lost his power of speech when Alice asked him seriously who had shaved the lions, being unable to account otherwise for their manes.")

By now Roosevelt was deep into politics, a New York State assemblyman determined to bring honesty to government. He was also a writer, whose early productions suggest the wide range of his interests: a history of the War of 1812 (begun in college) and a monograph on the short-tailed shrew. And in the fall of 1883, needing a rest from the political life, seeking relief from his recurrent asthma, but most of all drawn by a deep desire for adventure amid the vanishing wildlife of the West, he set out on a hunting trip in the Dakota Badlands. Determined to kill a buffalo while there were still some left to kill, he impressed his rugged young guide with his doggedness and apparent relish of the hardship encountered on the trail. The great herds were gone, but he finally got his trophy, to his almost hysterical delight. Before returning to New York he had decided to invest in a cattle ranch in this wild country he had come to love.

It was a wiser decision than he knew. The following winter he suffered a double blow: the death of his first wife in childbed and of his mother the same day. His life momentarily shattered, he sought solace in the western wilderness, to which he would return again and again for almost a decade thereafter. Here his passion for wild nature and his literary ambitions would both find fulfillment. He had a subject to write about which, in its union of natural grandeur and personal challenge, was ideally suited to his temperament. The result was three books: *Hunting Trips of a Ranchman, Ranch Life and the Hunting Trail,* and *The Wilderness Hunter.* More than a mere account of hunting adventures — though there is plenty of that — these volumes included both new observations on the life histories of the big-game animals and occasional eloquent passages on the beauties and esthetic appeal of the western wilderness.

Big-game hunting was for Roosevelt the epitome of the "strenuous life." His favorite species, both to study and to kill, was the bighorn sheep — the swift, wary denizen of the high ridges and mountain peaks. "No other kind of hunting does as much to bring out the good qualities, both moral and physical, of the sportsmen who follow it. If a man keeps at it, it is bound to make him both hardy and resolute; to strengthen his muscles and fill out his lungs." For Roosevelt, as for hunters before and since, there was no contradiction between the thrill of the successful chase and the quiet joy that one can find in nature. "All hunters," he wrote, "should be nature-lovers." The trilogy on his western trips contains vivid descriptions at each end of the scale. Here he is being charged by a wounded grizzly: "I held true, aiming behind the shoulder, and my bullet shattered the point or lower end of his heart, taking out a big nick. Instantly, the great bear turned with a harsh roar of fury and challenge, blowing the bloody foam from his mouth, so that I saw the gleam of his white fangs; and then he charged straight at me . . . He came steadily on, and in another second was almost upon me. I fired for his forehead, but my bullet went low, entering his open mouth, smashing his lower jaw and going into his neck . . . Through the hanging smoke the first thing I saw was his paw as he made a vicious side blow at me . . . He lurched forward, leaving a pool of bright blood where his muzzle hit the ground . . ." And so on.

While it is demonstrably true, as Roosevelt asserted, that the finest sportsmen are also nature lovers, one cannot help feeling that on occasion he pushed that paradox to the limit. Witness, for example, his diary for a month in the summer of 1884, when he sought surcease from the pain of his young wife's death in relentless killing, day after day. His "battery" consisted of a Colt revolver, a 10-gauge shotgun, and three high-powered rifles. Sample entries (there are few blank days):

Knocked the heads off two sage grouse.
   12 sage hens and prairie chickens, 1 yearling whitetail "through the heart."
   "Broke the backs" of two blacktail bucks with a single bullet.
   1 blacktail buck, 1 female grizzly, 1 bear cub, "the ball going clean through him from end to end."

As one reads this last entry, it is hard not to feel a certain inconsistency with his excoriation elsewhere of "the swinish game-butchers who . . . murder the gravid doe and the spotted fawn with as little hesitation as they would kill a buck of ten points." But bear cubs, of course, were "vermin." *

"I have never sought to make large bags," he states in *Hunting Trips of a Ranchman.* But "it is always lawful to kill dangerous or noxious animals, like bear, cougar, and wolf."

Despite their titles, the value of these books as nature writing does not depend on their hunting stories. Roosevelt knew how to evoke the spirit of a wild and spacious country soon to be subdued forever. "In hunting," he writes,

the finding and killing of the game is after all but a part of the whole . . . No one but he who has partaken thereof, can understand the keen delight of hunting in lonely lands. For him is the joy of the horse well ridden and the rifle well held; for him the long days of toil and hardship, resolutely endured, and crowned at the end with triumph. In after-years there shall come forever to his mind the memory of endless prairies shimmering in the bright sun; of vast snow-clad wastes lying desolate under gray skies; of the melancholy marshes; of the rush of mighty rivers; of the breath of the evergreen forest in summer; of the crooning of ice-armored pines at the touch of the

---

* Eighteen years later, while bear hunting in Mississippi, the President — quite naturally — refused to shoot a bear cub which his companions had captured and tied to a tree. A celebrated cartoon by Clifford K. Berryman of the Washington *Post* based on this incident led to the creation of the "Teddy-bear," mascot of the Republican party during Roosevelt's presidency and beloved by children ever since.

winds of winter; of cataracts roaring between hoary mountain masses; of all the innumerable sights and sounds of the wilderness; of its immensity and mystery; and of the silences that brood in its still depths.

In contrast to the fierce excitement of the chase is his quiet joy in the landscape, in the changing color of the hills, in the prairies and their wildflowers, and above all in the birds. Thus as he rests before the campfire he considers the various qualities of birdsong, comparing in his memory the song of Europe's nightingale with the American thrushes:

The nightingale is a performer of a very different and far higher order [than the skylark] yet, though it is indeed a notable and admirable singer, it is an exaggeration to call it unequalled. In melody, and above all in that finer, higher melody where the chords vibrate with the touch of eternal sorrow, it cannot rank with such singers as the wood thrush and hermit thrush. The serene, ethereal beauty of the hermit's song, rising and falling through the still evening under the archways of hoary mountain forests that have endured from time everlasting; the golden, leisurely chiming of the wood thrush, sounding on June afternoons, stanza by stanza, through sun-flecked groves of tall hickories, oaks, and chestnuts — with these there is nothing in the nightingale's song to compare.

The song of the western meadowlark he finds peculiarly evocative of the land he had come to love for its purity and peace as well as its call to high adventure.

The meadowlark is a singer . . . deserving to rank with the best. Its song has length, variety, power, and rich melody and there is in it sometimes a cadence of wild sadness, inexpressibly touching. Yet I cannot say that either song would appeal to others as it appeals to me, for to me it comes forever laden with a hundred memories and associations, with the sight of dim hills reddening in the dawn, with the breath of cool morning winds blowing across lonely plains, with the scent of flowers on the sunlit prairie, with the motion of fiery horses, with the strong thrill of eager and buoyant life. I doubt if any man can judge dispassionately the songs of his own country. He cannot disassociate them from the sights and sounds of the land that is so dear to him.

Roosevelt's highly developed sense of hearing — so evident in all his nature writing — apparently endured throughout most of his life. Long after his years on the prairie, he had a rare opportunity to compare English and American birdsong when he visited England en route home from his African safari. Before leaving America, he had arranged through the British Ambassador to spend a day in the country with Viscount Grey of Falloden, Britain's Foreign Minister and a keen amateur ornithologist. So occurred the now-famous bird walk in the valley of the Itchen and the New Forest, the two of them alone together, as Roosevelt had once been with John Muir in Yosemite, far from the official banquets and speeches and cheering crowds. Grey was astonished by his companion's knowledge of English birds, but even more by his highly developed sense of hearing:

We began our walk, and when a song was heard, I told him the name of the bird. I noticed that as soon as I mentioned the name, it was unnecessary to tell him more . . . He knew the kind of bird it was, its habits and appearance. He just wanted to complete his knowledge by hearing the song . . . He had one of the most perfectly trained ears for bird songs that I have ever known, so that if three or four birds were singing together he would pick out their songs, distinguish each, and ask to be told each separate name; and when, farther on, we heard any bird for a second time, he would remember the song from the first telling and be able to name the bird himself.*

Nor was this sensitivity to sound, so apparent in his prose, confined to birds. "Roosevelt's characteristic auditory effects resonate on every page," writes Edmund Morris in his admirable *The Rise of Theodore Roosevelt*, "from the 'wild, not unmusical calls' of cowboys on night-herd duty, their voices 'half-mellowed by the distance,' to the 'harsh grating noise' of a dying elk's teeth gnashing in agony. There are, to be sure, some vignettes that make non-hunters gag, such as that of a wounded blacktail buck galloping along 'with a portion of his

*From a speech delivered at Harvard University, December 8, 1919, eleven months after Roosevelt's death.

entrails sticking out . . . and frozen solid.' But the overwhelming impression left after reading *Hunting Trips of a Ranchman* is that of love for, and identity with, all living things. Roosevelt demonstrates an almost poetic ability to feel a bighorn's delight in its sinewy nimbleness, the sluggish timidity of a rattlesnake, the cool air on an unsaddled horse's back, the numb stiffness of a hail-bruised antelope."

The success of his western narratives led Roosevelt to think seriously of a literary career. Reviewers compared him to Thoreau and Burroughs. George Bird Grinnell, editor of *Forest and Stream,* was reminded of Francis Parkman's *Oregon Trail,** and the London *Spectator,* oddly enough, bracketed him with the gentle Isaak Walton and his *Compleat Angler.* But politics won out. A series of political offices, followed by national fame as the dashing leader of the Rough Riders, would lead to the governorship of New York, the vice-presidency, and, in the fall of 1901, to the presidency. Roosevelt was big-game hunting in the Adirondacks when he received news of McKinley's death by an assassin's bullet.

Throughout his career, and most conspicuously in the White House, Roosevelt not only maintained but strengthened his ties with the sportsmen, the professional naturalists, the nature writers, and — to use the new term that would include them all — the conservationists. He was in a position to put their knowledge to use, their ideas into action. His enthusiasm encouraged good nature writing, and his fury at the "nature fakers" discouraged bad.† Similarly, he helped to draw the line between the true sportsman and the "game hog." Though doubtless motivated in large measure by self-interest, the big-game hunters were among the first to realize the need for wildlife conservation. An outstanding example is a man who, as an editor, a writer, and a co-founder with Roosevelt of the famous Boone and Crockett Club, deserves to be better known: George Bird Grinnell.

* Some of Grinnell's own writing seems closer to Parkman. See pp. 119–121.
† See pp. 214–15.

Roosevelt's senior by nine years, Grinnell was born in Brooklyn, New York, in 1849. Like Roosevelt, he came from a distinguished family, whose pedigree included Betty Alden, the first white woman born in New England, and five colonial governors. And like Roosevelt he had an early bent toward natural science: later they would share a passion for big-game hunting in the still virgin areas of the West. Both were bird-lovers from childhood. If young Roosevelt enjoyed the unique privilege of learning taxidermy from a former companion of Audubon, Grinnell had already gone him one better. When Grinnell was eight years old, the family moved to Audubon Park on the Hudson, where his father bought a large tract of land from Audubon's widow. Here in the old Audubon mansion Madame Lucy Audubon conducted a small private school for children of neighboring families, and it was from her than young Grinnell first learned about birds. One moment in particular would forever stand out in his memory, as it did for John Burroughs and so many others: his first sight of that incredible phenomenon, the flocking of the passenger pigeon. He never forgot the morning when, as a small boy, he left the breakfast table to watch a cascade of these beautiful birds pour down from the sky upon the dogwood tree beside the house, till not a space remained along the laden branches, and latecomers crowded together in a living blue-gray carpet as they gleaned berries from the ground. Already such sights were becoming less common in the eastern states, though not yet in the Midwest — as witness the rejection by the Ohio Senate in 1857 of a proposed law to control the slaughter that had been going on since colonial days: "The passenger pigeon needs no protection. Wonderfully prolific, having the vast forests of the North as its breeding grounds, traveling hundreds of miles in search of food, it is here to-day and elsewhere to-morrow, and no ordinary destruction can lessen them, or be missed from the myriads that are yearly produced." By the time Grinnell reached middle age, the passenger pigeon would be rare. Decades before his death, it would be extinct.

The incredibly swift demise of the passenger pigeon was a warning, an extreme example of what was happening to many forms of wildlife as the country began to fill up. Henry Thoreau had already bewailed the disappearance of the great mammals that had once roamed the forests of New England, leaving a fauna that was tamed and emasculated, like "a tribe of Indians that had lost all its warriors." The western plains were now suffering a similar fate, as Grinnell would soon see for himself. Immediately after graduation from Yale, he joined the Peabody Museum's great paleontologist, Othniel Charles Marsh, on a fossil-collecting trip to the Far West. A few years later General George H. Custer chose him as the naturalist for an expedition to the Black Hills of South Dakota, the country that became so dear to Theodore Roosevelt.* But it was during a government survey of the birds and mammals of the newborn Yellowstone National Park — where hunting was still allowed — that he was struck most forcibly by the destruction of the big-game animals. To his official report he added a covering letter:

It may not be out of place here to call your attention to the terrible destruction of large game, for the hides alone, which is constantly going on in those portions of Montana and Wyoming through which we passed. Buffalo, elk, mule-deer, and antelope are being slaughtered by the thousands each year, without regard to age or sex, and at all seasons . . . It is certain that, unless in some way the destruction of these animals can be checked, the large game still so abundant in some localities will ere long be exterminated.

According to those who knew him well, Grinnell was a kind and courteous man, inclined to be self-effacing. This quality may explain the merely passing references he generally receives in histories of conservation. He possessed, in fact, that

---

*Fortunately Grinnell was too busy at the museum to go on Custer's fatal 1876 expedition, which would have ended his career then and there.

all-too-rare combination of talents: he was a trained scientist who could both write well himself and stimulate the writing of others. While still connected with Yale University, he accepted the position of natural history editor of the sportsman's magazine, *Forest and Stream*. Soon thereafter he became editor-in-chief, and during the next thirty years developed it into a journal notable for its scientific accuracy, to which leading naturalists were glad to contribute. One of his most successful crusades was in defense of Yellowstone National Park, which was constantly threatened with despoliation by local commercial interests and the railroad lobby. In 1892 he received a heartening letter from Roosevelt, then a member of the U.S. Civil Service Commission:

"I have just read your article, 'A Standing Menace,' printed in *Forest and Stream*, in reference to the attempts made to destroy the National Park in the interests of Cooke City. I heartily agree with this article. It is of the utmost importance that the park shall be kept in its present form as a great forestry preserve and a National pleasure ground, the like of which is not to be found on any continent but ours; and all public-spirited Americans should join with *Forest and Stream* in the effort to prevent the greed of a little group of speculators, careless of everything save their own selfish interests, from doing the damage they threaten to the whole people of the United States, by wrecking the Yellowstone National Park."

Grinnell once remarked to a friend and colleague that "the conquering of difficulties is one of the chief joys of life." As editor of an influential magazine in an age when the very concept of conservation was still suspect as somehow un-American, he had ample opportunity for such enjoyment. One of his early battles was on behalf of the birds. He had helped to found the American Ornithologists' Union (A.O.U.) — the distinguished offspring of William Brewster's Nuttall Club — and now he could use his position as a magazine editor to spread the gospel. He had long been appalled by the slaughter that was taking place — by game hogs and market gunners, by plume hunters, by egg collectors, by boys who killed songbirds just for fun. He urged his readers to form a protective association, in which each member signed a pledge not to molest the birds. The idea caught on instantly. Famous persons like Oliver Wendell Holmes, Henry Ward Beecher, and John Greenleaf Whittier lent their support, and membership in the first year (1886) rose to 39,000. Remembering his happy boyhood studies with Lucy Audubon, Grinnell named his brainchild the Audubon Society. To build up the Society, and to "foster the zeal of the thousands now on its rolls," he started a monthly publication, the original (though short-lived) *Audubon Magazine*. It ran articles on "How I Learned to Love and Not to Kill," "A Plea for Our Birds," "Maintaining the Balance of Life," and so on. The very first issue featured an impassioned essay by Celia Thaxter, the popular poet of the Isles of Shoals, attacking the heartless woman who insists on wearing plumes on her hat, who turns a deaf ear to all pleas and "goes her way, a charnel house of beaks and claws and bones and glass eyes upon her fatuous head." By contrast, "How refreshing is the sight of the birdless bonnet! The face beneath, no matter how plain it may be, seems to possess a gentle charm." It was a good start. Alas, Grinnell's rapidly mushrooming organization died, after two years, of its own success, having become too much of a load for a parent magazine that was published primarily for hunters and fishermen. But the seed had been sown.

 ❦

A year after Grinnell had introduced the idea of an "Audubon Society" in the pages of *Forest and Stream*, Theodore Roosevelt invited him and several other gentlemen sportsmen to dine with him at his New York residence to discuss a project that might seem almost the antithesis of saving "the feathered songsters of the grove." He proposed the formation of a club of American riflemen, to be known as the Boone and Crockett Club. Its objects were "to promote manly sport with the rifle," to explore wild and unknown parts of the country, to study wild animals and to further legislation for their protection. To be eligible for membership, one must have killed in fair chase an adult male of at least three species of American big-game animals. Roosevelt was the first president. He and Grinnell later edited a series of books in which members — including Roosevelt and an occasional professional writer like Owen Wister — described their hunting adventures and the habits of the game they pursued. Some of the best of these essays are by Grinnell himself, who seems to have been more interested in studying the animals than in killing them. In one of the last volumes, he looks back with nostalgia to the days when great herds of buffalo darkened the western plains:

On the floor, on either side of my fireplace, lie two buffalo skulls. They are white and weathered, the horns cracked and bleached by the snows and frosts and the rains and heats of many winters and summers. Often, late at night, when the house is quiet, I sit before the fire, and muse and dream of the old days; and as I gaze at these relics of the past, they take life before my eyes. The matted brown hair again clothes the dry bone, and in the empty orbits the wild eyes gleam. Above me curves the blue arch; away on every hand stretches the yellow prairie, and scattered near and far are the dark forms of buffalo. They dot the rolling hills, quietly feeding like tame cattle, or lie at ease on the slopes, chewing the cud and half asleep. The yellow calves are close by their mothers; on little eminences the great bulls paw the dust, and mutter and moan, while those whose horns have grown one, two, and three winters are mingled with their elders.

Not less peaceful is the scene near some river-bank, when the herds come down to water. From the high prairie on every side they stream into the valley, stringing along in single file, each band following the deep trail worn in the parched soil by the tireless feet of generations of their kind. At a quick walk they swing along, their heads held low. The long beards of the bulls sweep the ground; the shuffling tread of many hoofs marks their passing, and above each long line rises a cloud of dust that sometimes obscures the westering sun.

Life, activity, excitement, mark another memory as vivid as these. From behind a near hill mounted men ride out and charge down toward the herd. For an instant the buffalo pause to stare, and then crowd together in a close throng, jostling and pushing one another, a confused mass of horns, hair, and hoofs. Heads down and tails in air, they rush away from their pursuers, and as they race along herd joins herd, till the black mass sweeping over the prairie numbers thousands. On its skirts hover the active nimble horsemen with twanging bowstrings and sharp arrows piercing many fat cows. The naked Indians cling to their naked horses as if the two were parts of one incomparable animal, and swing and yield to every motion of their steeds with the grace of perfect horsemanship. The ponies, as quick and skilful as the men, race up beside the fattest of the herd, swing off to avoid the charge of a maddened cow, and, returning, dart close to the victim, whirling hither and yon, like swallows on the wing. And their riders, with the unconscious skill, grace, and power of matchless archery, are driving the feathered shaft deep through the bodies of the buffalo. Returning on their tracks, they skin the dead, then load the meat and robes on their horses, and with laughter and jest ride away.

After them, on the deserted prairie, come the wolves to tear at the carcasses. The rain and the snow wash the blood from the bones, and fade and bleach the hair. For a few months the skeleton holds together; then it falls apart, and the fox and the badger pull about the whitening bones and scatter them over the plain. So this cow and this bull of mine may have left their bones on the prairie, where I found them and picked them up to keep as mementos of the past, to dream over, and in such reverie to see again the swelling hosts which yesterday covered the plains, and to-day are but a dream.

Grinnell was writing in 1913, when the Boone and Crockett Club was twenty-five years old. During that quarter-century, the western frontier, symbol of abundance, wellspring of the so-called American dream, had passed into history. There were, of course, islands of wilderness still surviving amid the swirling tide of settlement that had reached the shores of the Pacific. But as Grinnell wrote, "the old wild frontier of the limitless prairie and of the steep and rugged unknown" was gone forever. From the start, the emphasis of the Club had been as much on conservation as on trophy hunting. The idea of game refuges originated with its members. The forest reserve system — that milestone in conservation history — owed much to their efforts, enhanced by the happy circumstance that a Club member, John W. Noble, was Secretary of the Interior in 1891, when the act creating these reserves came before Congress. Three years later the Club played a major role in the passage of the Park Protection Act, which, in the nick of time, saved Yellowstone from commercial development when the railroad extended its lines to the Park. As for Grinnell himself, perhaps his greatest monument, and a tribute to the persuasiveness of his pen, is Glacier National Park in the northern Rockies. With typical anonymity he writes: "In the early days of the Club's history, one of its members was a frequent visitor to a section in Montana, now well-known." In fact he had explored and hunted in this spectacular country before the Club was founded, and in 1901 he published an eloquent article in *Century* magazine entitled "The Crown of the Continent," urging that it be made a national park. Nine years later, his hope was realized.

Grinnell's enthusiasms were not confined to parks and wildlife. He may not have seen himself as a historian, yet buried in the Boone and Crockett Club's records are vivid vignettes of life in the old West, such as his eyewitness description of steamboating on the Mississippi and Missouri rivers. In addition to conservation, his major interest, and the subject of both his scholarly and popular books, was the Plains Indian. The two are, of course, inseparable. Almost a century before ecology became a common concept, Grinnell was aware of the contrast between the Indian who lived essentially in harmony with the land, and the white man whose goal was to conquer it. No armchair sentimentalist, he had risked his life on scientific expeditions through hostile Indian country; but he had also won the trust of friendly tribes, joined in their buffalo hunts, participated in their council meetings, earned the respect of their chiefs, and acted successfully as official government representative under both Cleveland and Roosevelt. Out of this experience came a series of short books on Indian life and folklore — beginning with *Pawnee Hero Stories* and *Folk Tales* — and a definitive study of the Cheyennes.

When the famous Harriman Expedition sailed for Alaska in the summer of 1899, George Bird Grinnell was among the distinguished company, which — it will be recalled — included John Muir and John Burroughs.* Though the three men came from very different backgrounds, they had much in common. Each was an articulate naturalist, shaping public opinion in his own way. But the meeting of East and West, personified by Burroughs and Muir, was in Grinnell's case the dynamic

* It is interesting to note how similar were the objectives — if not necessarily the motivation — of the Boone and Crockett and the Sierra clubs. Eight years earlier, when Robert Underwood Johnson of *Century* magazine, Muir, and others were organizing to defend the Sierra from exploitation, Grinnell had suggested that the Boone and Crockett Club might be a vehicle for the kind of "defense" Johnson had in mind. However, officers of the Club felt that their organization, with its headquarters in New York City, should restrict its attention to the Rockies: "Those especially interested in the Yosemite Park could form an association having for its object the maintenance of the California parks. When necessary this latter association could unite with the Boone and Crockett Club in any work in which they were both interested. Many members might belong to both clubs" (Holway R. Jones, *John Muir and the Sierra Club*, p. 8).

Can one imagine John Muir killing three species of big-game animals in order to qualify?

force within a single man's career. In the words of a contemporary, he was a prime representative of that group of "educated Easterners who went to the frontier in the buffalo and Indian days and devoted their lives to the welfare of the great West."

❦

Not every writer committed to saving America's wildlife was so self-effacing. Nor did these sportsmen-conservationists all come from the East. About the time that John Muir was breaking away from the family farm in Wisconsin, a child named William Temple Hornaday was getting his first impressions of the broad virgin prairies of Iowa — its windswept sea of grass, its vast numbers of passenger pigeons and prairie chickens that proclaimed the apparently limitless bounty of the frontier.

Again it was Audubon's great books — the *Birds of America*, the *Quadrupeds* by Audubon and Bachman — that led a young man into a naturalist's career. Inspired by Audubon's writings, which he came across as a college undergraduate, Hornaday taught himself taxidermy, and soon landed a job ideally suited to his adventurous, romantic temperament: a collecting expedition to India and Southeast Asia for Ward's Natural Science Establishment. From this experience came his first book, a fat volume which gave evidence, early in his career, that the author would never be at a loss for words. In his preface he writes:

He, at least, who loves the green woods and rippling waters, and has felt the mystic spell of life in "a vast wilderness," will appreciate the record of my experiences. I love nature and all her works, but one day in an East Indian jungle, among strange men and beasts, is worth more to me than a year among dry and musty "study specimens." The green forest, the airy mountain, the plain, the river, and the sea-shore are to me a perpetual delight, and the pursuit, for a good purpose, of the living creatures that inhabit them adds an element of buoyant excitement to the enjoyment of natural scenery, which at best can be but feebly portrayed in words.

A Naturalist in the White House   123

Some years later, Hornaday found another golden opportunity to pursue living creatures "for a good purpose." Appointed chief taxidermist for the U.S. National Museum, he suddenly realized the need for creating a "habitat group" — the first of its kind — of the American bison, before the species became totally extinct. In an article for *Cosmopolitan* magazine, entitled "Our Last Buffalo Hunt," he describes this adventure; thirty years later (while editing this same article for book publication), he mentions the qualms with which he undertook it. "If the reader of 1925 now should feel doubtful about the ethical propriety of our last buffalo hunt, and the killing that we had to do in order that our National Museum might secure a few good wild skins out of the wreck of the millions, let him feel assured that our task was by no means a pleasant one, and at the same time remember that the author has made some atonement to *Bison americanus* by the efforts that he has put forth since 1889 for the saving and the restoration of that species."

That sentence says a good deal about the change that the naturalist-authors, including Hornaday, had already wrought in the public's attitude toward wildlife. It also reflects the shift from unrestricted sport-shooting to preservation that Grinnell noted in the history of the Boone and Crockett Club. As for Hornaday himself, his revelation, if not quite comparable to Saul's on the road to Damascus, is expressed with all the passion of an evangelist. In the preface to *Our Vanishing Wild Life*, published in 1913, he writes: "I have been a sportsman myself; but times have changed, and we must change also." He recognizes that sportsmen could take credit for most game-protective laws: "For all that, however, every man who still shoots game is a soldier in the Army of Destruction!" "The earth is THE LORD'S," he reminds us; the wild things are not ours, but given to us in trust. Henry Fairfield Osborn, president of the American Museum of Natural History and friend of Theodore Roosevelt, compared *Our Vanishing Wild Life* to "the great bells in the watch-towers of the cities of the Middle Ages which called the citizens to arms to protect their homes, their liberties and their happiness."

As director of the New York Zoological Society,* as author of *American Natural History* (which had won warm praise from President Roosevelt) Hornaday preached from a lofty pulpit, and he made no social distinctions in his choice of candidates for eternal hellfire. They included "men posing as gentlemen" who were actually no better than game-hogs, fashionable ladies who insisted on wearing plumes in their hats, market gunners and the epicures who supported them, and the western sheep-herders "who want the entire earth all to themselves." He quotes with scorn the president of the powerful Wool-Growers Association, which fought against establishing a National Antelope Preserve on the grounds that "the proper place in which to preserve the big game of the West is in city parks, where it can be protected."

Though Hornaday's main mission was to halt wanton slaughter, he knew that saving wildlife habitat was equally important. His one blind spot — which he shared with most of his contemporaries — was his unawareness of the part played by what he terms "noxious predatory animals" in maintaining a healthy natural environment. For him there were "good animals" and "bad animals." The former should be protected; the latter, classed as "vermin," should be destroyed. "Vermin" included bears, mountain lions, wolves, coyotes, wildcats, and lynxes; and, among the smaller mammals, weasels, mink, foxes, and skunks — unless there is "positive evidence" that they destroy noxious rodents. There were also "several species of birds that may at once be put under sentence of death for their destructiveness of useful birds . . . Four of these are Cooper's Hawk, the Sharp-Shinned Hawk, Pigeon Hawk and Duck Hawk." With hindsight, based on modern research, it is easy to criticize this point of view, which often involved an anthropomorphic attitude toward wild nature. For all his love of wilderness, Theodore Roose-

* The New York Zoological Society had been founded in 1895, with nine Boone and Crockett Club members on its first board of directors. The zoo in the Bronx opened a year and a half later.

velt, for example, found the howling of wolves a sinister and mournful sound, "ever fraught with foreboding of murder and rapine." Predators like the mink he terms "bloodthirsty"; the ferret has an "insatiable blood lust" — though in the same breath he remarks on how it keeps down that "perfect bane to the cattlemen," the prairie dog. When during his presidency he arranged to visit Yellowstone Park, he had planned to hunt mountain lions there, "on the supposition that they are 'varmints' and not protected." The newspapers, however, set up a howl as fraught with foreboding as that of the wolves, calling him not an animal-lover but a game-butcher. So he had to leave his rifle behind and — perhaps as an earnest of his good intentions — he asked the gentle and benign Sage of Slabsides, John Burroughs, to accompany him on the trip.* As for Hornaday, his ambiguous attitude toward game protection is stated with unconscious irony in his *The Minds and Manners of Wild Animals.* "The great California grizzly is now believed to be totally extinct. The campaign . . . to secure laws for the reasonable protection of bears is wise, timely and thoroughly deserving of success because such laws are now needed." The big brown bears of Alaska, on the other hand, are still "unafraid, insolent, aggressive and dangerous. They need to be shot up so thoroughly that they will learn the lesson of the polars and grizzlies, — that man is a dangerous animal, and the only safe course is to run from him at first sight."

* Contrary to popular belief, Burroughs was not wholly averse to killing for sport; and when it came to predators, he shared the conventional wisdom of his time. In his account of that Yellowstone trip he wrote: "Some of our newspapers reported that the President intended to hunt in the Park. A woman in Vermont wrote me, to protest against the hunting, and hoped I would teach the President to love the animals as much as I did . . . She did not know that I was then cherishing the secret hope that I might be allowed to shoot a cougar or bobcat; but this fun did not come to me. The President said 'I will not fire a gun in the Park; then I shall have no explanations to make.'

"I have never been disturbed by the President's hunting trips," Burroughs continued. "Such a hunter as Roosevelt is as far removed from the game-butcher as day is from night; and as for his killing of the 'varmints,' — bears, cougars, and bobcats, — the fewer of these there are, the better for the useful and beautiful game."

Though modern naturalists would not agree with Dr. Hornaday's prescription for educating bears, there is no doubt that his militant campaigns and voluminous writings on behalf of wildlife educated a public that might not have heard a less strident voice. His friends agreed that "he had an uncommon faculty for making enemies," but he was doubtless happy to be judged in light of the enemies he had made. After all, as he once remarked, "Many men are both morally and intellectually lower than many quadrupeds."

❦

In 1912, when he wrote the foreword to Hornaday's *Our Vanishing Wild Life*, Henry Fairfield Osborn was president of both the New York Zoological Society and the American Museum of Natural History: an Olympian figure whose scientific attainments had brought him honors on both sides of the Atlantic, and whose "benevolently autocratic character" (in the words of his colleague, George Gaylord Simpson) was largely responsible for the fact that the museum he governed with such paternal pride had already become one of the greatest in the world. "A magnificent old devil," recalled Margaret Mead. "This was his dream, and he built it. He was arbitrary and opinionated, but I got my first view of many things from his books and the exhibits he sponsored."

Just one year older than Theodore Roosevelt, Osborn had also come into the world with social position and financial security; his parents were old New England stock, and J. P. Morgan, Sr., was "Uncle Pierpont." Coupled with this was an energy and drive that almost matched Roosevelt's. A fossil-collecting trip after graduation from college turned him toward the study of paleontology, as it had George Bird Grinnell seven years before. In London he studied under the great Thomas H. Huxley, who, on one memorable occasion, introduced him to Charles Darwin. The twenty-two-year-old Osborn was dissecting a lobster when he looked up and saw the two men enter the laboratory. "From the large number of students working there at the time, Huxley singled me out,

perhaps because of my early paleontological writing. I realized that I gazed steadily into Darwin's face and especially into his benevolent blue eyes, which were almost concealed below the overhanging brows, eyes that seemed to have a vision of the entire living world and that gave one the impression of translucent truthfulness."

Osborn had a pretty broad vision himself: no less than a definitive memoir on all the fossil mammals of North America. Like Agassiz, he was given to grandiose schemes. "He planned as if he were to live forever," writes Simpson, "and he laid out more work for himself than could have been completed in ten lifetimes." The bulk of his publications — and the bulk was enormous — took the form of technical monographs, but he had a flair for popular writing as well, and a missionary zeal for alerting the layman to the critical condition of America's heritage. In preaching conservation, he used arguments and concepts that he shared with men like Muir and Burroughs, and that have since become commonplace, such as the recognition of wilderness values as a part of our culture. "We no longer destroy great works of art . . . but we have yet to attain the state of civilization where the destruction of a glorious work of Nature, whether it be a cliff, a forest, or a species of animal or bird, is regarded with equal abhorrence." As for the cost of conservation, he points out the total investment in animal preservation would be less than the cost of a single battleship, which will soon be obsolete anyway. (So a half-century later the Sierra Club estimated that the cost of an adequate National Redwood Park would be equal to that of three days of highway construction.)

"Our animal fortune seemed to us so enormous that it never could be spent," Osborn told members of the Boone and Crockett Club in 1904. "Like a young rake coming into a very large inheritance, we attacked this noble fauna with characteristic American improvidence, and with a rapidity compared with which the Glacial advance was eternally slow; the East went first, and in fifty years we have brought about an elimination in the West which promises to be even more radical than that effected by the ice. We are now beginning to see the end of the North American fauna; and if we do not move promptly, it will become a matter of history and of museums." John Muir read Osborn's speech in Grinnell's *Forest and Stream*. "I found your Boone and Crockett address and have heartily enjoyed it," he wrote to his old friend. "It is an admirable plea for our poor horizontal fellow-mortals, so fast passing away in ruthless starvation and slaughter. Never before has the need for places of refuge and protection been greater." Muir's next comment would not have gone down so well with Club members: "The murder business and sport by saint and sinner alike has been pushed ruthlessly, merrily on, until at last protective measures are being called for, partly, I suppose, because the pleasure of killing is in danger of being lost from there being little or nothing left to kill . . ."

Osborn was more tolerant than Muir of his friends, the wealthy big-game hunters, whose contribution to wildlife preservation — for whatever purpose — he readily acknowledged. But his true passion was for educating the public. "It must not be put on the minutes of the history of America, a country which boasts of its popular education, that the Sequoia, a race 10,000,000 years old . . . was cut up for lumber, fencing, shingles, and boxes!" he told his Boone and Crockett Club audience. "It must not be recorded that races of animals representing stocks 3,000,000 years of age, mostly developed on the American continent, were eliminated in the course of fifty years for hides and for food [he refrained from mentioning sport] in a country abounding in sheep and cattle."

Osborn and Muir — the one a self-assured, somewhat bristly embodiment of the Establishment; the other a wanderer at home only in the wilderness — enjoyed a relationship as happy as that of the cactus with the cactus wren. Not the least of Osborn's contributions to the literature of conservation was his kindness in providing Muir in his later, productive years with ideal writing conditions in a cottage on the Osborn estate at Garrison-on-Hudson. Here, during the summer of 1911, Muir (then seventy-three) struggled to finish both his autobiography and his book on Yosemite before leaving for the Amazon. "I am now shut up in a magnificent room pegging away at that book," he wrote to John Burroughs, "and working as hard as I ever did in my life." The previous summer Muir had taken Osborn on a short trip to Yosemite, doubtless instructing him in geology: one of the few subjects, according to a colleague, of which his host had only a limited acquaintance. Soon thereafter Osborn threw his considerable weight behind Muir in the last vain battle to save Hetch Hetchy.

Osborn's museum (for that is the way his staff thought of it) has nourished a variety of scientists who, as Theodore Roosevelt put it, can take the facts of science and make them into literature. And who can guess how many of the millions of children who have swarmed through its halls got there a first glimpse of man's place in the great chain of life? As Robert Cushman Murphy, a former curator of birds, has written, "[Osborn] carried many profound discoveries of a scientific epoch into homes and schools throughout the world, changing 'dinosaur' from a high-brow to a household word and making Mesozoic dragons almost as familiar to children as the creatures of Noah's Ark . . ." Some of those children would grow up to be scientists themselves. Countless others would, as Osborn had hoped, learn to recognize the works of nature as no less precious and worth preserving than the works of man.

Osborn may have been autocratic, but on one occasion he encountered a will even stronger than his own. When Roosevelt, at the age of fifty-five, determined to lead a daring expedition through unmapped and particularly dangerous areas of the Brazilian jungle, his friend was horrified and sought to dissuade him. The risks were too great. Roosevelt refused to listen: "I have already lived and enjoyed as much of life as any nine other men I know; I have had my full share, and if it is necessary for me to leave my bones in South America, I am quite ready to do so."

Osborn's fears were justified. The first stage of the expedition went well, as the party — including two naturalists from the American Museum — penetrated deep into the Mato Grosso, that vast expanse between the Amazon and the La Plata river systems, to reach at last the headwaters of the River of Doubt,* which Roosevelt was determined they would descend. Here the trouble began. Thundering rapids, swamped canoes (one boatman was drowned), exhausting portages, hostile Indians, noxious insects, tropical disease — all together they brought the trip to the brink of disaster. Rushing into the current to save two capsized canoes from splintering on the rocks, Roosevelt suffered a leg wound, which became infected; shortly thereafter he was stricken with a severe bout of malaria. When, some six weeks and 1500 miles later, the expedition reached Manaos on the Amazon River, he had ample material for his last book of outdoor adventure, *Through the Brazilian Wilderness*. But he returned

---

* Now the Roosevelt River.

home prematurely aged, and his health was never fully restored.

The death of Theodore Roosevelt in 1919, and of John Burroughs two years later, might be said to mark the end of an era. With encouragement from the White House, a native literature of nature had come of age. Both professional and amateur naturalists, many of them personal friends of the President, were writing popular as well as technical books in their chosen fields. The most widely read, and most closely tied in with the newborn conservation movement, dealt with his own lifetime enthusiasm, the study of our native birds.

CHAPTER VI

Birds and Men

"We, too, are out, obeying the same law with all nature. Not less important are the observers of the birds than the birds themselves."
— Henry David Thoreau, JOURNAL

THE BOND between birds and men is older than recorded history. Birds have always been an integral part of human culture, a symbol of the affinity between mankind and the rest of the natural world, in religion, in folklore, in magic, in art — from early cave paintings to the albatross that haunted Coleridge's Ancient Mariner. Scientists today recognize them as a sure indicator of the health of the environment. And as modern field guides make identification easier, millions of laymen watch them just for the joy of it.

To the first settlers in North America, however, the amazingly rich avifauna was seen principally as a source of food or, in the case of "those mischievous birds called the Black Bird and the Crow," pests to be destroyed. By the end of the seventeenth century, the enduring symbol of Thanksgiving, the wild turkey, had almost vanished from New England. Two centuries later, when George Bird Grinnell launched the first *Audubon Magazine*, ornithology had become a respected branch of science, yet the slaughter of birds continued, on an even wider scale, by more sophisticated means and from more varied and complex motives. That many other species did not follow such magnificent birds as the passenger pigeon and the Carolina parakeet to extinction is owing in large measure to the writings of articulate scientists and gifted amateurs who, while pursuing their own professions or avocations, made the reading public aware of what was happening.

Among the professionals who established ornithology as a science, none is remembered today with more respect — almost with awe — than a complex, incredibly productive scientist and western historian named Elliott Coues. Coues, like Thoreau, was descended from a native of the Isle of Jersey, who came to America before the Revolution. He was born in Portsmouth, New Hampshire, in 1842 — the same year as Sidney Lanier and Clarence King — and grew up in Washington, D.C., where his father worked in the Patent Office. Here he attended college and medical school.

When the Civil War broke out, he enlisted as a medical cadet in the Union Army. Like most eminent ornithologists,

Elliott Coues had been an ardent bird-lover since childhood. And like John Burroughs, five years his senior, he later recalled the sudden moment of awareness that foreshadowed his future career. In his case it was his first sight of a common but dazzlingly brilliant bird, cousin to the gaudily colored species of the tropics: "More years have passed than I like to remember since a little child was strolling through an orchard one bright morning in June, filled with mute wonder at beauties felt, but neither questioned nor understood. A shout from an older companion — 'There goes a Scarlet Tanager!' — and the child was straining eager, wistful eyes after something that had flashed upon his senses for a moment as if from another world, it seemed so bright, so beautiful, so strange . . . That night the vision came again in dreamland, where the strangest things are the truest and known the best; the child was startled by a fall of fire, and fanned to rest again by a sable wing. The wax was soft then, and the impress grew indelible."

By the time the Civil War ended Coues, now in his early twenties, was firmly imprinted on birds. Oddly enough, it was the U.S. Army that inadvertently launched him on his unmilitary career. Assignments to various remote army outposts in the West (where official duties were apparently not onerous) gave him the chance to collect hitherto unknown bird species, and to compile a mass of new information that resulted in the famous *Key to North American Birds*, described by a contemporary as "one of the best if not *the* best bird book ever written." Published in 1872, it ran through five editions during three decades. It can hardly be called a work of literature. But one of the top bird men of the following generation, Frank M. Chapman, found it "an inexhaustible store of information, its technicalities so humanized by its author that they were made attractive and intelligible even to the novice . . . the work of a great ornithologist and a master of the art of exposition."

The army command did not know that it was doing Coues a lasting service when, toward the end of the war, it had assigned him to these godforsaken western outposts. But the *Key* established his scientific reputation, and in 1873 he was appointed naturalist to the United States Northern Boundary Commission, and subsequently to the Hayden Survey — an ambitious government project (initiated the same year as Clarence King's) covering the vast Western Territories. The following year he published *Birds of the Northwest*, a book that Roosevelt claimed no ranchman could afford to be without "if he cares at all for natural history."

A founder of the American Ornithologists' Union, originator of that ultimate authority in nomenclature, the *Check List of North American Birds*, Coues did not confine himself to ornithology.* He wrote on general zoology, on biology, on comparative anatomy; he became an authority on fur-bearing animals and produced a staggering total of almost a thousand papers and monographs during his lifetime.

If only he had stopped there! But as his friend D. G. Elliott wrote in *The Auk* at the time of his death: "First among his most eminent characteristics was his love of truth, and he was constantly striving with all the force of his energetic nature to search it out and take its teaching to himself wherever he might find it, careless where it might lead him . . ." It led him, of all things, into the arms of the world-famous Madame Helena Blavatsky, goddess of the Theosophical Society, whom he described — to the embarrassment of his scientific associates — as "the greatest woman of this age, *who is born to redeem her times.*" Never one to take a back seat, Coues promptly founded a branch of the Society in Washington, and helped organize the American Society for Psychical Research; he even tried to become the head of the whole movement in

---

* An accomplished classical scholar, Coues enjoyed tracing the Greek or Latin origin of the scientific name of each species. One which must have given him particular delight was *Falco sparverius isabellinus*, the "Isabel Sparrow Hawk" (then considered a subspecies): "The Lady Isabel, having confidence in her husband's prowess, vowed not to change her chemise until that warrior had taken a certain town. He was longer about it than she expected, and she wore the garment until it assumed a peculiar brown tint: hence the term 'isabel-color'; whence quasi-Latin *isabellinus*."

America. To his chagrin, he failed to be elected, whereupon the scholar in him took back the reins from the mystic. Already skeptical about the messages from the "world beyond," he had quarreled with the Society, which he now denounced as "Madame Blavatsky's famous hoax." A month later, he was formally expelled. For the rest of his life he focused on more worldly matters, devoting his incredible energies to editing some fifteen volumes of early western travel, beginning with the journals of Lewis and Clark. Characteristically, he was in the midst of a strenuous research expedition through the Southwest when he died at the age of fifty-seven, leaving to his successors the accomplishment of several ordinary lifetimes.

As a personality, Coues must have been a bit overpowering. Young Frank Chapman, newly elected member of the A.O.U., described the great man in his journal after their first meeting: "Confident, assuming, slightly pompous, his faith in his own ability undoubted . . . Tall, full beard, long wavy hair brushed back from a good forehead . . . pleasant spoken, unreserved and affable." Not a man to talk to, Chapman commented later, unless you have something to say.

Open-minded in argument, Coues was a generous but severe critic of other men's work. "He believed true criticism was to seek that which is praiseworthy rather than something to condemn," recalled his friend Elliott. "But no one could be more caustic in his treatment, nor wield a sharper weapon when he found that praise would be misapplied and it would be kinder to act as the skillful surgeon does, create wounds in order that the patient's recovery might be more sure and lasting." The patients' response to this treatment has not been recorded.

In his ornithological research Coues was, by modern standards, equally ruthless. Bird study and reliable bird records still depended solely on the gun; good field glasses, much less binoculars and color cameras, had not yet been developed. "I wish to urge a point, the importance of which is often overlooked," he writes. "It is our practical interpretation of the adage 'a bird in the hand is worth two in the bush . . .' How many birds of the same kind do you want? — *All you can get* — with some limitations; say fifty or a hundred of any but the most abundant and widely diffused species . . . If forced to reduce bulk, owing to limited facilities for transportation in the field (as too often happens) throw away according to *size,* other things being equal. Given only so many cubic inches or feet, eliminate the few *large* birds which take up the space that would contain fifty or a hundred different little ones. If you have a fine large bald eagle or pelican, for instance, throw it away first, and follow it with your ducks, geese, etc. . . ." In his *Natural History in America* (1977), Wayne Hanley of the Massachusetts Audubon Society comments on this passage: "The current decline among birds of prey is reflected in Coues's advice that included a 'fine large bald eagle' among the birdskins to be thrown away first for the sake of saving space. One may be imprisoned today for owning a fine, or even decrepit, bald eagle."

Coues was an ardent bird-lover all his life, both before and after he became a professional ornithologist. To the scientists of his day, there was no inconsistency in this attitude, any more than there is to the gunners who, now as then, kill for sport. Even the gentle John Burroughs admonished his novice bird students: "Don't ogle it through a glass. *Shoot it!*" As for the gunners, it should be remembered that most of the early conservationists first came to enjoy the outdoors and the world of nature as sportsmen. This is true of Roosevelt, of Grinnell, of Hornaday, and many others who, like Coues, are associated mainly with the West. It is also true of many — but not all — of the literary naturalists who found their inspiration in the mellower countryside of New England.

❧

If the New England Puritans were guided by the Old Testament view of nature, believing anything not "useful" to be somehow evil, their successors have done their best to right the balance. No corner of the continent has been so lovingly studied by naturalists as the Boston-Cambridge-Concord region, from Thoreau's time to the present. The nature essay which he developed remained a favorite literary form. One who practiced it with particular charm and humor was a well-born Boston bachelor named Bradford Torrey, who would eventually edit Thoreau's *Journal*. Like Wilson Flagg, Thomas Wentworth Higginson, and so many others, Torrey published his first nature essay, entitled "With the Birds of Boston Common," in the *Atlantic Monthly*. "Encouraged by this success, which had been quite unlooked for by him," wrote his birding companion Francis H. Allen, "he embarked on what finally became his life work as a writer of discursive essays on birds, flowers, and the world out of doors . . . His combination of enthusiasm with a humorous detachment was also one of his greatest charms as a writer, and one that made it possible for readers without any particular knowledge of or interest in birds to enjoy his writing almost as much as the confirmed bird-lover."

Torrey had little patience with his Puritan ancestors' attitude toward nature. "Why should men be so provincial as to pronounce anything worthless merely because *they* can do nothing with it?" he wrote in his first book, *Birds in the Bush* (1885). "The clover is not without value, although the robin and the oriole may agree to think so. We know better; and so do the rabbits and the humblebees." Birdwatching, however, had not yet become a respectable pastime. Early on a spring morning Torrey was standing at the side of "one of those delightful back-roads, half-road and half lane, where the grass grows between the horse-track and the wheel-track," listening to the song of a white-eyed vireo.

While I stood peering into the thicket, a man whom I know came along the road, and caught me thus disreputably employed. Without doubt he thought me a lazy good-for-nothing; or possibly (being more charitable) he said to himself, "Poor fellow! he's losing his mind." . . . Take a gun on your shoulder, and go wandering about the woods all day long, and you will be looked upon with respect. But to be seen staring at a bird for five minutes together — well, it is fortunate there are asylums for the crazy. Not unlikely the malady will grow upon him; and who knows how soon he may become dangerous?

For all his playfulness, Torrey was a competent observer, with a gentle and cheerful philosophy that reminds one less of Thoreau than of Wilson Flagg. Like Flagg, he sprinkled his prose with appropriate texts, though in his case from the Scriptures rather than the classics, as he struggled to reconcile the apparent cruelty of wild nature with the doctrine of an all-wise Providence. *Birds in the Bush,* which went into edition after edition, was followed by some ten more volumes of essays, on subjects ranging from New Hampshire's White Mountains to Florida and Texas. With his easy conversational style, his ability to combine science and esthetics, he doubtless converted thousands of readers who had hitherto considered birdwatchers to be at best mildly insane.

Of greater importance for our time was his editing, toward the end of his life, of the first complete edition of Thoreau's *Journal,* in fourteen volumes — one of the most seminal pieces of writing in American literature.*

ʏ

These New England writers were in the mainstream of a literary tradition that goes back to Gilbert White's *Selborne* and beyond: a lifelong celebration of nature as it reveals itself through intimate acquaintance with one cherished spot on earth. Such a place is the Concord River Valley, which still retains much of its original charm, as anyone with a canoe can see for himself.

"I think that I speak impartially when I say that I have never met with a stream so suitable for boating and botanizing as the Concord, and fortunately nobody knows it," wrote Thoreau in his journal in 1858. Plenty of persons know it today; the wildness and remoteness which he valued so

* Francis H. Allen, then an editor at Houghton, Mifflin & Company, was a co-editor of this massive project, though his name did not appear on the first edition.

highly — "which a single country seat would spoil beyond remedy" — have all but vanished. Yet there remain stretches of the river, from its source in the Westboro swamps to its confluence with the Merrimack at Lowell, where one can evoke some sense of the past, where one sees this singularly undramatic stream through the eyes of those who, through the qualities they brought to it, made it the vehicle for some of the best nature writing in our literature.

"This river of ours," wrote Hawthorne, "is the most sluggish stream that I ever was acquainted with." So it is at most seasons over most of its length, including the stretch he knew beside the Old Manse. But, a mile downstream, during the spring freshets, he might have sailed with Thoreau over the Great Meadows through "a tumultuous sea, a myriad waves breaking with whitecaps," under the dark, wind-driven clouds. Or, at the same season, he might have snaked his canoe up to the hidden pond where the river is born, as one can still do today. Here it is a narrow trout stream, scarcely wider than the canoe itself; dark, deep as the length of one's paddle, meandering through the marsh with a strong but silent current. As one labors upstream, sometimes paddling, sometimes poling, mayflies rise from the water, a spotted sandpiper teeters on a tiny mudflat, black duck, mallards, blue-winged teal explode from unseen puddles, and a pair of wood duck take wing with a shrill squeak — till suddenly one emerges on a broad cattail-bordered pond, alive with tree swallows skimming the surface and blackbirds calling from the shore. For a moment there is a sense of remoteness, of wildness, such as was felt by Thoreau and, a generation later, by that Gilbert White of the Concord River, William Brewster.

❧

Born in 1851, a descendant and namesake of the Pilgrim leader, Brewster was reared in the literary atmosphere of Cambridge; Longfellow, a family friend, lived just up the street. Poor health and weak eyesight during early manhood

kept him from going to Harvard, but he survived this depriva-
tion — which Thoreau might have termed a blessing — with
notable success. His boyhood friend, Daniel Chester French,
the future sculptor of Concord's famous Minuteman (and of
the statue of Starr King in San Francisco) had encouraged his
interest in nature, and particularly in birds. His father, who
liked shooting and fishing, had given him a gun. French's father, an amateur collector, supplied lessons in taxidermy.
"Will's father had Audubon's Ornithology and my father had
Nuttall's," French wrote many years later, "which we studied
with a thoroughness which would have put us at the head of
our classes if applied to our school books." When the French
family left town, young Will found another soul mate in a boy
named Henry Henshaw, whose frail health also kept him out
of college — but not out of the rough fields and forests that
still surrounded Cambridge in those days. "It was our custom
to start for the woods soon after daybreak, often afoot, sometimes in a buggy, for the Fresh Pond swamps (a favorite
haunt), or for Belmont, Waverley, Lexington, or Concord . . .
As a result of this activity Brewster's collection grew apace
until it ultimately became one of the largest private collections ever made in this country."

A trial period in the family bank quickly convinced both father and son that William was cut out to be a birder, not a
banker. In 1876, when only twenty-five, he organized
America's first bird club, the Nuttall Ornithological Club
(named for Thomas Nuttall, the great American ornithologist), with fewer than a dozen members. Seven years later,
at his urging, it gave birth to a national organization, the
American Ornithologists' Union (A.O.U.), one of whose members, George Bird Grinnell, would in turn found the first Audubon Society. So began a chain reaction of immeasurable
impact on the course of conservation history.

Meanwhile the Nuttall Club — to which Theodore Roosevelt was elected when he came to Harvard — continued to
meet in the private museum that Brewster built in his Cambridge backyard to house his burgeoning collection of bird-

skins and books. Later he took charge of the bird collection in Harvard's Museum of Comparative Zoology and became known as the foremost field ornithologist of his time. All of this activity resulted in literally hundreds of technical papers, and such standard books as *The Birds of the Cambridge Region*. The scientific community could be grateful that Will Brewster had shown no talent for banking. He himself apparently believed that he had little talent for popular writing either, but he was too modest. Here is his description, written in his youth, of a trip with Robert Ridgway to a cypress swamp in Illinois, in search of the beautiful prothonotary warbler*:

Towards the middle of the afternoon we reached Beaver Dam Pond, and embarked in an old weather-beaten dugout. Our guide, a half-breed Indian and a most accomplished woodsman, took his station in the stern, and, with a vigorous shove upon his long push-pole, sent the frail craft well out into the pond. Before us stretched a long, narrow sheet of water hemmed in on every side by an unbroken wall of forest trees. Around the margin grew a fringe of button-bushes, with a sprinkling of tall slender willows, while behind and above them towered the light-green feathery crests of numerous cypresses . . . Wood Ducks and Hooded Mergansers rose on every side, while their broods of downy ducklings scuttled off among the water-plants, sometimes huddling close together, a dusky mass of bobbing little forms, at others, when closely pressed, separating and diving like water-sprites. Overhead, Buzzards were wheeling in graceful, interminable circlings, while in their nests upon the tops of some gigantic sycamores, a little back from the shore, stood a number of Great Blue Herons, their tall, graceful forms boldly outlined against the sky. From the lower depths of the forest came innumerable bird-voices, — the slow, solemn chant of the Wood Thrush, the clear, whistled challenge of the Cardinal, the sweet, wild notes of the Louisiana Water Thrush . . . Higher up among the trees Woodpeckers rattled upon dead limbs, a Tanager sang at intervals . . .

* Robert Ridgway is one of the great figures in American ornithology, author of the monumental *Birds of North and Middle America* and many other standard works. He was a member of Clarence King's Fortieth Parallel Survey (see p. 48) and of the famous Harriman Expedition of 1899 (see pp. 14–15), a founder of the American Ornithologists' Union and for many years curator of birds in the United States National Museum.

The spaces between the living stems were filled with stumps in every stage of decay, and perforated with countless Woodpecker-holes, most of them old, and long since given up by their original tenants. That a locality so favorable in every way had not been over-looked by the Prothonotary Warblers was soon evinced by the pres-ence of the birds on all sides in numbers that far exceeded anything which we had previously seen, and careful search soon revealed a number of nests.* Probably not less than twenty pairs were here breeding in close proximity. In the larger holes and among the branches were the nests of a colony of Grackles . . . As we returned down the pond late in the afternoon the sun was sinking behind the tree-tops. The dying breeze still agitated the crest of the forest, but not a breath rippled the still water beneath. The lonely pool rested in deep shadow, save at its upper end, where the slanting sunbeams still lighted up the group of willows, bringing out their yellowish foliage in strong relief against the darker mass behind. The arches of the grand old woods were filled with a softened, mysterious light and a solemn hush and silence prevailed, broken only by the oc-casional hooting of a Barred Owl or the song of some small bird among the upper branches, where the rays of the setting sun still lingered.

Brewster nevertheless found writing hard, painful work. "It will surprise many who have admired his smoothly flowing periods and felicitous methods of expression," commented a contemporary, "to know that he wrote only with great dif-ficulty and labor." There is no reason for surprise. A great admirer of Thoreau, he had set himself high standards, and he came closer to meeting them than he knew. He told his old friend Dan French that he would frequently spend a whole af-ternoon in perfecting one sentence, and regretted that he could not write popular articles on natural history like some of his contemporaries. But after reading his Concord journals French felt that "no ornithologist who has ever lived in America" could compare with him "as a master of simple, dignified prose."

Perhaps it was from Thoreau that Brewster got the idea of

---

* "This is the only warbler in North America that is known to nest habi-tually in holes in trees" (Forbush, *Birds of Massachusetts*).

keeping a journal of his outdoor observations, but it was largely by chance that he came to live in Concord, and that the greater part of this journal should have been devoted to Thoreau's beloved Concord River. He knew the Concord region, of course; he had hunted ruffed grouse in its woods, listened to the flight-song of the woodcock in its meadows, and collected birds for his museum. He and his wife had spent two summers in Hawthorne's Old Manse. When he learned that a fine tract of land downstream, with hills and ancient pines, was about to be sold for timber, he bought it to save the woods from destruction. Subsequently he built several log cabins at the water's edge for weekends alone or with his friends; and purchased a colonial farmhouse which eventually became his home. Christened "October Farm," it would give its name to the first of two books drawn from his journals of life on the river: *October Farm* and *Concord River* — posthumous publications which have become classics of their kind. Despite resemblances in style and subject, their kind is not Thoreau's kind. Brewster was no mere imitator of Thoreau or anyone else. Like Thoreau he avoided the "fine writing" so typical of the early nature essay; but unlike him, he neither moralized nor intruded himself into the picture. It is perhaps an exaggeration to say, with Thomas Barbour, that Brewster and Thoreau "were in no wise kin," but it is true that, whereas "Thoreau's ego was always near the surface," Brewster, a modest man, was more concerned with nature itself than with his own reaction to it.

One trait they notably had in common. When he was twenty-four, Thoreau wrote in his journal: "Nothing can be more useful to a man than a determination not to be hurried." Once, for example, he spent a happy afternoon conversing with a woodchuck.* Forty years later, Brewster recorded a morning with a family of muskrats:

July 7, 1892

Spent the entire forenoon at the Buttricks' landing, watching the

* *Journal*, April 16, 1852.

brood of young Flickers and the Muskrats. There were four of the latter in my boat-house under my canoe and a fifth beneath the boathouse in the water. I drew out the canoe without disturbing them and then crawled in. When I was within about four feet of them, three scuttled across the house and plunged down through a crack between the boards into the water. The fourth remained perfectly still and presently began to scratch his head with his hind paw. I cautiously thrust out a long straw and assisted. He started and showed his teeth for a moment, turning on the straw as if to bite it, but soon quieted down again when, dropping the straw, I substituted my forefinger and, of course, now worked to much better advantage, at first giving the back of the head a thorough scratching, next taking the sides of the neck and finally stroking the back down to the tail. It was difficult to realize that I was actually handling a wild and perfectly free Muskrat for, after the first slight show of resentment, no kitten could have been gentler and more confiding. In a little while the eyes began to close and the animal gradually sank down on one side and was soon apparently fast asleep.

Though his name will always be associated with Cambridge and Concord, Brewster studied and collected birds from the Gulf of St. Lawrence to Florida; and in 1894 his friend Frank M. Chapman, curator of birds at the American Museum of Natural History, took great delight in introducing him to the birdlife of the tropics. "I expected to, and did, receive the greater part of my pleasure in seeing the response of his finely tuned, sensitive nature to a flora and fauna which I knew would arouse his utmost interest and enthusiasm." Brewster must have been the perfect companion, in his Cambridge study or in the field. After their first encounter at an A.O.U. meeting, Chapman noted in his journal: "Brewster leaves nothing to be desired either in appearance or actions. He is an ideal; handsome, frank . . . sincere, perfectly natural . . . Extremely pleasant, but not too much so; a man whose friends are to be envied." Thirty-three years later, when Brewster died in 1919, at the age of sixty-eight, Chapman's opinion remained unchanged: "No estimate of Brewster's work can be exact which does not take into account the character of the man . . . He loved all that is fine in human intercourse, and his thoughtfulness for others, his sympathetic appreciation of and interest in their work, their joys and their sorrows made his friendship one of life's best gifts." *

℞

For Brewster, the pleasure of a river trip was enhanced by the presence of a companion — of the right sort. For years he and his old friend Dan French never missed their "annual day" on the river, rain or shine. And then there was that extraordinarily attractive and gifted young man, the Secretary of Harvard University, Frank Bolles. Bolles had studied law to gratify his father, but he preferred journalism, and put in some years on a Boston paper before going to work for President Eliot, in an office that could have been deadly dull. Not so for Bolles. The "tall, rugged man with bearded face and friendly eyes" became one of the most popular men in Harvard Yard, a personal friend and adviser to the students, a link with the graduates; the spark plug of every new enterprise. All of which left him little time — in contrast to his friend Will Brewster — to enjoy his passion for the outdoors. But summer vacations he spent roaming the wilderness near New Hampshire's Mt. Chocorua; weekends and holidays he made a dash for the country around Cambridge. After each of these short excursions he would record his impressions while they were still vivid. Soon he was writing them up for the Boston *Post*, where they caught the eye of James Russell Lowell. As a result of Lowell's encouragement, *Land of the Lingering Snow: Chronicles of a Stroller in New England from January to June*, was published in 1891, and its companion volume, *At the North of Bearcamp Water*, two years later. Both as a naturalist and as a writer, Bolles was wholly self-taught, which may explain in part the freshness and almost naïve enthusiasm with which he records even the smallest outdoor adventure.

---

* It was Chapman's idea, after Brewster's death, to establish the Brewster Medal, the top award for books on American ornithology. Appropriately, the medal was designed by Brewster's lifelong friend and boating companion, Daniel Chester French.

No more than Brewster does he moralize, or concern himself principally with his own response. "Instead of suggesting the sentiments which a given scene called up in him," wrote a friend, "he paints the scene and leaves the reader to put in the sentiments." True, yet some of his best passages give a sense of excitement, of personal involvement in the life about him, which enable the reader to share his experiences as no merely factual description ever could. When he and Brewster were on the river together, they would occasionally record the same event in their journals. Take for example an encounter with a great horned owl, on an early spring camping trip. Brewster sets the scene:

It was very dark when we reached Fairhaven Cliff and Bolles began hooting like a Barred Owl. I followed with a feeble imitation of the Great-horned Owl which, after a few moments and to my infinite surprise, was answered by Bubo himself from the tall pines on the west bank of the river. We stopped paddling, of course, and I continued the conversation in the best Owl language that I could command. Bubo was prompt in his responses and presently appeared directly over our heads — a great shadowy bird with broad wings and big head, flapping at first, then sailing as majestically as an Eagle, finally descending in a series of undulations to the low trees on the shore . . .

A fire that we kindled seemed to attract him for he came into the top of a pine nearly over us and hooted steadily at intervals varying from ten to fifteen seconds. His voice was deep, yet soft and cooing like that of a Carolina Dove . . .

To Brewster, great horned owls were old friends, at home in the pine woods above his riverside cabin. But, as any camper knows, the first nighttime visit by one of these great birds is an eerie experience. Bolles describes this same incident in an essay entitled "A Voyage to Heard's Island":

Nearer and on our right was a grove of lofty white pines. There are few such trees in this part of New England; they are a fragment of the primeval woods, full of wind voices and memories of a lost race of men, and a vanishing race of birds and mammals. As we neared this grove a mysterious greeting came to us from its depths. A voice at once sad, deep, soft, and full of suppressed power seemed to question us. My friend responded in the stranger's language, and a few moments after a dark form floated over us, its great wings making no sound as they beat against the night air. Then from the foot of Fairhaven Hill the voice called to us again; and soon the form passed back over the river to the tops of the pines. Behind Fairhaven Hill the eastern clouds reflected a slowly increasing flood of yellow light. Over the rest of the sky night had settled. Bird voices were hushed, but from the river banks, as far as the ear could hear, the song of frogs rose and fell in irregular rhythm. The air was chilly, and a thin layer of white mist hurried over the surface of the water . . . At last the moon's rim showed through the trees on Fairhaven Hill, and the high pines close by us on the western shore were bathed in uncertain light. From their tops the mysterious voice still questioned us at intervals.

This pine grove was our chosen camping ground, and the light of the moon enabled us to select a landing place and to draw our canoes ashore . . . Instead of being alarmed by our landing, the light of our fire, and the sound of our voices, the dark phantom of the pines seemed to be attracted by these unusual interruptions. The voice grew louder and more distinct. Its winged source came nearer from tree top to tree top, until it settled in the tallest, darkest pine in the grove, almost immediately over our heads. It was unlike any other voice I had ever heard. It possessed a contralto quality; it was laden with intense emotion, yet it was calm and singularly regular both in its sounds and in its silences. In spite of its softness and the slight trembling in its tones, it suggested power, — a power sufficient to raise a trumpet note audible a mile away.

Ten o'clock came and went, and we sought our cocoons . . .

The scene of Frank Bolles's nature essays extended far beyond the Cambridge-Concord region. Witness his classic account of a night on the rocky summit of Mt. Chocorua in a raging thunderstorm — an experience as awesome as John Muir's in a storm-tossed treetop on the High Sierra, or Clarence King's in a Yosemite blizzard — which he describes with breathless excitement and touches of quiet humor. More essays were being prepared for publication when, in January of 1893, he suddenly died of pneumonia. He was only thirty-six. "In his death," wrote his friend William Thayer, "Harvard has lost a son than whom none was ever more devoted, and American literature has lost a writer who had already produced work of singular and lasting merit, and who, just reaching the fulness of his powers, gave promise of something still more precious."

⚜

Another friend of Brewster, who often stayed in his cabin on the Concord River, was a professional ornithologist and charming writer named Edward Howe Forbush. Forbush not only lived to fulfill his early promise, but remains a sort of patron saint of New England birders, a gentle, humorous, companionable saint whose finest legacy is the three-volume *Birds of Massachusetts and Other New England States.* He himself was a New Englander from way back. Born in 1858 — the same year as Theodore Roosevelt — he grew up in West Rox-

bury, Massachusetts, when it was still glorious country. "Throughout his boyhood" (wrote his colleague T. Gilbert Pearson), "this future naturalist exhibited an originality and venturesomeness that led him into various difficulties, such as falling into a cistern, breaking through ice and riding down the cellar stairs on a chair. He also learned some of the laws of nature when he dropped a lighted match into a bottle of gunpowder . . . His youthful inquisitiveness, however, led him into other fields of exploration which produced most interesting, if less startling, results." These fields included all of outdoor nature, but most of all birds. At the very time that young Roosevelt was solemnly donating his stuffed squirrel, bats, and birds' eggs to the American Museum in New York, Forbush was also teaching himself taxidermy. "At the early age of fifteen," he recalled, "I came to believe myself a hunter-naturalist, but even at that early age the excitement of the chase was sometimes followed by reaction and remorse at the death of the lovely creatures slain, as I fondly believed, in the interest of science." This was the period when natural history was still studied largely from museum specimens: skins, skeletons, and various bloated creatures pickled in alcohol, which had so revolted Henry Thoreau. Forbush of course recognized that study collections, to which he himself made extensive contributions, were essential, but they were not enough. "Some of the material used by students was very dead, having been so for fifty years or more. Such mummies have their uses, but later I came to see life, not death, would solve all riddles . . . and that it was more essential to preserve the living than the dead."

To learn and to preserve became his life work. When the family moved to Worcester, he joined the local natural history society, and soon found himself president. He conducted a summer camp for nature study, meanwhile supplementing his income by collecting trips as far west as the Washington Territories and as far south as Florida. In 1876 he made a trip on the Oklawaha River which Sidney Lanier had described so lovingly the previous summer. Both the poet and the professional naturalist were overawed by its lush beauty, and shocked by the ruthless behavior of their fellow passengers.

During the journey to southern Florida we saw what no man ever will see again. Along the upper St. Johns and the Oclawaha the Florida wilderness came down to the river banks and encroached upon and even overhung the stream. In many places on the Oclawaha the semi-tropical foliage with its drapery of Spanish moss entirely overarched the water, so that a steamboat plowing its way along the river, seemed to float in a tunnel of luxuriant verdure. Alligators in numbers swam in streams and ponds or rested on the shores. Uncounted swarms of waterfowl of many species inhabited the waters in innumerable multitudes. Great flocks of White Egrets and ibises, among them the lovely Roseate Spoonbills, possessed the land. Every turn in the river brought into view a new scene, to be scanned for novel forms of interesting life . . .
     Practically all tourists were armed with rifles, shotguns, revolvers, or all three. These armed men lined the rails of the steamboats and shot *ad libitum* at alligators, waterfowl or anything that made an attractive target. There were practically no restrictions on shooting, although the steamers never stopped to gather in the game, but left it to lie where it fell.

Forbush wrote entertainingly of his adventures — some of them quite hair-raising — in the pages of George Bird Grinnell's *Forest and Stream.* He became a leader in both the national and the Massachusetts Audubon societies, and simultaneously went to work for the state government, eventually as State Ornithologist. In fighting for stricter game laws, he instinctively realized that Americans still suffered from the Puritan philosophy that only those creatures "useful" to man were worth saving. His *Useful Birds and Their Protection* was a pioneer work in economic ornithology. Nor did he stop there. His hundreds of popular lectures on conservation, along with countless newspaper and magazine articles, must have had a lasting impact on the crustiest of New England farmers and businessmen. "He accomplished his ends with a minimum of effort," recalled his successor, John B. May, "as, tall, spare, and almost ascetic in appearance, he moved quietly about his chosen work."

Perhaps the most endearing thing about Forbush is the obvious joy with which he pursued his profession. Today's writers on natural history tend to draw a sharp line between the scientific study and the book for popular consumption. Not so in the past. Early works are full of what someone has termed "popular excursuses." Audubon lightened his huge *Ornithological Biography* with charming and often humorous "episodes" of frontier life. Thomas Bewick concluded each chapter of his classic *History of British Birds* with a woodcut depicting English rural life in vivid — sometimes macabre or bawdy — terms. In the *Birds of Massachusetts* Forbush kept to his subject, but he let himself go when the spirit moved him. Thus he begins his entry on the "Haunts and Habits" of the common crow:

The Crow "knows a good thing when he sees it." He seeks and finds for his home a land of plenty . . . where the fruits of the earth are spread before him. He seeks the bounty of the fields. On September 23, 1913, while sitting on a moss-grown ledge near the brow of a precipitous side-hill just east of the village of Stowe, Vermont, I viewed a splendid panorama of mountain, valley and sky. Below me lay the village, nestling amid its environment of autumnal foliage like a gem in its setting or a bird on her nest. The neat well painted houses and well kept yards, the tall white church spire pointing toward the sky and the American flag flying from its staff on the cupola of the public hall typified much that is best in American village life. The eye roved to wide meadows stretching down the valley, clothed in plush-like green. There the winding course of the stream was marked by a double border of green shrubbery, with here and there a row of willows, and some scattering elms and maples glowing in the sunlight with the rich primal colors of the season. Then the eye, lifting, passed on over bordering fields to upland pastures with their soft and changing tints, interspersed with groups and groves of trees — the whole a great park laid out as if by the hand of a master. Beyond the pastures on either hand rose the hills, and in the background towered mighty Mount Mansfield, the giant of them all, its slopes darkened and blued by distance. Over the landscape flamed the red and gold of autumn, toned and darkened here and there by drifting shadows, and above all arched the blue dome with its fleecy clouds. The warmth and peace of summer brooded gently over all. Crows cawed in the valley, where substantial farm-houses and well filled barns attested the prosperity of the people. This is indeed a country of the blest. Such are the favorite haunts of the Crow in New England . . .

Unfortunately for the Crow he has a bad reputation, and it must be admitted that there is some reason for the low regard in which he is held among men. First he is black, the color of evil; then, he knows too much; his judgment of the range of a gun is too nearly correct. If Crows could be shot oftener they would be more popular. Henry Ward Beecher once remarked that if men wore feathers and wings a very few of them would be clever enough to be Crows . . . We have to get up very early in the morning to get ahead of the Crow. Most of us rarely see the sun rise, and while the sluggards still slumber, the early Crow is up to some abominable mischief in the back yard. It irritates us to have this disreputable fowl take such a mean advantage of us, especially as we know that it would not have happened had we been up and about, as we know we should have been. Then, according to human standards, the Crow is a thief and a robber. He steals eggs, chickens, corn; he robs song birds of their eggs and young, and so he is vilified and anathematized, pursued and destroyed, at every opportunity; but all to little purpose, for we may well believe that there are more Crows in the country now than there were when the Pilgrims landed on Plymouth Rock. To-day then, the Crow is the great American bird . . . If a person knows only four birds, one of them will be the Crow . . . He is well worth knowing. Each Crow is a character. There is more difference in Crows than appears as they fly over.

He concludes with Thoreau's eulogy: "This bird sees the white man come and the Indian withdraw but it withdraws not. Its untamed voice is still heard above the tinkling of the forge. It sees a race pass away but it passes not away. It remains to remind us of aboriginal nature."

Forbush was writing at a time when almost everyone still thought in terms of "good animals" and "bad animals"; when hunters made a sharp distinction between the creatures they killed for sport and the hungry "varmints" who offered unwelcome competition for the same prey. His concern, however, was more with the farmers. Each chapter of his book ends with a section on "economic status," ranging from a bird like the downy woodpecker, whose appetite for "noxious insects" warrants it "complete protection at all times and places," to the Cooper's hawk, which he concedes "is not a bird to be protected by the farmer, poultry-man or game-keeper." But unlike Dr. Hornaday, the sometimes misguided sportsman-turned-conservationist, he did not call for its immediate extinction.

In writing about the grandest of New England's so-called game birds, the ruffed grouse or partridge, Forbush anticipates the shift in emphasis that was already occurring during his lifetime: from the thrill of the hunt to the esthetic pleasure in contemplation of the living bird.

Whir-r-r! What — why, the partridge! Where he came from I know not, but now right here by the wall at the foot of that big white birch . . . stands a lordly old grouse, his raised ruffs with their dark metallic sheen glistening in the sunlight, as with crested head drawn back and carried high, with bright and banded tail held high and widely spread, he stands alert . . .

Only a partridge! You may see dozens hung by the neck or heels in butchers' stalls next fall; mere wrecks of things that were. But as for me, I would not exchange my one sight of that crested, full-winged bird, in all the glory of his nuptial plumage, moving alert upon his native heath, his proud spirit untamed and free, his frame instinct with vibrating electric life and undaunted vigor drawn from our rugged New England hills, for all the keen joy of the sportsman as the mangled, bleeding form falls to his deadly aim, or the delights of the epicure as he revels in the luscious tender flesh of the slaughtered birds as they lie garnished upon the groaning table.

❧

Today those who go looking for birds with a field glass rather than a gun are no longer, as Bradford Torrey suggested, seen as candidates for the asylum, but in some circles they are quite rightly considered dangerous. *Per se* conservationists, they may frequently be found in sunlit meadows or in dismal swamps, blocking the path to Progress. For those who still believe in the frontier philosophy of unhampered exploitation, "birdwatchers," like "environmentalists," are natural enemies. The fact that they are taken so seriously today is an indication of how effective the articulate members of the fraternity have been during the past century in educating the public, in altering our basic attitude toward nature. As Louis Agassiz's Museum of Comparative Zoology set the pattern for the American Museum of Natural History, so the New England naturalists (particularly the ornithologists) helped lay the groundwork for what became a national movement. In getting this movement under way, no one was more effective than Brewster's young friend and admirer, Frank M. Chapman. In his own words, Chapman's life constitutes a "record of that period of our history when, through ignorance of their charm and value, we permitted the birds of our gardens and forests to be killed by countless thousands . . . to that time when we became aware of their existence and guarded their lives as we guard our own."

Chapman was born in rural New Jersey in 1864 — the year when George Perkins Marsh published *Man and Nature*, when Clarence King explored the High Sierra, when Abraham Lincoln signed the bill to preserve Yosemite Valley. His father was a Wall Street lawyer with a farm in rural New Jersey. The son learned to name the common birds as soon as he could talk, and knew most of their songs before he went to school. By the age of twenty he was reporting on bird migration for the A.O.U. A year later he read John Burroughs' *Wake-Robin* for the first time and was deeply moved by the passage in which Burroughs describes the emotions aroused by the song of the hermit thrush at evening in the hemlocks.*

"I for the first time found expressed my own response to the song of the wood thrush. I could not have told this to Burroughs, but so strong was my gratitude for his aid in self-revelation that I tried to express it in writing. He at once replied saying with what pleasure he learned that anything he had written possessed this potentiality." It was ten years before they met, and became close friends.

For young Chapman nature study was still an avocation, not a career. Like William Brewster, he went to work in a

* See page 10.

bank. But unlike his friend, he did quite well at it, and when after six years he suddenly resigned, his colleagues were mystified. They were unaware that he had not only been spending every free moment in the field studying the birds, but was already a member of the A.O.U. and of that distinguished company of naturalists, the Linnaean Society. "It became evident," he recalled, "that there would soon be a serious conflict between the bank clerk and the bird man . . . That the demand for ornithologists was limited, that their remuneration was but little above the vanishing point, were facts to which no real bird student gives serious attention." In 1888 he joined the staff of the American Museum as assistant to Dr. Joel A. Allen, recently of the Museum of Comparative Zoology in Cambridge. It was a time when "ornithology as a profession in this country was almost unknown."

Chapman was primarily a field ornithologist, a student of birds in nature, rather than a taxonomist. Above all he was a great popularizer — the greatest since Audubon. Taking charge of the Museum exhibits, he developed the now-familiar "habitat groups." No longer, in the words of the Museum's historian, Geoffrey Hellman, would the birds on display consist of "a lot of stuffed specimens arranged in a manner reminiscent of the grill of a college club." Birds must be real before we can see them as friends, and the first step toward friendship is recognition. To reach out to the public at large, Chapman produced his famous *Handbook of Birds of Eastern North America*, followed by a book for beginners, entitled *Bird-Life*, with illustrations by Ernest Thompson Seton. And in February 1899 he performed perhaps the most influential act of his life when he launched a new magazine named *Bird-Lore*, which he would edit for the next thirty-six years.

George Bird Grinnell's original *Audubon Magazine* had blossomed and died a dozen years earlier, but its seed had sprouted from Maine to California. Beginning with Massachusetts — which remained the spearhead of the movement — there were already seventeen state Audubon societies. One of their main concerns was the widespread use of wild birds in the millinery trade. On two late-afternoon walks in downtown New York City, Chapman had identified forty species, from grebes to grosbeaks, worn by female passersby, "few if any of whom knew that they were wearing the plumage of the birds of our gardens, orchards and forests." In Boston, the Massachusetts Audubon Society issued color charts of common birds and checked millinery in the stores, while working to restore the gull and tern colonies off the New England coast. The Pennsylvania Society won wide publicity for the Audubon cause by distributing in pamphlet form Celia Thaxter's emotional call to arms, "Woman's Heartlessness," which had appeared in the first issue of Grinnell's *Audubon Magazine*. Theodore Roosevelt, then Assistant Secretary of the Navy, joined the Washington, D.C., Society, and Chapman delivered its opening lecture, on "Woman as a Bird Enemy." So it went. The movement was achieving national recognition, but to be effective it must speak with a single voice. On his own initiative Frank Chapman, ex-banker and powerful persuader, raised the money for an official Audubon publication. So *Bird-Lore* (later renamed *Audubon Magazine*, and then simply *Audubon*) was born.

The first issue opened with an article by John Burroughs, "In Warbler Time"; the frontispiece, from a photograph by Chapman, showed the sage in his rocking chair beside the hearth at Slabsides. There were special sections for teachers and students and for "Young Observers," and a piece on bird photography, in which Chapman himself was a pioneer. The second number had a snapshot by Chapman of a chickadee feeding from the hand. Very cozy, sometimes corny, but deeply serious as well. Before its second year was out, Chapman had secured contributions from almost every well-known writer on birds, among them Ernest Thompson Seton, William Beebe, Robert Ridgway, Mabel Osgood Wright, Florence A. Merriam, William Brewster, Bradford Torrey. As the magazine grew, he was able to engage top-flight artists to match his writers. "Perhaps the most extraordinary single feature of the magazine," writes Roger Tory Peterson, "was the series of bird portraits by Louis Agassiz Fuertes, George Miksch Sutton, Allan Brooks, R. Bruce Horsfall, and others. For many years a frontispiece in full color graced each issue." Looking ahead Chapman could scarcely have envisioned today's *Audubon*, the most beautiful and literate of nature magazines. But had he done so, he would have recognized it as a logical extension of the standards he had set.

Bird-Lore was only a month old when Chapman received a warm letter from Theodore Roosevelt, "the beginning of an inspiring friendship," as he notes in his autobiography. "Spring would not be spring without bird songs," the future President wrote, anticipating by sixty-odd years the title of Rachel Carson's famous book, *Silent Spring*. Chapman was a perfect example of the sort of person that Roosevelt felt the country needed, someone able to take the facts of science and write of them with fidelity yet with an interpretative and poetic spirit. By the time Roosevelt had reached the White House, Frank Chapman had become perhaps the leading champion of nature and nature study in the country. An effective organizer and creative editor, he was also a talented author. Besides his many technical papers, he produced innumerable popular articles and no fewer than eighteen books, ranging from professional monographs to informal autobiographical volumes embodying in eloquent terms his personal enthusiasms, notably his passion for the birds and other wildlife of the tropics. In *My Tropical Air Castle*, published when he was sixty-four, he writes:

"We all have our 'Castles in the Air' but few of us, to use Thoreau's words, succeed in putting 'the foundation under them.' Ever since, as a boy, I read Bates' 'Naturalist on the Amazon' and Wallace's 'Travels in the Malay Archipelago' my castle has been in the tropics. For my own northern woods and fields I have the affection born of long and close association; but they lack the romance, the mystery, the enchantment, the inexhaustible possibilities of tropical forests and swamps. One forms a lasting and intimate friendship with nature in the north, but falls hopelessly in love with her in the south. But even while she lures she repels and perhaps herein lies her endless fascination. One is never quite sure of her. Her most winsome aspect may be deceptive, or it may be a dream of rare delight."

Of the many beautiful wild places that Frank Chapman had known during his travels, his favorite was the tropical research station on Barro Colorado Island in the Panama Canal Zone. Here he had his own "air castle" overlooking Gatun Lake:

It is in late December and early January, when the dry season is struggling for control, and the days are a succession of strongly contrasted and abruptly changing meteorological conditions, that the view across the lake presents its greatest interest. Over a blue sky clouds gather quickly; the lake becomes gray, squalls play on its surface; and suddenly the rain is on us. The Howling Monkeys roar a protest but their voices are literally drowned by the sound of the increasing storm. The lake becomes invisible; the world itself seems obliterated by walls of falling water. Then, quickly as it came, it passes; a bit of blue sky appears; the sun, like a searchlight, sends down brilliant streaming rays and soon floods the earth with golden cheerfulness. Again the vault is azure; great mountains of fluffy white clouds are banked on the horizon and the soggy earth and dripping, glossy, spangled leaves are the only evidence of the storm. In a few minutes it may be raining again, and this rapid shifting of the scenes between the two extremes creates a constantly changing panorama of great beauty. One morning a vivid bow faced the rising sun and through its center a Man-o'-War Bird, on set wing, sailed majestically.

By the year 1945, when Frank Chapman died at the age of eighty-one, our whole attitude toward birds and other wildlife had drastically changed, thanks in large measure to the writings of the articulate naturalists. Bird sanctuaries dotted the map of America from coast to coast. Birds and other animals were protected in national parks and federal wildlife refuges. Market-gunning had ceased, and the Migratory Bird Act had made slaughter of songbirds a federal offense. The annual "Christmas Census" — first suggested by Frank Chapman in 1900 — had replaced the locally organized "shoot."

Later Roger Tory Peterson's famous *Field Guide* made it possible to recognize birds through binoculars rather than by collecting them with a gun. So birdwatching grew to be a popular sport, with inestimable impact on the entire field of conservation. Protection of birds means protection of their habitat. Though the term "ecology" was not yet in common use in Chapman's day, there existed a new understanding of the interrelationship of all forms of life, including man. The foundation for today's environmental movement had been firmly laid.

When Frank Chapman received the Roosevelt Medal in 1928, the Brooklyn *Eagle* commented: "Nature interests millions today when formerly it interested thousands. The men who have had a part in this development have effected a fairly profound change in our habits of mind."

CHAPTER VII

Birds and Women

Audubon Society lady to E. B. White: "Mr. White, do
you watch birds?"
White: "Yes, and they watch me."

WRITING for the newly founded *Atlantic Monthly*, Wilson Flagg, it will be recalled, had recommended the study of flowers as a suitable outdoor recreation for the female sex who "cannot without some eccentricity of conduct follow birds and quadrupeds to the woods." Flagg was reflecting the mores of his time, but times were changing. True, one finds few women among the early American nature writers. This is not surprising. Many of our best naturalists began as sportsmen. Others, sponsored by the government or the natural history museums, found their inspiration in the frontier wilderness, in unclimbed mountains, unplumbed canyons, tropical rain forests. And though Louis Agassiz could enchant the young ladies of Cambridge with his lectures, few were to be seen in the laboratories or in the field. The world of science, with the technical training it required, remained largely a man's world. Serious field work, particularly in ornithology, still depended on the gun.

Yet there was another approach to nature, differing from the purely scientific in emphasis rather than in kind, which required no academic degrees, no far-flung expeditions, no killing. Thoreau, Burroughs, Flagg, Higginson, Torrey were in this tradition. So were a number of women writers who, unaware of any "eccentricity of conduct," followed the birds into the woods and wrote about them and other aspects of nature with understanding and enthusiasm. Their books, their essays in the literary magazines (and later in *Bird-Lore*), reached countless homes; their special talent for interesting young readers, and their emotional commitment when the Audubon societies were just getting under way, had an immeasurable impact on the whole conservation movement. Among the most memorable are Olive Thorne Miller, Mabel Osgood Wright, and Florence A. Merriam (who led an outdoor life as rugged as any man's).

In 1875, the year that Sidney Lanier published his enchanting guidebook to Florida and Wilson Flagg his culminating work on *The Birds and Seasons of New England*, there appeared in Boston a nature book for children, entitled *Little*

Folks in Feather and Fur. The author, Olive Thorne Miller,* was a contemporary of John Burroughs, and she shared with him an ability to reach the young. The folksiness of the title is deceptive; Mrs. Miller did not "write down" for children, either in this or in a long series of subsequent volumes based on observations from the coast of Maine to southern California, where she spent the final years of her life. Her nature books, which cover a period of no less than forty years, were directed mainly to children, and of these, her bird books were her best. They include *Bird-Ways, In Nesting Time, A Bird-Lover in the West, The First Book of Birds, With the Birds in Maine,* and *The Children's Book of Birds*, published three years before her death at the age of eighty-seven. By then she had long been a member of both the A.O.U. and the Linnaean Society. Like Celia Thaxter she had made the most of her popular following by joining the Audubon fight against the slaughter of birds for women's hats. Man's defacement of the natural scene also roused her fury. Her comments on dumping and littering, made at the turn of the century, have a surprisingly modern ring. She recalls how a lovely wooded ravine, "the only beautiful retreat for miles around," was used by the neighbors "as a common dumping-ground for all human waste. I cannot defile my pages with a list of the things that turned it into a most repulsive place . . ." One summer morning at her "Beloved Island" on the coast of Maine, she found her favorite spot for birdwatching "a scene of desolation. The sea had not risen and washed it away; no storm had displaced it — but a party of human beings had been there — ladies perhaps. The rocks far around were strewn with lobster- and egg-shells, crusts of bread, a tin can or two, and a great greasy newspaper . . . One half hour's visit from a thoughtless party had destroyed the charm of a month's study. I turned and left, and visited it no more." She is dismayed by "the spirit of lawlessness which seizes many of us in the country. Persons at home honest, well-bred, and thoughtful in dealing with oth-

---

*A pen name. Her real name was Harriet Mann Miller.

ers, suddenly blossom out into devastators and thieves." Ladies "who would not dream of taking a neighbor's purse" destroy valuable wildflowers and denude Maine's lovely balsam-firs. Elsewhere she contrasts the way nesting birds blend into their surroundings with the devastating impact of man. "How different our way! We cannot put up even a tent without changing the whole neighborhood, beginning at once to deface and destroy. Nay, we cannot even walk through the woods without leaving it strewn with our wreckage."

In a happier mood, she tells of an early summer morning which brought her an unexpected joy:

A quiet retreat in New Hampshire, in sight of Chocorua, made famous by our lamented Frank Bolles, offered me a peculiar and more musical morning attraction, — nothing less than the song of the barn-swallow. Not the low, sweet utterance we are familiar with from our bird of the hayloft, but strangely loud and clear, and poured out with all the freedom and abandon of a bobolink. It was such an exhibition of this bird's musical ability as I have seldom heard. The reason seemed to be that in that neighborhood he had to sustain almost the entire burden of song, the only other bird common about the place being the cedar-waxwing, who rarely speaks above a whisper. This being the case, the barn-swallow rose to the occasion and assumed his rôle with spirit, not only showing himself social and lively about the house, but blossoming out as a really brilliant singer, capable of furnishing a morning song to enchant the most critical audience. Perching himself on the peak of the roof over a dormer window and standing up very straight on his tiny black legs, — contrary to the family custom of sitting, — one would sing his quaint and charming song for half an hour at a time without pause, in so loud a tone that I hardly recognized it at first.

(This agrees with Forbush's description of the barn swallow's song as "a succession of twittered notes; a low chattering trill often followed by a clear liquid note." It is doubtful, however, that Mrs. Miller's swallows were singing from a sense of social obligation.)

Like Burroughs, Mrs. Miller wrote "less in the spirit of exact science than with the freedom of love and old acquaintance." One cannot fairly say of her, as was said of him, that she created "an army of nature students," but she was a pioneer in a field she made her own: the fine art of fostering a love of nature in the young.

❦

By the following generation, women were writing of nature with enthusiasm and professional competence. In 1839 the New York *Evening Post* printed an essay entitled "A New England May Day" — a charming, evocative piece of writing on a literary level considerably higher than Mrs. Miller's. The following year this reappeared as the opening chapter in a small, handsomely printed volume called *The Friendship of Nature*, dedicated to "S. O." The author was Mabel Osgood Wright, daughter of Samuel Osgood, a New York City clergyman and scholar and member of William Cullen Bryant's literary circle. He had encouraged her writing and her interest in nature from early childhood, and when she married and moved to Fairfield, Connecticut, she found plenty to write about in the New England countryside at every season of the year. Shortly after *The Friendship of Nature* came *Birdcraft*, with a subtitle that foreshadowed today's field guides: "A Field Book of Two Hundred Song, Game, and Water Birds." Frank Chapman gave both books a warm welcome. The first, he said, "records a loving intimacy with birds and flowers and seasons with the charm of one who sees keenly, feels deeply, and writes eloquently and sincerely." The second is "one of the first and most successful of the modern bird manuals."

Mrs. Wright was an early exponent of the doctrine that all living creatures, not just human beings, had their natural rights. Her next book, written jointly with none other than the awe-inspiring Elliott Coues, announced this conviction in its title, *Citizen Bird*. (This volume was also notable on other grounds: it was illustrated with the first substantial series of drawings by one of our greatest bird artists, Louis Agassiz Fuertes, who would later illustrate Forbush's *Birds of Massachusetts*.) These and her later books had, in Chapman's words, an "incalculable influence" in promoting an interest in birds and their protection. Nor did she stop there. She was a mainstay of *Bird-Lore* from its birth, a founder and the first president of the Connecticut Audubon Society, a director of the National Association, a member of the A.O.U., and finally — in practical application of her forceful ideas on conservation and education — the originator and guiding spirit of one of the earliest bird sanctuaries. The idea for Birdcraft Sanctuary, as she christened it, came from her father "in the 1860's, when I ran loose about the ten wild acres at the edge of the village . . . back at those days when we took birds as matters of course in the plan of nature, to be eaten if we so desired (Robin broth being considered a luxury for invalids), or used for decorative purposes, a Hummingbird or a Blue Jay being much in fashion for hat-trimming, or else to be listened to in the early hours of dawn and twilight when the notes of the Wood Thrush or Song Sparrow carried one away from earth and made the present a waking dream of the worth while."

Birdcraft opens with an appeal to the reader: "It is to the *living bird* in his love-songs, his home building, his haunts, and his migrations that I would lead you. The gun that silences the bird voice, and the looting of nests, should be left to the practical hand of science; you have no excuse for taking life, whether actual or embryonic, as your very ignorance will cause useless slaughter and the egg-collecting fever of the average boy savours more of the greed of possession than of ornithological ardour." *Birdcraft* combines the essential facts of a manual with personal recollections and anecdote, as Forbush was later to do on a far greater scale. Like John Burroughs, Walt Whitman, Theodore Roosevelt, and Olive Thorne Miller, Mrs. Wright was bewitched by the song of the hermit thrush, America's rival to the nightingale:

I made its acquaintance, several years ago, in the lane back of the garden, and had watched its rapid, nervous motions during many migrations before I heard it sing. This spring, the first week in May, when standing at the window about six o'clock in the morning, I heard an unusual note, and listened, thinking it at first a Wood

Thrush and then a Thrasher, but soon finding that it was neither of these I opened the window softly and looked among the nearby shrubs, with my glass. The wonderful melody ascended gradually in the scale as it progressed, now trilling, now legato, the most perfect, exalted, unrestrained, yet withal, finished bird song that I ever heard. At the final note I caught sight of the singer perching among the lower sprays of a dogwood tree. I could see him perfectly: it was the Hermit Thrush! In a moment he began again. I have never heard the Nightingale, but those who have, say that it is the surroundings and its continuous night singing that make it even the equal of our Hermit; for, while the Nightingales sing in numbers in the moonlit groves, the Hermit tunes his lute sometimes in inaccessible solitudes, and there is something immaterial and immortal about the song. Presently you cease altogether to associate it with a bird, and it inspires a kindred feeling in every one who hears it.

Mrs. Olive Thorne Miller tells delightfully of her pursuit of the Hermit in northern New York, where it was said to be abundant, but when she looked for him, he had always "been there" and was gone; until one day in August she saw the bird and heard the song and exclaims: "This only was lacking . . . This crowns my summer."

Mrs. Wright had referred briefly to the hermit thrush in her first published essay, "A New England May-Day." Here it appears in the context of the changing seasons, of the whole world of nature which she had known and loved since girlhood:

Look at the bank where the sun, peeping through, has touched the moss; there is saxifrage, and here are violet and white hepaticas, pushing through last year's leaves; lower down the wool-wrapped fronds of some large ferns are unfolding. The arbutus in the distant woods is on the wane, a fragrant memory. At the shady side of the spring are dog-tooth violets; and on the sunny side the watercourse is traced by clusters of marsh-marigolds, making a veritable golden trail. On a flat rock, almost hidden by layers of leaf mould, the polypody spreads its ferny carpet, and the little dicentra — or Dutchmen's breeches, as the children call it — huddles in clumps. The columbines are well budded, but Jack-in-the-pulpit has scarcely broken ground. On the top of the bank the dogwood stands unchanged, and the pinxter flower seems lifeless.

A brown bird, with reddish tail and buff, arrow-speckled breast, runs shyly through the underbrush, and perching on a low bush, begins a haunting, flute-like song. It is the hermit thrush. Its notes have been translated into syllables thus: "Oh speral, speral! Oh holy, holy! Oh clear away, clear away; clear up, clear up!" — again and again he repeats and reiterates, until seeing us he slips into the bushes . . .

We must turn homeward now, for the birds are hurrying to shelter, the wind is rising, and the sound of the waves on the bar, two miles distant, is growing distinct and rhythmic. Big drops of rain are rustling in the dry beech leaves, the smoke of burning brush has enveloped the spring and shut off the meadow. The logs blazing on the hearth will give us a cheery welcome, for the mercury in the porch registers only ten degrees above freezing . . . This is the first of the Moon of Leaves, the May-day of Old England, and we have gathered violets and daffodils, and we have heard the hermit thrush singing in the lane.

ᗥ

On a visit to Washington in 1906, John Burroughs wrote in his journal: "I lunched with Mrs. Bailey (Florence Merriam)." He had also been lunching at the White House with a distinguished company: "The President and Mrs. Roosevelt were very cordial. Ten or a dozen people there. Secretary Root and Dr. Merriam . . . one governor . . ." Florence Merriam Bailey and Dr. C. Hart Merriam, the first chief of the Bureau of Biological Survey, were brother and sister.* They had grown up in northern New York State, in the shadow of the Adirondacks. Their father, a prominent banker and congressman, was also an outdoorsman, with a more than superficial interest in the mountains; during the summer of 1871 he had gone west to visit John Muir in Yosemite Valley, and Muir had subsequently written him a long letter on the subject of glaciation.† Though theirs was not a literary family like the

---

* Dr. Merriam was one of the country's leading biologists. He was particularly outspoken in defense of predators and their part in maintaining the balance of nature, decades before this concept was generally understood.

† "I have been haunting the rocks of this region for a long time, anxious to spell out some of the great mountain truths which I felt were written here, and ever since the number, and magnitude, and significance of these Yosemite glaciers began to appear, I became eager for knowledge concerning them and am now devoting all my time to their history." The rest of the letter is an abridged version of a technical article which constituted (in the words

Osgoods, their mother was a college graduate and Florence herself attended the college for women recently established by Sophia Smith at Northampton, along a beautiful stretch of the Connecticut River. With a brother, and later a husband, both wildlife biologists, it is not surprising that she took to nature writing at an early age.

By happy circumstance, George Bird Grinnell, editor of *Forest and Stream*, had founded the original Audubon Society during Florence's senior year at Smith. Why not organize such a society among her fellow students? She checked with Grinnell; he would be happy to have her use the Audubon name. There was one other bird-minded girl in her class who would help. And so, she later recalled, "the two amateur ornithologists of the student body laid deep, wily schemes. 'Go to,' said they. 'We will start an Audubon Society. The birds must be protected; we must persuade the girls not to wear feathers on their hats. We won't say too much about hats, though. We'll take the girls afield and let them get acquainted with the birds. Then, of inborn necessity, they will wear feathers never more.' " The plot worked, better than they could have dreamed. They were barely organized when a milliner in town "inquired anxiously if the college authorities had forbidden the use of birds, so many hats had been brought in to her to be retrimmed." Soon thereafter came the ultimate accolade: a visit to their club from none other than the Sage of Slabsides. John Burroughs, who never shrank from the company of attractive and adoring young women, spent three happy days in Northampton, and the future of the Society was assured. "He took us out in classes of ten to forty, whenever we could get away from recitations." One afternoon Burroughs and thirty girls climbed Mt. Tom. "The strong influence of Mr. Burroughs' personality and quiet enthusiasm gave just the inspiration that was needed. We all caught the contagion of the woods."

---

of W. E. Bade) "the first published statement of the ice erosion theory to account for the origin of Yosemite."

Florence was determined that the contagion should spread beyond the college campus. Grinnell's *Audubon Magazine* offered the perfect outlet for her work. Beginning with the very first number, she contributed a series on "Fifty Common Birds and How to Know Them." Her opening paragraph suggests that she still has young ladies in mind. "When you have saved a man's life you naturally take a new interest in him; and so it is with the birds the Audubon Society has been trying to rescue. You are so in the habit of discriminating between men, and studying their individual peculiarities, that it appears a comparatively easy matter to know them; but with birds the case is entirely different. There are so many kinds . . . at first the difficulties you meet are almost overwhelming." Yet, as she goes on to demonstrate in a series of vivid sketches, there is no need for despair. Each species, like each man, has its own field marks and patterns of behavior by which it may be identified.

When still in her mid-twenties, Florence Merriam developed these articles into a book for Houghton Mifflin's Riverside Library for Young People. Entitled *Birds Through an Opera Glass*, it aimed at helping "not only young observers but also laymen to know the common birds they see about them."

So far so good. But in the eighteen-nineties woman's rôle was still in the home; a girl was supposed to be on the lookout for the right man, not the rare warbler. Olive Thorne Miller, for example, published her first nature stories only after she had raised four children, and even then under a pseudonym. Mabel Osgood Wright, in the sentimental romances that unfortunately followed her nature books, railed against the "new woman" who seeks "what she calls 'recognition' and 'identity' . . . outside the protecting walls of her natural affections!" * Florence Merriam does not appear to have been

___

* In the words of Robert H. Welker, "Mrs. Wright, herself something of a career woman, nevertheless displays an interesting ambivalence, with sympathy and awareness on the one hand, and shrill attacks on feminism and careerism on the other. Nearly always she resolves the problem in conven-

worried about either recognition or identity, but neither was she much taken with the charms of domestic life. A few months after leaving Smith College she wrote to her classmates: "I have been doing Audubon work combined with that most abhorred and abhorrable occupation of plain sewing, with housekeeping and bookkeeping, and am taking a P.G. course in business with my father." Soon she was involved in social work, after the pattern of Jane Addams' famous Hull House, but she developed tuberculosis and went west for her health. The result was two more books, one about her summer in a Mormon village of Utah; the other, laid in southern California, entitled *A-Birding on a Bronco*. Back at her brother's home in Washington, D.C., her health restored, she gave "bird talks," worked for the Women's National Science Club, and produced yet another book, *Birds of Village and Field*. With color keys for field identification and drawings by Louis Agassiz Fuertes and Ernest Thompson Seton, it appeared in 1898, shortly after Mrs. Wright's *Birdcraft* and Dr. Chapman's *Bird-Life*.

So by the turn of the century thousands of families were discovering the delights of birdwatching, thanks in large degree to the women writers who, not surprisingly, had a special talent for bringing the love of birds into the home. At the very moment when Frank Chapman was delivering his lecture on "Woman as a Bird Enemy" in the nation's capital, a group of enlightened and articulate women were spreading his gospel and supporting his crusade with deep emotional commitment.

As for Florence Merriam, she had barely started on her career. The year following publication of *Birds of Village and Field*, she married an energetic young naturalist who worked for her brother Hart in the Biological Survey, and a new phase of her life began. She and Vernon Bailey made a perfect team. For thirty years they took field trips together through-

---

tional and even saccharine terms of marriage to a proper male — or, failing that, virtual madness."

out the West, he studying and collecting mammals, birds, reptiles, and plants, she concentrating on observing the birds and writing about them. As Paul H. Oehser recalls in *The Auk:* "She was no 'woman tenderfoot,' and the wagon trips across the prairies and the pack-outfit travel in the western mountains, in those early days of the century, were not to be laughed off. Though not a robust woman, and as a girl threatened with tuberculosis, she developed a wonderful vitality, both physically and mentally." Only three years after her marriage she produced a western companion volume to Chapman's classic *Handbook*. "My first knowledge of Mrs. Bailey," wrote the late great naturalist, Olaus Murie, "was my purchase of her *Handbook of Birds of the Western United States* . . . Throughout the book, following the necessary technical descriptions, are delightful informal accounts of birds, accounts that help to make each bird something of flesh and blood, a living thing." Her great love was the Southwest, and in 1928 appeared her *magnum opus, Birds of New Mexico*, in recognition of which she became the first woman to win the Brewster Medal.* More books followed; her last, *Among Birds in the Grand Canyon National Park*, was published when she was over seventy-five. Throughout her long career, she never lost sight of the young. Both she and her husband, Murie recalls, were always delighted at the discovery of a young person of promise. "Leaven the lump!" she liked to say. Well she might. A gentle but yeasty character, she had been doing exactly that all her life.

ଙ

Not all the women who were writing about nature at the turn of the century possessed the professional knowledge of Florence Merriam or the authority and literary talent of Mabel Osgood Wright. This deficiency, however, did not nec-

* This medal is awarded for original scientific work in ornithology, as distinguished from the Burroughs Medal, where the stress is more on the literary quality of the book in question.

essarily hinder sales of their books. As the frontier receded and America became more and more urbanized, there had developed a romantic nostalgia for the country and the world of the outdoors. Of this world birds, in their beauty and freedom, were a living symbol. Stimulated by the Audubon movement, bird books had quite suddenly come into fashion. In 1897 and 1898 one could find on the bookstore counters, alongside *Birdcraft* and *Birds of Village and Field*, two handsome volumes with colored plates, entitled *Bird Neighbors* and *Birds That Hunt and Are Hunted*. The author was Neltje Blanchan, wife of the famous publisher Frank N. Doubleday. Inspired no doubt by the literary atmosphere around her, she had taken to nature writing, and that benign master of the art, John Burroughs, had given her a proper send-off by describing her work as "reliable" and "written in a vivacious strain by a real bird lover." Vivacious it was, and reasonably accurate — if a bit chatty and moralistic. Her aim was to stimulate a "personal, friendly acquaintance with the live birds, as distinguished from the technical study of the anatomy of dead ones," to make us realize "how marvelously clever they are, and how positively dependent agriculture is on their ministrations." Only when she came to the predators did she go off the deep end. Prime targets, of course, were the Cooper's hawk, which "lives by devouring birds of so much greater value than itself that the law of the survival of the fittest should be enforced by lead until these villains, from being the commonest of their generally useful tribe, adorn museum cases only." The feeding habits of his smaller cousin, the sharp-shinned hawk, aroused her to new heights of anthropomorphism; he is a villain who derives "fiendish satisfaction" from killing his "little prey." The ways of the great horned owl were horrible, and were not eagles perhaps guilty of carrying off small children? By dividing the world of nature into good and bad animals she was, of course, reflecting the common view, embellished by her own imagination. When she wrote on wildflowers for her husband's ambitious and successful nature series — which would include W. J. Holland's classic volumes on butterflies and moths — she was on sounder ground.

❦

By today's standards, writers like Neltje Blanchan may seem sentimental and moralistic, but it took a friend of hers, one of her husband's best-selling authors, to transmute the veneration of nature into something close to a religion. Gene Stratton-Porter was born in 1863 — Neltje Blanchan's senior by two years — and when she died in 1924 her books had sold

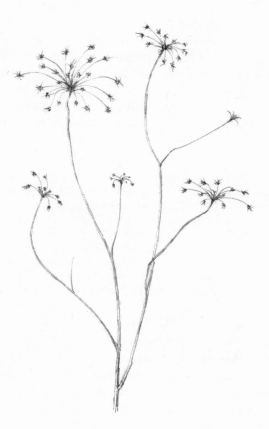

between eight and nine million copies. Though it was her novels rather than her strictly "nature books" that amassed these staggering sales (her publisher, Frank Doubleday, persuaded her to alternate the two genres) everything she wrote was steeped in nature worship. In the words of her daughter and biographer, "she considered intimacy with all outdoors and nature one of the best pathways to God." Her father, an Indiana farmer and Methodist preacher, apparently concurred. As a child she was allowed to roam the woods and fields, studying the wildflowers, watching over the nesting birds, catching butterflies, and bringing home the cocoons of moths. The last, a hobby that continued after her marriage, resulted in her popular *Moths of the Limberlost*. Her daughter recalled that "many nights, when she was expecting a moth to emerge, she pinned the cocoon close to her pillow and the scraping of the moth's feet as it broke through the cocoon awakened her so that she could watch it develop." Limberlost Swamp — named for an unlucky hunter named Limber who vanished in it — was a favorite haunt near her home, which she describes with near ecstasy:

Flashing through the treetops of the Limberlost there are birds whose colour is more brilliant than that of the gaudiest flower lifting its face to the sunlight. The lilies of the mire are not so white as the white herons that fish among them. The ripest spray of goldenrod is not so highly coloured as the burnished gold on the breast of the oriole that rocks on it. The jays are bluer than the calamus bed they wrangle above with throaty chatter. The finches are a finer purple than the ironwort; while for every clump of foxfire flaming in the Limberlost there is a cardinal glowing redder on the bush above it.

The latter became the subject of her first book, *The Song of the Cardinal*, which has been described in a biographical sketch by Beatrice K. Hofstadter as "a humanized account of bird-life somewhat in the manner of *Black Beauty*." This was followed by *Freckles*, the novel that eventually sold a million and a half copies and won her an international reputation. The hero is a poor but pure young man who guards the Limberlost Swamp against poachers and wins a lovely rich girl for his pains, their union made socially acceptable by the fact that he turns out in the end to be the son and heir of an Irish lord. Her picture of swamp life is more convincing. As Miss Hofstader writes: "In *Freckles*, as in her other books, Mrs. Porter's interest is not in human nature but in wildlife as a source of moral virtue." In some ways she is surprisingly modern. Unlike her friend Neltje Blanchan, she finds no villains in the wild, despite occasional provocations to do so. Though she is greatly distressed at the depredations of a pair of great horned owls on the songbirds around Limberlost Cabin, she nevertheless writes to a friend: "You know, I have a theory that one must not upset the balance of nature. One must leave her in her natural state to work out her own salvation."

To her increasing annoyance, few critics took Gene Stratton-Porter's work seriously as literature. But the flood of fan mail engendered by *Freckles* and its successor, *A Girl of the Limberlost*,* helped to heal her wounded pride. Modestly, yet almost defiantly, she tells why she writes as she does, and how her work has affected the lives of her readers. "I am a creature so saturated with earth, water, and air that if I do not periodically work some of it out of my system in ink, my nearest and dearest cannot live with me. When such a time overtakes me, I write as the birds sing, because I must, and

---

* The heroine, like the writer herself, is an avid collector of moths (including the magnificent Cecropia), and pays her way through school by selling them to dealers. This aroused the ire of Dr. Frank E. Lutz of the American Museum of Natural History, author of the classic *Field Book of Insects*, in which he writes: "I hope my children's children will call it Cecropia even though it was nicknamed something else by a lady who wrote very good fiction but did immeasurable harm to unalloyed love of nature by encouraging the commercial viewpoint. People forget that the Limberlost stories are fiction, and my mail was for some time filled with letters from people, ranging all the way from an eight-year-old boy, who wanted to sell a battered Luna so that he could get a pony, to invalids who wished to get money to buy medicine by selling the moths that came to their bedside lamps. Permit me to say that he who goes to Nature with money in his eyes will not only be blind to her truths, her glories, and the real benefits that she offers to those who love her, but he will be disappointed as to his financial returns."

usually from the same source of inspiration." She cites letters "from every class and condition of people, all the way from northern Canada to the lowest tip of Africa, all asking for more of the outdoors ..." There was the hospital nurse, whose bedridden patients would lose themselves for hours in her pictures of swamp and forest; the warden of a state reform school who "wrote that fifteen hundred sin-besmirched little souls in his care, shut for punishment from their natural inheritance of field and wood, were reading my books to rags because they scented freedom and found comfort in them." There was the American soldier who read her on the road to Verdun; the London banker who found a new interest in nature; the schoolteachers grateful for her influence on their pupils, and so on and on. However one classifies them, her books obviously helped to make outdoor nature a part of everyday life. Freckles may be as unlikely a creation as Rousseau's noble savage, but he won the hearts of millions of readers who were convinced by his creator's comfortable philosophy that wildness, far from being evil as the Church had once assumed, was one with God.

CHAPTER VIII

Figs from Thistles

"Nature is a part of our humanity, and without some awareness and experience of that divine mystery, man ceases to be man."
— Henry Beston, THE OUTERMOST HOUSE

IN THE AMERICAN LITERATURE of nature, it is seldom the gentle, picturesque scene that evokes the strongest writing. As a source of inspiration, our remaining wild areas have little to do with the English literary tradition of Gilbert White's beloved Selborne, of William and Dorothy Wordsworth's Lake Country, of W. H. Hudson's downland. Probably our most forbidding landscape, yet fascinating on closer acquaintance, is the southwest desert. Here I have chosen two writers as representative of different approaches to this complex environment. The first is Mary Austin, who wrote in the early years of this century: an extraordinary woman whose nature books (which deserve to be better known) have been ranked with those of Thoreau and Muir. The second is Joseph Wood Krutch, the urban professor turned nature writer, whose life could not have been more different from hers.

Except for the polar regions, the desert is surely the environment that offhand seems least hospitable to man. Yet in America as elsewhere, this apparently lifeless land has given rise to profound insights into the nature of the living world. So it has always been. In the semi-arid regions where Christianity was born, the desert — synonymous with "wilderness" — was not merely a devil-ridden wasteland; it was also a place of trial and testing, and ultimately of revelation.

Unlike friendlier, lusher landscapes — well-watered valleys, grasslands, lakes, and forested hills — desert country, for many of us, arouses at first sight a sense of alienation rather than of affection. Only as we live with it for a while do we begin to recognize its unique qualities, endlessly various but having in common the sense of fundamental reality, of a world stripped down to the bone. Here, as in the high Arctic, we feel as if we were on the frontier of life's ingenious campaign to colonize, in some form or other, every available square inch of the planet. Not that there is any sense of crowding, as in wooded country; on the contrary, these arid lands often give a curious parklike impression. Where competition among plants is for water rather than for light, they tend to stand apart, rather than seeking to overtop one another. The battle for existence goes on largely underground. One way to visualize the plant life of a desert is to turn the whole landscape upside down in your mind's eye. The roots then become a tangled web of interlocking branches in a nightmare forest as luxuriant as the visible desert is sparse.

The desert landscape, writes Paul Shepard, is esthetically abstract. "Its forms are bold and suggestive. The mind is beset by light and space . . . The desert sky is encircling, majestic, terrible . . . infinitely vaster than that of rolling countryside and forest lands." The most awesome landforms of the arid West, such as the canyons of the Colorado River, shocked early explorers like Powell and Dutton into rare bursts of eloquence. But it would take a woman of genius of a later generation to immortalize the less obviously spectacular, yet intrinsically beautiful desert country which "lies between the high Sierras south from Yosemite — east and south over a very great assemblage of broken ranges beyond Death Valley, and on illimitably into the Mojave Desert."

On November 2, 1902, Messrs. Houghton, Mifflin & Company of Boston received an extraordinary document in response to their routine request for biographical information from a young writer new to their list. Her name was Mary Austin. Her first book, which she had entitled *A* (later *The*) *Land of Little Rain*, was scheduled for publication the following spring. She had already sold stories and articles to most of the monthly magazines including the *Atlantic* (then owned by Houghton, Mifflin) and she felt sure that she could get favorable comments from editors and friends in the West, among them John Muir. "I have written the biographical sketch in the third person," she remarks,

to avoid the use of so many 'I's' which always makes me miserable. Born Mary Hunter in Carlinville, Illinois [she omits the year, 1868], she began to be familiar with the English classics as soon as she could read, and the study of them and an intimate acquaintance with nature occupied most of her years until the end of her university work. At that time very serious ill-health drove her to California, and a friendly destiny provided that she should settle in the new and

untamed lands about the Sierra Nevadas and the desert edges . . . All of Mary Austin's work is like her life, out of doors, nights under the pines, long days watching by waterholes to see the wild things drink, breaking trail up new slopes, heat, cloud bursts, snow; wild beasts and mountain bloom, all equally delightful because understood.

At this point the typed biography stops. "I can't do it . . . ," she continues by hand. "There is really nothing to tell. I have just looked, nothing more . . . Then I got so full of looking that I had to write to get rid of some of it . . . I was only a month writing *A Land of Little Rain* but I spent twelve years peeking and prying before I began it." She includes a brief, wholly convincing self-portrait: "You are to figure to yourself a small, plain, brown woman, with too much hair, always a little sick, and always busy about the fields and mesas in a manner, so they say in the village, as if I should like to see anybody try to stop me."

She says nothing about her early life, which up to then had been a series of tragedies. Rejected by her mother from infancy, she had found comfort in her love for her father — a lawyer of literary tastes whose health had been shattered in the Civil War — and her sister Jennie who, she recalled years later, "was the only one who unselfishly loved me." But both had died when she was ten. (Shortly after her sister's death, she overheard her mother remark to a friend: "If only it could have been Mary!") A brilliant child, with a gift for writing — much influenced by Emerson — she was considered odd and perverse. When she entered Blackburn College — a small school in Carlinville — everyone who knew her expected that she would major in English, but she chose science instead; she could read by herself, but science required a laboratory and a teacher. And what could she learn from these English professors? "They've never written any books!" She was, however, elected class poet. "I spare you mercifully all quotations," she writes in her autobiography.

A week or two after Mary's graduation the family left the Midwest to take up a homestead in southern California. So began her love affair with the desert, the source of her most enduring books.

For Mary the desert wilderness was both a passion and a refuge from a world where she did not belong. Her aggressive intellect and fierce independence made her something of a misfit in conventional small-town society. Her early experiences with men, for example, were inauspicious. "When we went places," she recalled, "they usually came home mad. Either I had more attention than they did, or I had to tell them to shut up and let me talk, and they came away mad." Eventually she found herself trapped in a bleak and loveless marriage with a feckless young man who may have let her talk but — she felt — made no attempt to understand her, and who would without explanation leave her for long periods while he pursued abortive irrigation projects and other unsuccessful business enterprises. Their only child, a daughter, turned out to be hopelessly retarded and was sent to an institution. When the couple finally separated, their pious, straight-laced neighbors laid all the blame on Mary. But by then she could defy them. In the desert country of southern California's Owens Valley she had created a new life of her own. These "desert years" lasted from 1891 to 1905. Here she was able to give full expression to her unique talent.

Three decades later, when she came to write her autobiography, Mary Austin recalled how she was "consumed with interest as with enchantment" on her first encounter with the life of the desert. "Her trouble was that the country failed to explain itself . . . Its creatures had no known life except such as she could discover by unremitting vigilance of observation; its plants no names that her Middlewestern botany could supply . . . She was spellbound not to miss any animal behavior, any bird-marking, any weather signal, any signature of tree or flower." On nights when she could not sleep (she was apparently suffering from malnutrition) "Mary would sit out among the dunes in the moonlight . . . watching the frisking forms of field mouse and kangaroo rat, the noiseless passage of the red fox and the flitting of the elf owls at their mating." A poet and a mystic, Mary Austin also had a naturalist's passion for facts. Like Henry Thoreau, she would have scorned "the mealy-mouthed enthusiasm of the mere lover of nature." She was, in her own words, one of those people plagued with an anxiety to know.

The essays that make up *The Land of Little Rain* were written at white heat: a bursting forth and crystallization of material that she had been absorbing and refining for more than a decade. Like any lover, she was fierce in defense of the object of her love. To know this country only superficially, yet claim to understand it, would have been to her a desecration. "The real heart and core of the country are not to be come at in a month's vacation. One must summer and winter with the land and wait its occasions. Pine woods that take two and three seasons to the ripening of cones, roots that lie by in the sand seven years awaiting a growing rain, firs that grow fifty years before flowering — these do not scrape acquaintance."

The title essay sets the stage in the opening paragraphs:

East away from the Sierra, south from Panamint and Amargosa, east and south many an uncounted mile, is the Country of Lost Borders.

Ute, Paiute, Mojave, and Shoshone inhabit its frontiers, and as far into the heart of it as man dare go. Not the law, but the land sets the limit. Desert is the name it wears upon the maps, but the Indian's is the better word. Desert is a loose term to indicate land that supports no man; whether the land can be bitted and broken to that purpose is not proven. Void of life it never is, however dry the air and villainous the soil.

This is the nature of that country. There are hills, rounded, blunt, burned, squeezed up out of chaos, chrome and vermillion painted, aspiring to the snow-line. Between the hills lie high level-looking plains full of intolerable sun glare, or narrow valleys drowned in blue haze. The hill surface is streaked with ash drift and black, unweathered lava flows. After rains water accumulates in the hollows of small closed valleys, and, evaporating, leaves hard dry levels of pure desertness that get the local name of dry lakes. Where the mountains are steep and the rains heavy, the pool is never quite dry, but dark and bitter, rimmed about with the efflorescence of alkaline deposits . . . The sculpture of the hills here is more wind than water work, though the quick storms do sometimes scar them past many a years's redeeming. In all the Western desert edges there are essays in miniature at the famed, terrible Grand Canyon, to which, if you keep on long enough in this country, you will come at last . . .

Here you find the hot sink of Death Valley, or high rolling districts where the air has always a tang of frost. Here are the long heavy

winds and breathless calms on the tilted mesas where dust devils dance, whirling up into a wide, pale sky. Here you have no rain when all the earth cries for it, or quick downpours called cloudbursts for violence. A land of lost rivers, with little in it to love; yet a land that once visited must be come back to inevitably. If it were not so there would be little told of it.

Mary Austin could be prickly in her personal contacts with those who resented her intellectual superiority and who obviously disapproved of her independent ways. Not so with the Indians or with the settlers from Old Mexico. All her life she would be an interpreter and ardent champion of Indian culture. A rebel against the narrow formalized religion of the Methodists among whom she was raised, unable to accept the doctrine of original sin, she responded wholeheartedly to the Indian view of the world, to its poetry and its mysticism. The Paiute and Shoshone medicine men and dancers, she wrote, "are the only poets I personally know . . . I get nearer to the roots of the poetic instinct among these simple hearted savages than any other where." One is reminded of Henry Thoreau, who found among the Indians of the Maine Woods that same sense of kinship with the wild nature which the white man has all but lost. Toward the end of her life she expressed her conviction in words that Thoreau might have used: "Man is not alone or helpless in the universe; he has toward it and it toward him an effective relation." Or as she wrote to a friend when she was living, somewhat uneasily, as a literary celebrity in New York City: "It is in nature that I recognize God."

As for the Spanish-American settlements in the California desert, they were to Mary Austin not so much a source of inspiration as of pure delight. These families had moved north across the Mexican border during the silver-mining boom, bringing with them their ancient customs. Mary found their merry, generous, carefree nature — and their simple piety — a welcome contrast to those "people whose creeds are chiefly restrictions against other people's way of life." In El Pueblo de Las Uvas — the Town of the Grape

Vines — "singing is the business of the night . . . as sleeping is for midday. When the moon comes over the mountain wall new washed from the sea, and the shadows lie like lace on the stamped floors of the patios, from recess to recess in the vine tangle runs the thrum of guitars and the voice of singing." This, as much as the chirping of the linnets, the night songs of the mockingbirds, the harsh croak of ravens, was to her the voice of the desert. "Your earthborn," she wrote in the concluding chapter of *The Land of Little Rain*, "is a poet and a symbolist . . ."

At Las Uvas every house is a piece of earth — thick-walled, white-washed adobe that keeps the even temperature of a cave; every man is an accomplished horseman and consequently bowlegged; every family keeps dogs, flea-bitten mongrels that loll on the earthen floors. They speak a purer Castilian than obtains in like villages of Mexico, and the way they count relationship everybody is more or less akin. There is not much villainy among them. What incentive to thieving or killing can there be when there is little wealth and that to be had for the borrowing! If they love too hotly, as we say "take their meat before grace," so do their betters. Eh, what! shall a man be a saint before he is dead? And besides, Holy Church takes it out of you one way or another before all is done. Come away, you who are obsessed with your own importance in the scheme of things, and have got nothing you did not sweat for, come away by the brown valleys and full-bosomed hills to the even-breathing days, to the kindliness, earthiness, ease of El Pueblo de Las Uvas.

Mary Austin was a mystic, from earliest childhood. At the age of five, as she stood beneath a walnut tree, she had experienced an "ineffable moment" during which she felt in communication with God. To her, as she later explained, God was "the experienceable quality of the Universe." After death our awareness would be broadened, our horizons lifted. (Hence the title of her autobiography, *Earth Horizon*.) Her identification with nature was complete. "Man is not himself only . . . He is all that he sees; all that flows to him from a thousand sources . . . He is the land, the lift of its mountain lines, the reach of its valleys." She also identified herself with the *Chi-*

sera, the rainmaker, and — like the people of the Findhorn community in Scotland today — she believed that "there is no good reason to believe why a plant may not be, in its own degree, aware of man" and capable of cooperating with him.

Three years after the publication of *The Land of Little Rain*, Mary Austin left the country she loved so dearly in bitterness and sorrow. The notorious rape of Owens Valley to provide water for growing Los Angeles, accomplished through lies and deception, came to her as a brutal shock. "Mary did what she could," she writes, "And that was too little . . . She was stricken; she was completely shaken out of her place." (Over twenty years later, as a delegate to the Seven States Conference, she would fight bitterly but futilely against the diversion of Colorado River water to Los Angeles.) By now permanently separated from her husband, she moved to Carmel and joined the Bohemian group that included Ambrose Bierce and Jack London. Thereafter her literary output was prodigious. During the following three decades she produced some twenty-five volumes: Indian legends, romances, religious works, poetic dramas, essays on socialism, and didactic novels about women's rights.* On a visit to London she found herself a celebrity. She hobnobbed with George Bernard Shaw and members of the Fabian Society, she visited Joseph Conrad and listened sympathetically to the personal problems of H. G. Wells, who declared her to be the most intelligent woman in the United States. Back in New York she became involved with writers and critics, suffragettes and social reformers. But the urban East was not for her. "It was not simple nor direct enough," she wrote. "It lacked freshness, air and light. More than anything else it lacked pattern

---

*In the preface to *The Arrow Maker* (1911) she writes: "To one fresh from the consideration of the roots of life as they lie close to the surface of primitive society, this obsession of the recent centuries that the community can only be served by a gift for architecture, for administration, for healing, when it occurs in the person of a male is only a trifle less ridiculous than that other social stupidity, namely, that a gift of mothering must not be exercised except in the event of a particular man being able, under certain restrictions, to afford the opportunity."

. . . I liked the feel of roots, of ordered growth and progression, continuity, all of which I found in the Southwest." So in 1924 she built herself a Spanish adobe house in Santa Fe, New Mexico, where she spent the final decade of her life. (It was in this house that Willa Cather wrote *Death Comes for the Archbishop* — a book that distressed Mary because it sympathized with the building of a French cathedral in a Spanish town, which she termed "a calamity to local culture.")

Mary Austin was well aware that, of all her varied writing, it was the nature books that would last. "I knew that my work which was essentially of the West, like *The Land of Little Rain*, *The Flock,** and *The Land of Journey's Ending*, had a permanent hold on the future." In fact it has proved almost as timeless as the work of Henry Thoreau, with whom she had much in common. She went to the desert for the same reason he declared he went to Walden woods: "To live deliberately, to front only the essential facts of life . . ." In her words, "the secret charm of the desert is the secret of life triumphant." A triumph, like her own career, over seemingly insuperable odds.

❦

One thinks of Mary Austin as a child of the desert, deeply rooted as a creosote bush, venturing into the urban literary world only when she had a firm hold on the soil that nourished her. By contrast, Joseph Wood Krutch, desert philosopher *par excellence*, was already an established literary figure in New York City before he so much as glimpsed his first saguaro or Gila woodpecker. Born in Knoxville, Tennessee, in 1893, Krutch studied and later taught dramatic literature at Columbia University. He wrote scholarly books on the

---

*Published in 1906, *The Flock* was recognized as a classic account of sheepherding in arid country. Though written in poetic, evocative prose, it was so full of information that President Theodore Roosevelt sent an expert from the U.S. Forest Service to get Mary Austin's advice on government regulations for grazing on national forest lands.

history of the novel, biographies of Edgar Allan Poe and Samuel Johnson — that most urban of characters — and a pessimistic philosophical study entitled *The Modern Temper*, in which he deplored the incompatibility of modern science with the human spirit. As an editor and drama critic for the *Nation*, he moved in the most sophisticated intellectual circles — thereby giving the lie to his acerbic friend H. L. Mencken, who doubted that anyone could "come all the way from Tennessee to civilization in one generation."* His articles on contemporary history and politics were praised by men like Aldous Huxley and Albert Einstein. And when eventually he returned to Columbia as a full professor, he was launched on a distinguished academic career.

* Krutch and Mencken had both covered the notorious "monkey trial" in Dayton, Tennessee, in the summer of 1925, when John Scopes was found guilty of teaching evolution in the public schools.

But to borrow the title of his autobiography, Joseph Krutch was to have "more lives than one." The phrase is Henry Thoreau's. Krutch first read *Walden* in 1930, when he was already thirty-seven years old. It made, he recalled, "a tremendous impression . . . I was drawn to *Walden* no more by its criticism of the social system than by the way in which it illuminated my own growing interest in the world of nature as a spectacle, refuge, and teacher of lessons." Soon thereafter, he and his wife Marcelle acquired a country refuge in Connecticut. Invited to contribute to a series of biographies of American writers, he chose Thoreau. If one were looking for a turning point in Krutch's career, this would be it. "One winter night," he recalls, "shortly after I had finished *Thoreau* I was reading a 'nature essay' which pleased me greatly and it suddenly occurred to me for the first time to wonder if I could do something of the sort." The result was *The Twelve Seasons:* a charming little book that, like Mary Austin's *The Land of Little Rain*, just poured itself out, and was finished in a month. Here was Krutch the humanist and philosopher wedded to Krutch the budding naturalist. In nature — particularly in man as a part of nature — he found new faith to supplant the pessimism of *The Modern Temper*. He became convinced that, for him, the Good Life meant a natural as opposed to a wholly man-made world. When one adds to this his chronic allergies to city air, the decision of the Krutches to move to Tucson, Arizona, in the spring of 1952 appears less baffling than it did to their incredulous New York friends. They knew where they were going and what they would find. Vacation trips through the Southwest had already provided material for *The Desert Year*, a volume of essays that has the freshness of any first encounter. In it he recalls the shock of delight on his initial exposure to the charms of this "great, proud, dry and open land." The trip, he writes, was "undertaken without much enthusiasm. I had got off the train at Lamy, New Mexico, and started in an automobile across the rolling semidesert toward Albuquerque. Suddenly a new, undreamed of world was revealed. There was something so unexpected in the combination of brilliant sun and high, thin, dry air with a seemingly limitless expanse of sky and earth that my first reaction was delighted amusement. How far the ribbon of road beckoned ahead! How endlessly much there seemed to be of the majestically rolling expanse of bare earth dotted with sagebrush! How monotonously repetitious in the small details, how varied in shifting panorama! Unlike either the Walrus or the Carpenter, I laughed to see such quantities of sand."

The Desert Year, which won the John Burroughs Medal, was among the first of almost twenty books that Joe Krutch published during the last two decades of his life. "These books," in the words of Mark Van Doren,* "classified him as a naturalist, but he was a naturalist with a difference, for like Thoreau, of whom he wrote the best biography, he was a philosopher and a moralist; and latterly he became a prophet crying in the wilderness of man's brutality to the very world on which his own existence depends."

Krutch takes as a motto for one of his books Thoreau's well-known remark: "The man of science studies nature as a dead language. I pray for such inward experience as will make nature significant." By "significant," however, neither he nor Thoreau was suggesting, as did Emerson, that man's moral law lies at the heart of nature; neither did he share the assumption of many nineteenth-century poets that poetry flies out the window at the mere touch of cold fact. "The modern nature writer . . . believes that reality is quite as likely as fantasy to provide powerful aesthetic and emotional experiences." Krutch found his principal inspiration in the reality of the desert and its elaborate patterns of life which are largely hidden to the casual observer. Like Mary Austin, he knew that "one must summer and winter with the land and merit its occasions." June, when the broiling sun rose almost to the zenith, was his favorite month. This was the time to

* Mark Van Doren — poet, critic, and gifted teacher of literature at Columbia University — was almost precisely Krutch's age, and his closest friend for over forty years. Though different in their approach, they shared the same basic values, and Krutch found him "the perfect intellectual companion."

learn what the desert is really like, "the time to decide once and for all if it is, as for many it turns out to be, 'your country.' " Krutch's country was not confined to his home ground on the outskirts of Tucson, where from his window one could watch the Gambel's quail and white-winged doves and lizards come to drink, and where, he said, the bold cactus wrens would even invade the house in search of material for their nests. It included the Grand Canyon, and extended as far south as Baja California. The "forgotten peninsula," as he entitled it in one of his most engaging books, became his special love. Having traveled the length of the peninsula — twice the length of Florida — by four-wheel-drive truck, he realized that it was not for everybody.

To some the desert is repellent and even frightening. Such will probably find Baja even "harder to take" than Arizona. Both its landscape as a whole and the plant features which contribute to it are grotesque, though far from ugly. It is certainly not pretty in the usual sense, any more than some of the greatest works of art are pretty. But it should inspire awe and it can, for many at least, come to have that something-quite-different which we call "charm." The

more one comes to understand that the queerness is not mere queerness, that every seeming abnormality of the desert plant means something, the less one thinks of it as queerness at all. It is, instead, a manifestation of what used to be called "the wisdom of God manifest in the works of His creations," though it is nowadays more often thought of as an example of the astonishing success of living organisms when faced with the necessity of adapting themselves to the conditions of their environment. In any event, there is no oddity of stem, or leaf, or thorn which is not "functional." And if beauty consists, as some say it does, in the fitness of a means to an end, then the most grotesque of the plants of Baja is also beautiful.

Krutch had a scholarly delight in the oddities of nature. What first brought him to Baja California was the desire to see that queerest of all trees, the boojum, in its native habitat. He was not disappointed. "Even knowing very well what to expect," he writes, "it was still difficult not to experience the rustic-seeing-his-first-giraffe syndrome." In fact the simplest form of a boojum does suggest the neck of a giraffe projecting straight up out of the ground, tapering skyward from a thick base, sometimes with a bunch of flowers bursting from its head. Other specimens are more complicated, sprouting arms and hooks like surrealist hatracks. To Krutch, however, they were more than a spectacle. In *The Forgotten Peninsula*, for example, he delves with the zeal of a trained botanist into the mystery of the boojum's origin, and the reason that it is found only in two isolated spots on earth.*

Jouncing in his truck over spine-jarring sand tracks and breathtaking mountain passes, Krutch had come a long way from the classrooms of Columbia University, the offices of the *Nation*, and the first nights on Broadway. In the process he had brought to nature writing a variety of intellectual experience which is, so far as I know, unique. He appreciated the part that literature and philosophy have played in sharpening our powers of projection, our ability to see ourselves as

---

* In Baja California, between approximately the twenty-seventh and the thirtieth parallels, and in one spot on the Mexican mainland, directly opposite across the Gulf of California.

part of the living landscape. He did not react to the desert with the intensity, the poetic insight, and mystical vision of Mary Austin, nor did he approach it as a professional scientist. Rather he was an "amateur of nature," in the root sense of that phrase. He had a passion for learning the facts, but he knew that bare facts were not everything, and that the sort of writing he and other nature writers did had a practical purpose: "It resists the tendency to think of man as a machine and the determination to manipulate him as such. It is also an indispensable ally of the effort to conserve some of the earth's natural beauties. That effort cannot succeed unless sustained by the very 'love of nature' which the scientist sometimes distrusts."

This distrust, I like to think, is largely a thing of the past. The best of today's "nature writers," whether professionally trained or not, maintain a scientific discipline in their field observations and in their interpretation of what they see. In fact it has been suggested that, as the life sciences become more and more specialized and increasingly oriented toward the laboratory, these writers have taken over the role of the so-called old-fashioned naturalist. Certainly they have had a profound influence in creating a scientifically literate public. As Krutch points out, they have been an "indispensable ally" of the conservation movement. For it is obvious that we fight to preserve only what we have come to love and understand.

CHAPTER IX

Nature Lovers and Nature Fakers

"The grand leap of the whale up the Fall of Niagara is esteemed by all who have seen it, as one of the finest spectacles in nature."

— Benjamin Franklin (teasing the English for their ignorance of America)

THE LOVE OF NATURE, which Joseph Wood Krutch saw as a necessary corrective to a purely mechanistic view of the world and an "indispensable ally" of the conservation movement, had been a favorite subject of popular writers for many years past. The last decade of the nineteenth century was rich in nature writing. Countless articles appeared in the best magazines, and hardly a year went by in which readers were not offered one or more new nature books. In 1898 alone appeared works by Chapman, Merriam, Blanchan, and the first book of a man whose name remains a household word, Ernest Thompson Seton, chief progenitor of the "nature story." Now almost forgotten figures such as Ernest Ingersoll, Witmer Stone, William Everett Cram — all of them read with approval by Theodore Roosevelt — were making wild creatures a familiar part of everyday life. When Roosevelt entered the White House in 1901, he could rely on an ever-growing reading public to understand and support his commitment to preserving some remnant of wild America.

Many important measures, of course, had already been taken. Yellowstone and Yosemite parks, after youthful travails, were firmly established. The year 1885 saw the birth of the Adirondack Forest Preserve in New York, and, in Washington, the founding of the agency that became the U.S. Biological Survey. The Forest Reserve Act, establishing the national forests, was passed by Congress in 1891; the Sierra Club, destined to become a nationwide conservation organization, was founded the following year. In 1900 the Lacey Bill, banning interstate traffic in birds killed in violation of state laws, gave a shattering blow to the millinery trade.*

What part did the nature writers play in all this? In the case of well-publicized campaigns, such as that on behalf of the birds, it is clear enough. Earlier examples of the power of the pen, though perhaps not so obvious, are equally valid. Yosem-

---

* The *coup de grâce* was delivered a decade later by the Bayne Law, forbidding possession or sale of wild bird plumage in New York, the center of the millinery trade. This was followed by the Federal Tariff Act, making illegal the importation of skins or plumes for other than scientific or educational purposes.

ite Valley, as we have seen, was saved for posterity by the written word; first by Starr King and others who made its wonders nationally known, later by John Muir, whose articles led to its becoming the core of a great national park. The preservation of the Grand Canyon was directly related to the writings of Powell and Dutton. Similarly, if Grinnell had been inarticulate, would we now have Glacier National Park? And so on. But the contribution of these writers was far broader and deeper than the preservation of specific areas. Each in his own way enlarged our understanding of the natural world and strengthened our sense of kinship with it.

Take, for instance, that devoted disciple of John Muir, Enos A. Mills, who almost single-handedly created Rocky Mountain National Park. A native of Kansas, Mills moved to Colorado for his health while still in his teens, became a professional mountaineering guide and — following a chance encounter with John Muir — a literary interpreter of the wildlife of the Rockies. At Muir's urging he also explored Yosemite (the same year as Muir's historic meeting with Robert Underwood Johnson), Death Valley, and Yellowstone, and made two trips to Alaska, camping opposite Muir Glacier, and on one occasion tramping more than two hundred miles through uncharted wilderness when he was deserted by his Indian guides. Back in Colorado, he built a rural hotel for nature lovers and mountaineers. A daring climber himself, he barely escaped death one day on a sheer rock face of Long's Peak, saving himself only by the desperate feat of riding an avalanche down the mountainside.

Perhaps no one but John Muir had such adventures to write about. In his early thirties, Mills began publishing in national magazines: factual accounts of his own exploits, and scholarly articles interpreting the Colorado wilderness. His principal cause was the preservation of our forests and their wildlife. In 1906 alone he made more than fifty speeches from Pueblo, Colorado, to Boston, Massachusetts, where he was introduced by Bliss Perry, editor of the *Atlantic Monthly*. To any modern conservationist, his remarks in Boston have a remarkably familiar ring: "A Bill has been before Congress for years to preserve the White Mountains and Appalachian forests and add them to the national forest reserves, and one man only has prevented its passage. That man is Speaker Cannon, who also prevents the preservation of the Big Trees of California. You can save them if you will express yourselves." Call it the Wilderness Bill, substitute the chairman of the Committee on Interior and Insular Affairs for the Speaker of the House, and it all fits perfectly, over half a century later. *Plus ça change . . .*

In 1907 President Roosevelt personally appointed Mills Government Lecturer on Forestry. Two years later Houghton Mifflin Company published his *Wild Life on the Rockies*, dedicated to John Muir, and containing his classic essay, "The Story of a Thousand-Year Pine" — as impressive a performance, in its quiet way, as Muir's dramatic "Stickeen."

Mills always had young readers in mind, and when he related an adventure, he let out all the stops. The wolf in his time was still the symbol of savagery. "One day," he writes,

I was walking along slowly, reflectively, in a deep forest . . . Suddenly two gray wolves sprang from almost beneath my feet and faced me defiantly. At a few feet distance they made an impressive show of ferocity, standing ready apparently to hurl themselves upon me . . .

The two wolves facing me seemed to have been asleep in the sun when I disturbed them. I realized the danger and was alarmed, of course, but my faculties were under control, were stimulated, indeed, to unusual alertness, and I kept a bold front and faced them without flinching. Their expression was one of mingled surprise and anger, together with the apparent determination to sell their lives as dearly as possible. I gave them all the attention which their appearance and their reputation demanded. Not once did I take my eyes off them. I held them at bay with my eyes. I still have a vivid picture of terribly gleaming teeth, bristling backs, and bulging muscles in savage readiness.

They made no move to attack. I was afraid to attack and I dared not run away. I remembered that some trees I could almost reach behind me had limbs that stretched out toward me, yet I felt that to wheel, spring for a limb, and swing up beyond their reach could not be done quickly enough to escape those fierce jaws.

Both sides were of the same mind, ready to fight, but not at all eager to do so. Under these conditions our nearness was embarrassing, and we faced each other for what seemed, to me at least, a long time. My mind working like lightning, I thought of several possible ways of escaping. I considered each at length, found it faulty, and dismissed it. Meanwhile, not a sound had been made. I had not moved, but something had to be done. Slowly I worked the small folding axe from its sheath, and with the slowest of movements placed it in my right coat-pocket with the handle up, ready for instant use. I did this with studied deliberation, lest a sudden movement should release the springs that held the wolves back. I kept on staring. Statues, almost, we must have appeared to the "camp-bird" whose call from a near-by limb told me we were observed, and whose nearness gave me courage. Then, looking the nearer of the two wolves squarely in the eye, I said to him, "Well, why don't you move?" as though we were playing checkers instead of the game of life. He made no reply, but the spell was broken. I believe that both sides had been bluffing. In attempting to use my kodak while continuing the bluff, I brought matters to a focus. "What a picture you fellows will make," I said aloud, as my right hand slowly worked the kodak out of the case which hung under my left arm. Still keeping up a steady fire of looks, I brought the kodak in front of me ready to focus, and then touched the spring that released the folding front. When the kodak mysteriously, suddenly opened before the wolves, they fled for their lives. In an instant they had cleared the grassy space and vanished into the woods. I did not get the picture.

Enos Mills was at once an unabashed idealist and the archetype of the successful lobbyist. If he lacked John Muir's fire, he accomplished his ends by applying a steady heat to the custodians of our public lands. Thus it was that he created Rocky Mountain National Park, by mobilizing public opinion to overcome the bitter opposition of the U.S. Forest Service. Muir was proud of his disciple: "I shall always feel good when I look your way: for you are making good on a noble career," he wrote in 1913. "I glory in your success as a writer and lecturer and in saving God's parks for the welfare of humanity. Good luck and long life to you." Muir was then deep in the losing battle to save Hetch Hetchy. The year after, as his strength began to fail, he received a letter from Mills: "I shall leave for Washington in a few days to help set things moving for the conservation of scenery . . . As you well know, it is the work that you have done that has encouraged me . . . in the big work that I am planning to do. If you will push along another book or two these books will help the cause more than you can imagine." Muir would write no more books. But in January 1915, less than a month after his death, the U.S. Congress passed the bill creating Rocky Mountain National Park. And the following January, the National Park Service came into being.

In the concluding sentences of his essay on "The World without Firearms" Mills expressed his faith in the spiritual influence of wilderness on mankind: "The forests of the earth are the flags of Nature. They appeal to all and awaken inspiring universal feelings. Enter the forest and the boundaries of nations are forgotten. It may be that some time an immortal pine will be the flag of a united and peaceful world." *

༜

By the first decade of the present century the nature essay was in full flower as a popular literary form. "Nature-writing and the automobile business have developed vastly during the past few years," wrote Dallas Lore Sharp — clergyman, English professor, an editor of *Youth's Companion* — himself one of the most prolific and beguiling practitioners of the art. He was thinking not only of the nature essay, but also of a literary phenomenon as new, and as potentially hazardous in the wrong hands, as the automobile itself. This was the "nature story." Its greatest practitioner — one might almost say its inventor — was Ernest Thompson Seton.

The contrast between Seton and the nature essayists — the followers of that low-keyed homebody, John Burroughs — could hardly be sharper. Seton was romantic, proud, a talented artist, a superb storyteller whose passion for nature ranged from the art schools of London and Paris to the re-

---

* Four decades and two world wars later, E. B. White, in a memorable *New Yorker* editorial on World Federalism, would suggest the Wild Flag for this purpose.

motest wilderness of the Canadian Northwest. Born in northern England in 1860, he was of Scottish ancestry — less humble than John Muir's, since he claimed kinship with a Jacobite earl. When he was six years old the family moved to a farm in Ontario, and later to Toronto. His father, like Muir's, was a stern Calvinist: tight-fisted, bigoted, personally indolent but relentless in driving his children. "He was, I think," writes Seton in his autobiography, "the most selfish person I ever heard of or read of in history or in fiction." Whenever he could, the boy escaped to the nearby woods. "From my earliest years I longed to be a naturalist. I thought I had a mission — to be the prophet of outdoor life. My father said: 'No, there is no opening, no future, for such a calling. You have artistic gifts, and an artist you are going to be.' "

That prospect, Seton later admitted, was far from unpleasant; actually this decision by his imperious father determined his future career. His drawings, not his writings, would give him entrée to the scientific community and a means of self-support. And the happy union of words and illustrations by the same hand would make his books virtually unique.

Seton was twenty-two years old when he "gladly said goodbye" to his father's house and joined his brother in Manitoba. Behind him lay a brief period of study at London's Royal Academy, cut short by ill health and undernourishment. Now at last he was in what he called the land of his dreams. "We were now on the Great Plains of the Souris," he notes in his journal, "and although birds had abounded before, they now seemed multiplied by ten ... There were small flocks of brown cranes, and occasionally pairs of white cranes — glorious creatures — trumpeting in the sky, or sometimes seen on a prairie ridge where three or four of them would do a wonderful minuet, flapping their wings, bowing and chassezing in circles around each other, to the accompaniment of a loud bugling* ... Wild geese went over in long strings or V-

---

* During his childhood in Ontario he had watched with wonder a pair of migrating white cranes (now called whooping cranes). It was as memorable a

shaped bands. Prairie chickens were seen on nearly every little knoll . . ." Here on the prairie potholes he developed a
simplified system of drawing which, by stressing pattern and
field marks rather than detail, enabled him to identify ducks
at a distance and hawks overhead. Fifty years later, these
drawings would become the inspiration for Roger Tory Peterson's epoch-making *Field Guide to the Birds*.

For Seton the one curse of this glorious country was the
mosquitoes — "the stinging blood-sucking, plague-bearing
mosquitoes." Their swarms seem to have clouded his scientific perception. After describing how they attacked the helpless cattle, he remarks with apparent approval: "Since this
was written, the terror of the mosquitoes in the North-west
has been greatly reduced through drainage of the swamps
and ponds, some by natural drying and some by man's carefully planned efforts." On a later visit he notes sadly —
without making the connection — how things have changed:
"The million little lakes, from Winnipeg to the Rockies, had
so dwindled, so dried up, that the ducks had nearly disappeared . . . no more to be seen on the lonely prairie lands of
the Assiniboine."

But in these early days the Canadian West was a naturalist's paradise. For five years young Seton explored the virgin
forest and the tall-grass prairie: observing and sketching;
hunting elk and deer, wolves and coyotes and foxes; learning
to read animal tracks and to recreate the story of their lives
from the record of the snow. Here he gathered material for his
first scientific publication, *The Birds of Manitoba*, and for a
series of bird studies in *The Auk*. And here his career as a big-
game hunter reached its climax — and its end — with the

---

moment as John Burroughs' first sight of the black-throated blue warbler.
"The noblest thing that flies," he wrote sixty-odd years later. "The ring triumphant of that stirring trumpet call still echoes in my heart . . . Alas, I am
old now, and that glorious bird is gone — gone forever!" Happily, Seton was
wrong. Strictly protected in its wintering grounds on the Texas coast and its
breeding area in far northern Alberta, the tiny remnant population, of which
he was unaware, is slowly and precariously building back.

killing of a moose. Once more, the sportsman had turned conservationist.

After travelling three hundred miles on foot, through the snow, during nineteen days of toil, I kept my hunting vow and I killed the grandest beast of chase that roams America's woods. But another thought possessed me as I gazed on that superb animal, turned into a pile of butcher's meat, for the sake of a passing thrill of triumph. The thought was much like remorse — so that I then and there made a vow, which I have lived up to ever since — that so long as they are threatened with early extermination, I will never again lift my rifle against any of America's big game . . . Eighteen eighty-four must ever stand out in memory as the climax of my Golden Age, blessed now as I was with exuberant health, strength, and spirits.

But there was also a living to earn. Fortunately, C. Hart Merriam was seeking an illustrator for his monumental work on American mammals. Seton called upon him at his home in the Adirondacks. Here "I made the acquaintance of his charming mother and his father, Senator Merriam, also of his beautiful sister Florence, home from college * for spring vacation." To test the young artist's skill, Dr. Merriam gave him pen and ink and a shrew pickled in alcohol. When Seton had finished his drawing (he recalls in his never modest autobiography) Merriam "said that it easily gave me first place among animal illustrators in America." Seldom has a shrew cast so long a shadow. A few years later, Frank Chapman commissioned Seton to illustrate both the *Handbook* and *Bird-Life*. His living was secure.†

Despite all his far wanderings, Ernest Thompson Seton is invariably associated in our minds with the American South-

___

* Where she was about to found the Smith College Audubon Society. See p. 172.

† Wayne Hanley, editor for the Massachusetts Audubon Society and author of *Natural History in America*, writes me as follows:

"When I was a boy, Seton was my idol. I was surprised at many of the same Seton passages read later as an adult! In spite of himself, Seton was a top flight mammalogist and a rather impressive naturalist. His cartoons, or page-edge line drawings, are superb, especially for a sort of Oriental quality in which a few lines impart far more information than one might expect."

west. For good reason; it is the scene of the story that made him famous. Returning from a year's art study in Paris — during which he had painted what Theodore Roosevelt called "the best wolf picture I ever saw" — he accepted, of all things, a job trapping and poisoning wolves on a cattle ranch in the Currumpaw Valley of New Mexico. "Very soon I learned that the cowmen of the Currumpaw believed the wolf bands to be led by an immensely big strong wolf of supernatural cunning." For four months Seton, despite all his animal lore, was outwitted by the wily beast. Then he devised a devilish stratagem. Managing to trap the great wolf's mate, he used her carcass to make footprints in the snow, leading to the trap. For once Old Lobo, the King Wolf, was reckless; his "fidelity" was his doom. Out of this episode Seton fashioned his best-known story, "Lobo, the King of Currumpaw" — a superb tear-jerker that appeared first in *Scribner's* magazine and subsequently as the lead chapter of *Wild Animals I Have Known*. Illustrated with dramatic wash drawings and charming marginal sketches, the book became an immediate bestseller. In Seton's own words, it "founded the modern school of animal stories, that is, giving in fiction form the actual facts of an animal's life and modes of thought." After this initial success, "my books appeared as rapidly as I could write and illustrate them."

Seton believed that "natural history has lost much by the vague general treatment that is so common," that the life and personality of the individual animal is more interesting than the ways of the race in general. His stories are frankly anthropomorphic, as he sought to show that we can find in animals "the virtues most admired in Man." They "are creatures with wants and feelings differing in degree only from our own." Interpretation is one thing, observation another. Seton went far out in ascribing human traits to other animals, but his fund of knowledge about how wild creatures actually behave, gained through years of wilderness experience, gave an immediacy and excitement to his stories that few writers could match. They had an enormous appeal to young readers, and their message is clear. "Have wild things no legal or moral rights?" he cries out as Redruff, the ruffed grouse, is hanging helpless in a snare. "What right has man to inflict such long and fearful agony on a fellow-creature, simply because that creature does not speak his language?"

Later on, partly as the result of the so-called nature controversy, Seton turned away from fiction to produce the massive work on which his scientific reputation chiefly depends. This was the four-volume *Lives of Game Animals*, which won the John Burroughs Medal and which, he records in his autobiography, "was acclaimed as a masterpiece." But it is his animal stories that won him such a huge following. In the words of a fellow naturalist, they "have caused tens of thousands of people who never cared for nature before, to become interested in out-of-door life." They also, for a brief period, came close to getting him into trouble.

❧

Seton had always venerated John Burroughs. "He was one of my ideals," he recalls in his autobiography. "Imagine my feelings, therefore, when in *The Atlantic Monthly* for March, 1904 [actually 1903], Burroughs came out with a furious attack on me and on my disciples, especially reviling one William J. Long. There were six pages of denunciation, calling me a fraud, a faker, a sham naturalist, etc., etc." Thus began the "nature-faking" controversy: a bitter if sometimes ludicrous squabble in which even the President of the United States eventually became involved, and which did little credit to any of those concerned.

Burroughs began his article with a comment on the popular demand for nature books of every sort, including animal stories and animal romances, some good, some bad, some indifferent. A very small number "are valuable contributions to our natural history literature." Others are simply exploiting "the popular love for the sensational and the improbable." Whereupon he launched his attack on two best-selling authors: "Mr. Thompson Seton" and "his awkward imitator, the Rev. William J. Long." Long was the young pastor of a church in Connecticut, with degrees from Harvard and Heidelberg universities; a student of philosophy and a skillful writer who also claimed to be an experienced naturalist from many years spent in the northern forests. His romantic animal stories, such as *The School of the Woods*, were adored by schoolchildren. To Burroughs, they were ridiculous; he was the "Münchausen of our nature-writers." Burroughs suggests that the northwoods guides and trappers from whom the gullible young man got much of his material were pulling his leg; he scoffs at the idea that animals "teach" their young. The creatures Long writes about "are simply human beings disguised as animals."

Seton, for all his great reputation, does not come off much better. Burroughs observed that his book should have been entitled *Wild Animals I* ALONE *Have Known*. He "says in capital letters that his stories are true . . . True as romance . . . true in their power to entertain the young reader, they certainly are; but true as natural history they certainly are not." Burroughs cites some apparent absurdities, including the fox who deliberately led the hounds to the railroad trestle just in time to be killed by a passing train ("the presumption is that the fox had a watch and a time-table upon his person") or the compassionate mother fox who brings poison to her captured and suffering cub when she fails to free him from his chain. And so on, at tedious length.

The *Atlantic*'s editor, Bliss Perry, found the article a bit peevish and ill-natured, and suggested — not very helpfully — that the author alter his frown to "the smile of sarcasm." Burroughs himself had qualms about it even before it was printed. "Poor devil!" he said of Long. "I begin to feel sympathy for him. I'm sorry the article is so blunt and savage, but I couldn't deal with him in any other way." Reassurance soon came with a letter from the White House. Roosevelt was delighted; these writers who confuse fact with fiction do positive harm. (But he goes on to criticize some of Burroughs' own assertions.)

As for Long, he was not easily put down. Two months later he replied to Burroughs in the *North American Review*. Earlier writers "also were vilified and insulted for their observations . . . Mr. Burroughs has not seen these things on his farm, and therefore they must be false." Animals are as much individuals as are people. "The truth is, that he who watches any animal closely enough will see what no naturalist has ever seen." Elsewhere he inveighs, somewhat inconsistently, against what he calls "the tyranny of facts" as opposed to "the liberty and truth of the spirit." "The study of Nature is a vastly different thing from the study of Science."

The battle was joined. Nature fakers like Long, as Frank Chapman pointed out, thrive on criticism; the publicity stimulates sales. "It was Long's literary ability that made his writings so pernicious . . . Moreover, he was so aggressive in his own defense that editors were loath to give space to exposure of his errors." When a scientist questioned Long's story of a woodcock that mended its broken leg with a splint and a mud-cast dried in the sun, his furious reply "apparently so alarmed the publishers of that magazine that they closed the discussion then and there."*

Long kept fighting and raking in the royalties, but Seton and Burroughs were soon reconciled. Chapman told Burroughs that his attack on Seton was unjustified, that the latter was a sound observer and not to be classed with his would-be emulators. Shortly thereafter he brought the two men together in his home, for what turned out to be the beginning of a lasting friendship. Seton's account is more dramatic. At a formal literary dinner given by Andrew Car-

* "I recall," wrote Chapman, "another incident in which Long did not fare so well. As a resident of Stamford, he made the welcoming address at the annual meeting for the Connecticut Audubon Society, held in that city May 25, 1901. It was the first time I had met him and he at once placed me on the offensive by an uncalled-for, savage criticism of Ernest Seton's bird pictures. At the conclusion of the meeting he was introduced to Mabel Osgood Wright, president of the Society. 'Wright, Wright,' he said, 'you're the bird woman, aren't you? It seems to me that I have a letter from you at home, but I haven't read it yet.' 'Well, it couldn't be from me,' Mrs. Wright replied with icy clearness, 'for I never heard of you before' " (*Autobiography of a Bird-Lover*, p. 183).

negie — among the guests were Mark Twain, William Dean Howells, and Hamlin Garland — Seton arranged to sit next to Burroughs and baited him about his article until "poor old John broke down and wept." "One result of this interview," he recalls in his autobiography, "was a public apology for the attack, in which Burroughs wrote: 'Some are nature students, dryly scientific, some are sentimental, some are sensational and a few are altogether admirable. Mr. Thompson Seton, as an artist and a raconteur, ranks by far the highest in this field; he is truly delightful.'" In recounting his triumph, Seton conveniently omits the key phrase in Burroughs' "apology." Before "he is truly delightful," Burroughs had written "to those who can separate the fact from the fiction in his animal stories." Or, one might add, in his autobiography.

"Poor old John" may or may not have wept with remorse over his treatment of Seton, but he kept hammering away on what he called the "quack nature writers" and the gullible magazine editors who printed their stuff. Many of their "observations" were pure fake and deserved to be exposed. But occasionally Burroughs got carried away, as when he excoriated Harold S. Deming's "Briartown Sketches" in *Outing* magazine as a tissue of falsehoods, intentionally faked from beginning to end. In the heat of the chase he not only distorted Deming's text, but made a number of dogmatic generalizations about animal behavior that Deming and his supporters easily refuted. One of them concerned the nest of the hummingbird:

"Mr. Burroughs states that 'the nests are *always* neatly thatched with lichens': and with this as his scientific premise, he *deduces* the result that I lie when I write that I saw on a grapevine a hummer's nest thatched with bits of grapevine bark. If he will look in 'Birdcraft,' by Mrs. Mabel Osgood Wright, a well-known writer, he will find record of a hummer's nest, in a tall spruce, 'covered with small flakes of spruce bark, instead of the usual lichens.' This accords ill with the omniscience of Mr. Burroughs as to humming birds." Burroughs himself did the cause a disservice by lump-ing together the shameless fakers with the honest observers who — though sometimes in error, as he was himself — were simply reporting what they had seen.

Meanwhile, President Roosevelt was itching to get into the fight, though aware that in his position he should avoid public controversy. But when Long published a fantastic and impossible story of a white wolf, claiming in the preface that every statement "is minutely true to fact," it was too much. "I know that as President I ought not to do this," he wrote to Burroughs, "but I was having an awful time toward the end of the session and I felt I simply had to permit myself some diversion." He was referring to an article in *Everybody's Magazine* entitled "Roosevelt on the Nature Fakirs." In the form of an interview, it consisted of pungent comments by the President on fake natural history, beginning with Jack London's *White Fang* and zeroing in on Long's account of his white wolf biting through the chest walls of a caribou to its heart: "[The reader] will get a clear idea of just what the feat would be if he will hang a grapefruit in the middle of a keg of flour, and then see whether a big dog could bite through the keg into the grapefruit." What angered Roosevelt most was the impact of such nonsense on young readers. "The preservation of the useful and beautiful animal and bird life of the country depends largely upon creating in the young an interest in the life of the woods and fields. If the child mind is fed with stories that are false to nature, the children will go to the haunts of the animal only to meet with disappointment. The result will be disbelief, and the death of interest."

When Long read the article he must have felt, in the words of the journalist Mark Sullivan, "like a dove shot at by an elephant gun." But he quickly recovered his poise and shot back in two open letters to the President, whom he described as "a man who takes delight in whooping through the woods killing everything in sight . . . Who is he to write 'I don't believe for a minute that some of these nature writers know the heart of a wild thing.' As to that I find that after carefully reading two of his big books that every time Mr. Roosevelt gets near the heart of a wild thing he invariably puts a bullet through it. From his own records I have reckoned a full thousand hearts which he has thus known intimately . . ." Citing some of the bloodiest hunts, he concludes, "If it is charged that I do not understand nature as Mr. Roosevelt does, I stand up and plead guilty; yes, guilty in every page, every paragraph, every sentence."

Long won a good deal of sympathy from persons who were not happy about a President of the United States making a personal attack on a private citizen. So the inglorious conflict simmered on until, a few months later, a member of the Biological Survey arranged for a symposium of professional naturalists to express their views on nature-faking, in a long article to which Roosevelt himself contributed. They responded with enthusiasm. William T. Hornaday, the volcanic director of the New York Zoological Society, opened with heavy sarcasm: "Contrary to the rule of indignant naturalists generally, I must say a good word for William J. Long. His books . . . have furnished me much amusement . . . Whenever he enters the woods, the most marvelous things begin to happen." Dr. C. Hart Merriam explained that "the Rev. Dr. Long is possessed of that rare gift . . . called Creative Memory . . . A nature writer blessed with the Creative Memory does not have to go about wasting valuable time waiting and watching for animals to appear and do something." Despite the labored humor that these scientists seemed to think was required, there was enough hard evidence submitted to discredit Long once for all. Thereafter he would devote himself to more scholarly and less vulnerable literary pursuits.

Nature-faking would continue, but henceforth writers would be a bit more responsible; editors and their readers more discriminating. And the effect of honest nature writing would be enhanced. For as Roosevelt wrote, after praising some of our best literary naturalists, "the surest way to neutralize the work of these lovers of truth in nature-study, is to encourage those whose work shows neither knowledge of nature or love of truth."

Some time after the unseemly spat with Burroughs, Ernest Thompson Seton was giving a series of lectures for children as part of the American Museum's educational program. On one occasion when he had to cancel an engagement, the Museum invited as a substitute speaker a young nature writer from Cape Cod, Massachusetts, named Thornton W. Burgess. The fee was one hundred dollars. "Although I badly needed it," Burgess recalls in his autobiography, "the money meant little . . . This was the first direct recognition of my work by authorities in the field of natural science." Up to now he had been working alone, "lacking acquaintance with any naturalist or scientist of note . . . striving not to allow imagination to overstep the exacting bounds of truth and fact with the inevitable penalty of being branded a 'nature faker.' "

As seen through his own eyes, Burgess's career has a sort of Horatio Alger quality: the moral precepts learned on his mother's knee, the courage to say "yes" whenever opportunity knocks, the long climb up the ladder from obscurity to fame. His first book, *Old Mother West Wind*, published in 1910, had been written for his small son, while he supported himself with hack journalism, advertising writing, and — most important — a series of nature articles for *Country Life* magazine which had to pass under the critical eye of professionals like Frank M. Chapman. In 1913 he launched the "Bedtime Story Books," with the now-classic drawings of Harrison Cady, a well-known illustrator for the original *Life* magazine. (Burgess generously attributed a large share of his initial success to Cady's drawings.) So Johnny Chuck, Reddy Fox, Jerry Muskrat, Peter Cottontail, and their friends in the Green Meadow came on stage, never to leave it. Meanwhile his stories were being widely syndicated in the daily press. And at his suggestion *People's Home Journal* established a "Green Meadow Club" for children who signed a pledge to be kind to birds and other animals. Whether he realized it or not, he was following the pattern of the first Audubon Society that George

Bird Grinnell had founded, a generation earlier, in the pages of *Forest and Stream*.

Two events advertised the fact that Burgess had been accepted by the scientific community. One was the publication of his *Bird Book* with illustrations by Louis Agassiz Fuertes. "It rings true," wrote Dr. Hornaday, "and is by far the best bird book for children that we have ever seen. In fact it is the very book that anxious mothers, the children, and the booksellers have been waiting for for twenty years." Burgess's other great moment came when, at the annual meeting of the New York Zoological Society, he was presented with the gold medal of the Wild Life Protection Fund. Soon thereafter he joined the conservationists in the bitter battle, led by Hornaday, against the duck hunters, whose blood pressure rose with each new installment of the heartrending *Adventures of Poor Mrs. Quack*.

Every Burgess story has a moral, but he knew enough not to preach. "It is as natural for the average boy to throw a stone at a bird or to chase a rabbit or a squirrel as it is for him to draw his breath. To tell him that it is wrong or cruel is a waste of breath . . . But in that same average boy is inherent a peculiarly strong sense of justice. Arouse his interest in the daily lives of the lesser creatures . . . and he at once becomes their friend and champion."And every story must be credible. "It is permissible for Peter Rabbit to talk because the child understands that in all probability there is some form of communication between animals. But it is not permissible for Peter Rabbit to climb a tree or to ride a bicycle." Burgess never underestimated the young child's ability to recognize the phony. Perhaps that is one reason his stories have survived. Reviewing his autobiography, the *New York Times* commented: "Mr. Burgess actually belongs to a long line, one that reaches at least as far back as Aesop. But he won't discuss this in his autobiography. One wishes he had. Then one remembers that he really is Peter Rabbit and has been Peter Rabbit for a long time."

"Nature," Thornton Burgess reminds us, "was the first

teacher of the human race." He was passionately concerned with the neglect of what he felt should be the foundation of our educational system. Of all his countless fan letters the one he treasured most was from Dr. Clyde Fisher of the American Museum, on the occasion of the publication of his ten-thousandth story: "What an achievement! It would be difficult if not impossible to overestimate the value of your work in nature education and in conservation."

CHAPTER X

The "Old-Fashioned Naturalist"

"I should like to keep some book of natural history always by me as a sort of elixir, the reading of which would restore the tone of my system and secure me true and cheerful views of life."

— Henry David Thoreau, JOURNAL

IN A TECHNICAL, computerized age, one may be excused for looking back with nostalgia to a time when the President of the United States could concern himself so passionately with the biting powers of a wolf. Wild nature, whether embodied in the questionable anecdotes of William J. Long, the patient observations of John Burroughs, the thrilling tales of Ernest Thompson Seton, or the bedtime stories of Thornton Burgess, was an endlessly fascinating and romantic subject. Yet one often hears it said that the "old-fashioned naturalist" — as contrasted with the specialists and laboratory scientists of our day — is a figure of the past. The molecular biologists, the geneticists, have taken over the frontiers of knowledge; the taxonomy of birds, Roger Tory Peterson once remarked with a touch of hyperbole, can now be studied by analysis of the albumen in the egg, without the researcher even having seen the bird in flight. On the other hand there exists today a strong countercurrent in the recently popularized science of ethology, which is concerned with the behavior of the living animal. Whirlpools occasionally form in professional circles when these two currents come into conflict. To most writers and readers of nature books, however, this is of little concern. Some of the finest nature writers of our time, such as Joseph Wood Krutch and Edwin Way Teale, are in the mainstream of a tradition that goes all the way back to Henry David Thoreau — a man who preferred live creatures to dead specimens and was wholly unfamiliar with the electron microscope.

Before our age of specialization, many professional scientists were also "naturalists" in the broadest sense of the term. The archetype is probably Louis Agassiz, whose interests ranged from the Alpine glaciers to the Amazon, from fossil fish to the snapping turtles of the Concord River. One can think of a number of later figures who have had a like far-ranging view. I have chosen two for special comment — William Beebe and Robert Cushman Murphy — mainly because of their strong literary bent. But this is an arbitrary choice. For instance, one might equally well take that engaging character, Thomas Barbour, fourth in succession to Louis Agassiz as Director of Harvard's Museum of Comparative Zoology. An impressive figure, almost six-foot-six and upward of three hundred pounds, Barbour had, in the words of an old friend, "that mysterious quality that used to be called magnetism, in his case a blend of geniality, friendliness, enthusiasm, humor. He did nothing by halves. His likes were keen, his dislikes robust."* By any measure, he was a pungent character. (When he asked President Lowell of Harvard why the present generation failed to produce any of the curious figures that once stalked across the Harvard stage, Mr. Lowell replied, "Buy a mirror.") Barbour saw himself "by inclination an old-fashioned naturalist, many tell me the last of the breed. My colleagues prefer to know more and more about less and less and so are infinitely more erudite than I." The range of his travels and of his knowledge is staggering; he chose well in calling his autobiography *Naturalist at Large.*

Barbour's friend and mentor, the great oceanographer Henry B. Bigelow, would also qualify as an old-fashioned naturalist. So would David Fairchild, author of the classic *The World Is My Garden.* No one, Barbour claimed, could write more delightfully charming English than Fairchild: "Every sentence he writes is crammed with unbelievable grammatical errors, yet everything he writes holds one's breathless attention." There are many others: John C. Phillips, the ideal sportsman-naturalist, author of the monumental *Natural History of the Ducks;* or Donald Culross Peattie, a gentle character who preferred the binocular to the gun and had a statue of St. Francis in his garden — a sensitive (and highly successful) writer with a poetic approach to nature and the American Scene. Or, going back to an earlier time, the world-famous entomologist, Samuel H. Scudder, who studied under Louis Agassiz and became an authority on fossil insects and the author of a number of scientific and popular volumes on butterflies unsurpassed for their scholarship and their literary

* His dislikes included Henry Thoreau. See p. 146.

charm. More recently, in the same field, there is W. J. Holland, whose standard works on American butterflies and moths are leavened by engaging, half-humorous essays in courtly prose, and peppered with quotations from the poets. One could go on indefinitely. But none was more colorful (some scientists thought a bit *too* colorful) or more productive of best-selling books than Dr. William Beebe.

Born in 1877, William Beebe lived until 1962, the centenary of Thoreau's death and the year of Rachel Carson's *Silent Spring*. An all-around naturalist, he is probably best remembered as the first human being to explore the ocean depths, thereby adding a whole new dimension to the field of nature study. The popular image — and he enjoyed enormous popularity in his day — was that of a slim, daring, middle-aged scientist deep beneath the waves in his "bathysphere," while on the deck of the mother ship a bevy of sun-tanned beauties eagerly await his return to the surface. The picture is accurate, but limited. True, Beebe was a romantic adventurer from childhood, steeped in the writings of Jules Verne, Rudyard Kipling, John Buchan. He was also a distinguished field naturalist and a talented author. At the early age of twenty-two he was appointed curator of ornithology at the Bronx Zoo, and his first books dealt with his search for birds and wilderness in the heart of Mexico. Somewhat depressed after serving as an aviator in World War I, he sought spiritual refreshment in the jungles of British Guiana (now Guyana); the resulting book, *Jungle Peace*, published in 1918, was warmly praised by Theodore Roosevelt in one of the last book reviews that he wrote. Eight years later Beebe's magnificent *Pheasants of the World*, which had involved eighteen months of field work in Asia and the East Indies, won him the first John Burroughs Medal.

Beebe had a gift for taking the reader with him to the ends of the earth. Among the pheasants a favorite was the junglefowl, ancestor of all our domestic poultry, which he studied throughout its range in southeast Asia: "As often as I heard the red Junglefowl in various Eastern countries, it was always with a start at such familiar, barnyard sounds coming from the jungle, where sometimes I knew there were no human dwellings within a distance of many leagues." At earliest dawn he would conceal himself in a thicket near where the birds were calling, preferably one "free of the hordes of leeches which infested the surrounding foliage, and which made stationary observation elsewhere an impossibility." Hour after hour, he would watch their antics and listen to the crowing of a cock or the cackling of a hen, analyzing the notes and their meaning with a subtlety that reminds one of Konrad Lorenz translating the language of the jackdaws in *King Solomon's Ring*. Sometimes the cock's crowing, preceded by resounding smacks of the wings, was a clear challenge that rang through the jungle. "But at another time . . . I had the good fortune to watch and listen to a bird which was crowing and yet not challenging . . . The Jungle cock was on a fallen log, and his whole demeanor was of assured peace . . . His crowing was intermittent, uttered at a lower pitch, and did not have the tang and abruptness of the challenge. It had a hint of the domestic drawl, and after each effort he sang to himself the low content song with which we are so familiar in the barnyard hen — Waaaaaaaak — waak — Waaaaaaa! The whole seemed to me a real song, to be compared with the tempered notes of a thrush who perches near his mate on her nest and gives this vent to joy in the success of his life."

In sheer production, Beebe almost matched Burroughs, giving birth to a new book every year or two. But while Slabsides was world enough for Burroughs, the surface of the planet barely sufficed for Beebe. Sandwiched in between his jungle books appeared *Galapagos: World's End*. (The thousands of tourists who have since visited these enchanted islands may find his subtitle out of date, but his account still whets the palate as few such books can.) And in the late twenties he began diving in the waters off Bermuda, launching a new underwater career — the forerunner, as it were, of Jacques Cousteau. As described in *Half Mile Down* (1934), the world he watched through that heavy glass porthole, stage-lit by powerful headlights, was the world of Jules Verne translated from fantasy into fact. Struggling to put into words the experience of his first deep-sea dive Beebe, with uncanny prescience, compares his own sensations with those of some future astronaut in outer space:

A certain day and hour and second are approaching rapidly when a human face will peer out through a tiny window and signals will be passed back to companions, or to breathlessly waiting hosts on earth, with such sentences as:

> *We are above the level of Everest.*
> *Can now see the whole Atlantic coastline.*
> *Clouds blot out the earth.*
> *Temperature and air pressure have dropped to minus minus.*
> *Can see the whole circumference of Earth.*
> *The moon appears ten times its usual size.*
> *We now . . .*

Both by daylight and by moonlight I have looked from a plane down on the earth from a height of over four miles, so I know the first kindergarten sensations of such a trip. But until I actually am enclosed within some futuristic rocket and start on a voyage into interstellar space, I shall never experience such a feeling of complete isolation from the surface of the planet Earth as when I first dangled in a hollow pea on a swaying cobweb a quarter of a mile below the deck of a ship rolling in mid-ocean.

As the hollow steel globe sank beneath the waves, Beebe and his assistant, Otis Barton, felt themselves entering another world:

We were lowered gently, but we struck the surface with a splash which would have crushed a rowboat like an eggshell. Yet within we hardly noticed the impact, until a froth of foam and bubbles surged up over the glass and our chamber was dimmed to a pleasant green. We swung quietly while the first hose clamp was put on the cable. At the end of the first revolution the great hull of the barge came into view. This was a familiar landscape which I had often seen from the diving helmet — a transitory, swaying reef with waving banners of seaweed, long tubular sponges, jet-black blobs of ascidians, and tissue-thin plates of rough-spined pearl shells. Then the keel passed slowly upward, becoming one with the green water overhead.

With this passed our last visible link with the upper world; from now on we had to depend on distant spoken words for knowledge of our depth, or speed, or the weather, or the sunlight, or anything having to do with the world of air on the surface of the earth.

As they sank deeper, the light coming in through the porthole took on an eerie quality:

We were the first living men to look out at the strange illumination — and it was of an indefinable translucent blue quite unlike anything I have seen in the upper world . . . the blueness of the blue, both outside and inside our sphere, seemed to pass materially through the eyes into our very beings. This is all very unscientific, quite worthy of being jeered at by optician or physicist, but there it was. I was excited by the fishes that I was seeing perhaps more than I have been by other organisms, but it was only an intensification of my surface and laboratory interest; I have seen strange fluorescence and ultraviolet illumination in the laboratories of physicists; I recall the weird effects of color sifting through distant snow crystals on the high Himalayas; and I have been impressed by the eerie illumina-

tion, or lack of it, during a full eclipse of the sun; but this was beyond and outside all or any of these. I think we both experienced a wholly new kind of mental reception of color impression. I felt I was dealing with something too different to be classified in usual terms.

At the deepest point of the dive, Beebe experienced a sense of almost mystical revelation:

I was curled up in a ball on the cold damp steel, Barton's voice relayed my observations and assurances of our safety, a fan swished back and forth through the air, and the ticking of my wrist watch came as a strange sound of another world.

Soon after this there came a moment which stands out clearly, unpunctuated by any word of ours, with no fish or other creature visible outside. I sat crouched with mouth and nose wrapped in a handkerchief and my forehead pressed close to the cold glass — that transparent bit of old earth which so sturdily held back nine tons of water from my face. There came to me at that instant a tremendous wave of emotion, a real appreciation of what was momentarily almost superhuman, cosmic, of the whole situation: our barge slowly rolling high overhead in the blazing sunlight, like the merest chip in the midst of ocean, the long cobweb of cable leading down through the spectrum to our lonely sphere, where, sealed tight, two conscious human beings sat and peered into the abyssal darkness as we dangled in mid-water, isolated as a lost planet in outermost space. Here, under a pressure which, if loosened, in a fraction of a second would make amorphous tissue of our bodies, breathing our own homemade atmosphere, sending a few comforting words chasing up and down a string of hose — here I was privileged to peer out and actually see the creatures which had evolved in the blackness of a blue midnight which, since the ocean was born, had known no following day; here I was privileged to sit and try to crystallize what I observed through inadequate eyes and to interpret with a mind wholly unequal to the task. To the ever-recurring question, "How did it feel?" I can only quote the words of Herbert Spencer: I felt like "an infinitesimal atom floating in illimitable space." No wonder my sole written contribution to science and literature at the time was, "Am writing at a depth of a quarter of a mile. A luminous fish is outside the window."

And no wonder Beebe's accounts of his adventures caught the imagination of thousands of readers. Certain critics —

possibly envious of his success with the public — may have felt with justification that he was a bit of a showman, and that he tried too hard to make literature of everything he wrote. But if so, this did not affect his keen appreciation of good nature writing by others. Witness his anthology, *The Book of Naturalists*, which concludes with a selection from a volume recently published but virtually stillborn entitled *Under the Sea Wind.* Its author was an obscure young employee of the U.S. Fish and Wildlife Service named Rachel Louise Carson. So began a friendship that grew as Rachel Carson worked on the manuscript of her next book, *The Sea Around Us*, which was to have such a sensational success. "I had a grand visit with him," she wrote as this ambitious project, after years of struggle, was at last approaching completion. "As a result of our talk, I don't dare finish this book without getting under water, and he has me practically on the way to Bermuda, where he will make all sorts of advance arrangements so that I'll be sure of meeting the proper sharks, octopuses, etc." Actually she settled for a modest dive off the Florida coast, but at least he got her head under water. Subsequently he helped to keep her head financially above it when — together with Edwin Way Teale — he recommended her for a literary fellowship, during those lean years before the royalties for *The Sea Around Us* began to pour in. Alas, he did not live quite long enough to witness the immense influence of her *Silent Spring* in helping to save the living world that he had loved and studied for so many years, and which — when in his eighties — he still viewed, as she did, with a sense of wonder.

I could not help thinking of Dr. Beebe when I attended the First World Conference on National Parks, which was held in Seattle in 1962, the year of his death, and which brought together delegates from over seventy nations. One of the most original proposals came from Dr. Carleton Ray of the New York Aquarium. The time had come, he said, to establish a worldwide system of underwater parks to save our choicest coastal areas from exploitation and pollution, our coral reefs

from vandalism. A few decades earlier such a notion would have seemed fantastic. No longer. With the advent of snorkeling and scuba diving, the hitherto hidden world beneath the waves had become a part of our common experience. Here were forests composed not of trees but of coral and kelp, among which browsed fishes brighter than the brightest of birds. And thanks to modern technology, the eerie life of the depths was now a familiar sight in every living room — depths greater than even Beebe had plumbed. But he was the pioneer.

ॐ

Robert Cushman Murphy, successor to Frank M. Chapman as curator of the bird department at the American Museum of Natural History, was ten years younger than William Beebe, and a lifelong friend. Bob Murphy became an almost legendary figure before he died in 1973, in his eighty-fifth year. He had taken his first job at the museum the year that Burroughs published his account of camping with President Roosevelt in

The "Old-Fashioned Naturalist"

Yosemite Valley. When Muir's *My First Summer in the Sierra* appeared, Murphy was in the Antarctic as naturalist on the last of the whaling voyages under sail. And more than a half century later, thousands heard him on the radio demolishing the slanderous attacks on Rachel Carson that followed the publication of *Silent Spring*. Later still, having returned on a Navy icebreaker to the scene of his early voyage, he threw himself into one of today's great crusades, the battle to save the whales.

While I had the pleasure of meeting Dr. Beebe only in his later years — his charm and his enthusiasm still wholly intact — I had my first sight of Dr. Murphy (one can hardly call it a meeting) when I was a schoolboy in New York City and he was lecturing on his recent expedition to South America to study the mysterious Humboldt Current and the famous guano islands off the Peruvian coast, which he would describe so vividly in his *Bird Islands of Peru* (1925). Murphy's interest in the sea dated back to his childhood on the shores of Long Island and, as Dr. Dean Amadon of the American Museum points out, that early voyage in Antarctic waters on the whaling brig *Daisy* shaped his future career as a scientist: "His bookplate bears the likeness of a South Georgia elephant-seal, and his researches there on the King Penguin and other marine birds channeled his interests for the remainder of his life." Many years later he would immortalize that two-year voyage in his captivating, often humorous, *Logbook for Grace*, based on letters to the young bride whom he had left behind. (For energetic, intrepid Grace Barstow Murphy, once was enough. Hereafter she would go along, as readers of her *There's Always Adventure* know well.)

In 1936 the museum brought out Murphy's monumental *Oceanic Birds of South America*, with magnificent color illustrations by Francis Lee Jaques. These two fat volumes are living proof that the most exhaustive scientific studies can also make splendid reading. Here, for example, is his portrait of that favorite of Antarctic explorers, the Adélie penguin, during its nesting season on the edge of the ice:

After change of guard at the nest, the freed penguins proceed to gather in groups on the ice foot, where they frolic and chatter and chase each other about in high spirits. The one object of each bird appears to be to make some other dare the first plunge. As soon as one takes a header, the others follow like shot poured out of a bottle. Then all is silence until they bob up at the surface, 20 to 30 meters out, and start rolling and splashing while they clean themselves. Their chaffing at this time sounds like that of a crowd of boys. Returning later to the rookeries with glistening plumage, they often mingle with dirty birds bound for sea and show what social animals they are by standing together in small groups chatting. The sea and its ice are their playground. Here the bands of birds play tag and also use the floes in the tideway as excursion boats. Sometimes they crowd on, amid much bantering, until the embarking of each new bird means the pushing off of another on the far side. The tidal current at Cape Adare flows by at a rate of 5 to 6 knots, and when the crowded ice-pans have been carried a kilometer or so, the penguins all plunge into the water and come up easily against the current, perhaps to board a new raft for another joy-ride . . .

In clear water one can see that they constantly go so deep that they are out of sight from the crow's nest of a ship. In the swimming position their black soles are turned upward, thus completing the perfect system of countershading. They wing their way with powerful strokes, often in a zigzag course, especially if frightened. It is no rare feat for them to pass beneath an ice-pan a hundred meters across.

Elsewhere Murphy remarks that, to capture penguins, "you have to seize them from behind and cradle them in your arms." It makes a pleasant picture: the tall, handsome, courtly gentleman clad in his oilskins, gazing down with paternal affection at the stylish, somewhat comic-looking bird with its white shirt front and upraised, flipperlike wings.

On more formal occasions, Murphy could be somewhat intimidating. Trained in education, he had a powerful voice on the lecture platform and (in Dean Amadon's words) "he tended, like Dr. Johnson, to come through equally strong in private. I suspect this was the result of his wife's increasing and eventually total deafness. Shy or uncertain individuals were often uneasy or a bit put off in his presence. They missed the twinkle in his eye and the fact that he was always eager to help others, old and young. When it came to selecting research assistants, he thought, like his friend William Beebe, that attractive young ladies make the best helpers."

Murphy also shared with Beebe one essential quality of the "old-fashioned naturalist": he was never, in the narrow sense of the term, a specialist. Every aspect of nature fascinated him, and he was methodical beyond belief in recording his observations, including a unique diary covering some forty years of outdoor life on Long Island. Following in the path of Frank Chapman, he developed the fine art of education in natural history through museum exhibits. He wrote with authority about Audubon and other artists. Above all, his literary gift made him a force for conservation from the Antarctic oceans to his beloved Long Island, threatened with death by urban sprawl. In 1964 he published a delightful but disturbing little book that only he could have written. The title, *Fishshape Paumanok* (the Indian name for Long Island) is taken from Walt Whitman. "I might call it," he wrote, "the history of a detached fragment of Atlantic coastal plain . . . between the retreat of the Wisconsin ice sheet and the building of Levittown!" It concludes with the central issue of our time: "There is much that is ominous and awry. We amplify and beautify the centers of congregation for fast redoubling human populations without giving equivalent thought to the living space of man's fellow creatures, or the soil and ground water which are limiting 'trace elements' of existence. Shall those who come a few generations after us be able to look anywhere on a luxuriant, vital, and fecund, yet uncrowded world, such as Walt Whitman pictures so stirringly in his myriad verses?" This was the basic question with which writers younger in years — but years only — than "Robert of Paumanok" had been wrestling for at least the previous three decades. Beginning in the early nineteen-thirties, with another Roosevelt — another conservationist — in the White House, the basic beliefs of our nature writers about man's relation to the land had become a national issue. Their views could never again be ignored as theoretical and academic. To act upon them had become a practical matter of survival.

CHAPTER XI

Conservation in Action

"They tell in Gascony of a peasant plowing who picked up a handful of soil from the furrow, and cried, 'Behold, it is France!'"
— Russell Lord, BEHOLD OUR LAND

T HE VISION of the future that so concerned Dr. Murphy was based on well-known facts. Yet owing perhaps to their very magnitude, their significance had been slow to dawn on us. This was not for lack of warning; George Perkins Marsh's *Man and Nature* preceded the first Earth Day by more than a century. But he and conservationists ever since his time have had to contend with the frontier philosophy of limitless abundance, the deification of "free enterprise," the idea that planning — even for the sake of our own descendants — is somehow a contradiction of the American dream. When he got to the White House, Theodore Roosevelt did his best to shake us out of this belief by making conservation of natural resources an official government policy, and appointing men like Gifford Pinchot to put it into effect. His efforts, however, were hampered by a dearth of scientific knowledge about types of land and their response to human use. Though recognized as far back as Washington and Jefferson's day, the effects of uncontrolled exploitation of natural resources, especially of man-made erosion and depletion of the soil, were not yet fully understood. Nor was the public at large greatly disturbed about the future. No one was going to starve. Surely modern technology would see to that.

Only a major economic crisis, and a dramatic outcry from the wounded land itself, could shatter this complacency. By good fortune, the inevitable awakening occurred when another Roosevelt was entering the White House. The Great Depression that followed the stock-market crash of 1929 had done a good deal to destroy the myth of limitless abundance and unplanned prosperity. And the point was driven home by the explosion of the western "dust bowl" following several years of drought. Summer after summer, Americans could see the source of that abundance and prosperity literally blowing away.

In an era of bold far-sighted political leadership, even such disasters as these can have long-term positive results. Franklin D. Roosevelt, who took office on March 4, 1933, was a country squire with a deep love of the land. Only a few weeks after his inauguration, he presented Congress with an imaginative scheme for furthering the cause of conservation while taking hundreds of thousands of young unemployed Americans off the relief rolls. The Civilian Conservation Corps — or CCC for short — was an immediate success. "By the middle of June," writes Arthur M. Schlesinger, Jr., "1300 camps were established; by the end of July over 300,000 boys were in the woods. They discharged a thousand conservation tasks which had gone too long unperformed. They planted trees, made reservoirs and fish ponds, built check dams, dug diversion ditches, raised bridges and fire towers, fought blister rust and pine-twig blight and the Dutch elm disease, restored historic battlefields, cleared beaches and camping grounds, and in a multitude of ways protected and improved parks, forests, watersheds, and recreational areas.

"They did more, of course, than reclaim and develop natural resources. They reclaimed and developed themselves."

In 1935 the CCC had an annual enrollment of over half a million. That same year Congress for the first time accepted the prevention of soil erosion as a national responsibility by establishing the Soil Conservation Service (SCS). Appointed to run it was Hugh H. Bennett, a member of the Department of Agriculture who had spent thirty years studying and defending America's topsoil, and striving to convince a stubborn bureaucracy of the importance of his findings. A hearty, slow-spoken Southerner, "Big Hugh" shocked the nation with his claim that a third of America's best farmland was already ruined or seriously degraded. Dedicated and articulate, he gave a congressional committee a graphic example of what had happened to a huge area in southern Georgia, once rich in crops, now reduced to worthless gullies. "Some of the gullies," he said, "are the deepest I have ever seen. The largest of them, locally known as Providence Cave, is eight miles west of Lumpkin, Georgia . . .*

* Many of these Georgia gullies were more than half a century old. See Sidney Lanier's comment, p. 76.

"Last year I talked with a gentleman who went to school in a schoolhouse that stood in the center of Providence Cave. If the schoolhouse were there now it would be suspended 200 feet in the air. It has toppled into the gully, and along with it has gone a tenant house, a barn, a church, and most of a churchyard with fifty graves."

Aware that his land-saving program could succeed only with public support, Bennett mobilized both writers and photographers to document and publicize this mighty effort, supplementing the work of the technicians in the field. One of the first writers to be approached was Bennett's friend and admirer, Russell Lord, a staff member of *The New Yorker* in its youth and, like his colleague E. B. White, a graduate of Cornell. Lord loved the land and he loved the people on it; he was down-to-earth, humorous, and could work anywhere, but maybe best on trains. In the words of the famous Kansas editor William Allen White, he was among "the few American writers who treat America with what may be called geographical intelligence." He wrote and edited for the magazines, especially farm journals, and solicited poetry as well as prose from his contributors. Now he was asked by the SCS to go out over the country and write its first national bulletin, *To Hold This Soil*. The experience gave an immediacy and a sharp focus to a new book Lord was planning for general publication. *Behold Our Land* appeared in 1938, and to many readers it represented a new way of looking at our country. Over forty years later it still makes rewarding reading, for Russ Lord was reporting directly from the field. "All the time now," he writes,

farm migrants, up against it, are shifting from one place to another at a rate which makes precise count impossible. Month after month farms which probably ought never to have been cleared, and which had been given over in despair by experienced farmers accustomed to frontier conditions, are being reoccupied by newcomers. Some are farmers who have failed elsewhere. Some are inexperienced city people. And they all expect to make a living. I do not deny that the occasional new pioneer on worn land may come out of it a better man and happier. (I feel far sorrier for the women.) Last winter in Idaho and Oregon I saw penniless refugees from the Dust Bowl trying to get started again. The land there still is rich. The best of it sells for as much as five hundred dollars an acre. I was told of one Dust Bowl migrant, a man with a wife and three children. When he first came, he bought a nickel sack of tobacco and shoplifted a bag of flour from the store. The sheriff, notified, trailed him home, saw him enter his tent, propped against a truck, saw his three little girls tear open the flour sack and claw into it hungrily, eating the flour raw. The sheriff took up a collection and got this pioneer some day work. That was two years ago. The family is established and has more than a hundred dollars in the bank there now.

The more Lord learned, the greater became his admiration for members of the Soil Conservation Service. They were well trained, doing their job with zeal and patience, convinced that if the plain facts were brought before the people, the people would stop mutilating the land: "In my travels and thought the past three years," he wrote, "I have attained at times and places the same faith; but, looking back over the whole experience now, I don't know . . . There is so little time . . ."

❦

Three years before publication of *Behold Our Land*, when the Soil Conservation Service was just getting under way, a gifted young scientist had explained to the layman, in clear and eloquent terms, the underlying causes of the crisis with which the Service was striving to deal. Paul B. Sears, author of *Deserts on the March*, is an ecologist and former professor of botany at the University of Oklahoma whose interests range far beyond the plant kingdom. A gifted writer himself, he deplored the failure of most scientists to impart their knowledge to the general public, to bridge the gulf between what C. P. Snow later called "the two cultures": "Among those who have achieved professional distinction by their original work, it is the honorable exception who has taken pains to explain to the man on the street what he is trying to do. Yet the greatest have never been ashamed to do this . . ."

Sears's message could not have been better timed. National planning, if it was to succeed, required the technical knowledge of the professors; it also relied on public understanding of its purpose. "The ecologist," wrote Sears, "with all of his professional training, should be chosen with some regard for his talents as a publicist. People no less than plants and animals are a part of his material . . . Unless the general citizenry catch an understanding of the whole scene of which they are part, they will not be fitted to participate in a solution of their own problems." Sears saw great hope in the newly created Soil Conservation Service. "Yet we must not forget that this unit, like the Forest Service, has to operate in a democracy and cannot develop effective strength beyond that which public sympathy and support will confer upon it." The scene of *Deserts on the March* ranges from the vanished civilization of the ancient Mayas to the floods and denuded landscape of modern China, coming to a focus on the dust storms that were darkening the skies of America from Kansas to the East Coast as he began work on his manuscript:

It is twenty-two years after the disastrous flood of March, 1913. The meticulous Ohio housewife, whose gentle weekly dusting had always been sufficient to keep things trim between housecleanings, suddenly finds herself unable to deal with the ubiquitous, curiously ruddy dust that is settling down out of the upper air and filtering through her tightly built establishment. She knows that dust is one of the normal tribulations of her sisters who live in the West. She had heard of the old physician in southwestern Nebraska whose diary, after his death was found to contain the following entry, "Wind forty miles an hour and hot as Hell. Two Kansas farms go by every minute." Now her radio tells her of great dust clouds in New York and Washington. The stories of the old school geography about the sandstorms of the desert had always seemed somewhat too fantastic, describing as they did the camels with their funny trapdoor nostrils and the Arab with his scarf ever ready to serve as a dustmask. Here is today's paper, saying that out on the Great Plains, where that red dust on her library table comes from, a child has been found stifled in a windrow of dust. And wirephotos show school children with faces veiled like little Fatimas as they trudge along the country roads, out West. Pulmonary troubles, especially pneumonia, are reported on the increase because of the dust. One little town, where funerals are rare events, has four in one week and hospitals near the stricken area are having plenty to do. People are reported to be moving out with their household goods on trucks. Each day's conditions are chronicled in terms of visibility — one block, a quarter-mile, or on better days, perhaps a mile.

Slow at first to catch on, *Deserts on the March* was later rediscovered with the help of the Book Find Club and recognized as a landmark in its field. It was the first of a series of books for the layman which Paul Sears somehow found time to write while pursuing an active academic career, culminating in the decade 1950–1960, when he served as chairman of Yale University's new graduate program in the conservation of natural resources. In his inaugural address as president of the American Association for the Advancement of Science, he suggested that "our future security may depend less upon priority in exploring outer space than our wisdom in managing the space in which we live."

᭝

Sears and Lord had focused attention principally on the soil itself. Meanwhile the whole complex problem of conservation, above ground and under, social, political, and economic, was becoming a major political issue. The plight of those living close to the soil was depicted in two outstanding works of literature, *Let Us Now Praise Famous Men* (1941) by James Agee and Walker Evans, a report on the Alabama sharecroppers, and John Steinbeck's novel about migrant farm workers, *The Grapes of Wrath* (1939). The first was virtually ignored on publication but later became a modern classic; the second was an immediate best-seller.

In 1936 Stuart Chase, economist and prolific author, published *Rich Land Poor Land: A Study of Waste in the Natural Resources of America*. For the past decade Chase had been concerned with what he termed "the American concept of infinity" — a delusion well expressed by a pioneer when he first beheld the western grasslands: "It seemed that all the flocks and herds in the world could find ample pasturage on these unoccupied plains and mountain slopes beyond." Today, Chase comments, it takes patient search to find any virgin grasslands. The frontispiece of this book depicts that same gigantic gully in Georgia described by Hugh Bennett before the congressional committee — a frightening vision of the future if abuse of the land should continue unchecked. "Some day," he hopes, "we may become a land-conscious rather than a land-blind people." Chase was less concerned with esthetic and spiritual values of nature than he was with the bedrock question: "Can we find a new ecology which respects nature and still permits technical progress?" His book takes the form of a vast dramatic balance sheet, couched in terms that the layman can understand — a document such as God might produce if He were a certified public accountant. Chase ends on an almost hopeful note. In terms of conservation, more had been accomplished during the first three years of Franklin Roosevelt's presidency than during the previous three decades. "No more exciting and rewarding work is going on in America. I speak of all the forces of conservation, administration or nonadministration. These services are fighting for our homeland, attacking enemies as destructive as invading armies from beyond the seas."

In 1942, six years after publication of *Rich Land Poor Land*, there appeared another stock-taking book, entitled *America's Natural Wealth*. The author, Richard Lieber, was the Director of Conservation in Indiana, the organizer of her famous system of state parks. In describing our use and abuse of the land, he did not pretend to present facts unknown to scholars; his aim was "to attract the interest and to arouse the fighting spirit of intelligent laymen and laywomen" and "to speed up . . . the realization that the imperative need for conservation is NOW!" A first-rate workmanlike book, *America's Natural Wealth* probably got less attention than it deserved. By the time it reached the bookstores, "attacking enemies . . . from beyond the seas" had brought the country into a second world war. Once more, as during World War I, our natural resources would be put under a heavy strain, and our human resources temporarily diverted to national survival.

༒

The war years brought new pressures to bear on the public domain, new threats to the national conservation program which had taken hold so firmly during the early years of the Roosevelt administration. Private interests were quick to seize the opportunity of exploiting public property under the sacred banner of patriotism as, for example, when the logging companies attempted to invade the magnificent rain forest of Olympic National Park. The Air Force, they claimed, needed the Sitka spruce, ignoring the fact that more than enough was available outside the Park.* Fortunately the National Park Service, backed by conservation organizations, was able to resist this attack, which would have created a fatal precedent. Yet by the end of the war, bills had been introduced in Congress that would have opened vast areas of the West to private use free of all government regulation, regardless of the fact that the dust continued to blow and the rivers to run heavy with silt from denuded watersheds. The momentum that the national conservation movement had achieved under the aegis of the New Deal, the *esprit de corps* of agencies like the Soil Conservation Service, were on the decline and, in respect to the federal government, even worse lay ahead. Fortunately, at the same time, private conservation associations were multiplying and the public was being educated by some of the most forceful and well-informed writing so far published on behalf of a livable world — books that extended our

---

* The creation of this park, located on the Olympic Peninsula west of Seattle, is an illustration not only of President Roosevelt's interest in saving our wilderness, but of his extraordinary grasp of the geographical details involved in such an undertaking. When my wife and I first went camping in the Olympics in the summer of 1956, we were greeted by Irving Clark, a Seattle lawyer and mountaineer who had spent a lifetime working to establish the Park and who was at Roosevelt's elbow when the boundaries were drawn up. Roosevelt, he told us, had visited the area just once; but now, with a pencil and a map before him, he was able to trace the boundary line in exact detail, aware of the reasons for every twist and turn.

horizons beyond our borders to encompass critical issues common to the entire planet. In these terms, 1948 was a banner year. Two such books appeared almost simultaneously: Fairfield Osborn's *Our Plundered Planet* and William Vogt's *Road to Survival.**

❦

Fairfield Osborn, president of the New York Zoological Society, was born in 1887, the son of that "magnificent old devil" (in Margaret Mead's phrase) Henry Fairfield Osborn, paleontologist and beneficent autocrat of the American Museum of Natural History in its early days. Young Osborn had a love of science and natural history bred in his bones. "Ever since I was old enough to see or sense anything," he recalled in 1948, "the mysteries of the natural world have possessed my soul." Like so many naturalists, he took an initial fling at the financial world, but Wall Street — which he found "artificial" and "baffling" — was not for him. The Zoological Society notably was. Fairfield Osborn had a strong bent for both organization and showmanship, as no one who attended the Society's annual meetings can ever forget. And he was able to reach a worldwide audience, thanks to his ability to distill large complex issues into readable form, to convey the sense of urgency that he felt so strongly himself.

Our Plundered Planet (which was translated into eight languages) was not, in the author's words, "written primarily for any aesthetic or ethical purpose." The doctrine he preached was one of sheer survival. "There would seem to be no real hope for the future," he wrote, "unless we are prepared to accept the concept that man, like all other living things, is a part of one great biological scheme." If such a statement seems somewhat obvious thirty years later, that is because

---

* This was also the year of Louis Bromfield's *Malabar Farm*, in which he reminds us that agriculture is the "oldest profession," and that "there is as much original sin in poor agriculture as there is in prostitution." Bromfield demonstrates from his own experience how worn-out land can be redeemed by intelligent farming. To be sure, in his case, the initial costs of redemption were met in part by royalties from a long list of best-selling books.

writers like Osborn have made it so. Unfortunately, much of his book is still far from obsolete. On the contrary, some of the problems he deals with are even more acute today. Our technology continues to give us ever greater power, to make us specialists rather than generalists, increasingly detached from the earth.

Through the development of the physical sciences, funneled into vast industrial systems, [man] has created and continues to create new environments, new conditions. These extensions of his mind-fertility and his mind-restlessness are superimposed, like crusts, on the face of the earth, choking his life sources. The conditions under which he must live are constantly changing, he himself being the cause of the changes. In this metamorphosis he has almost lost sight of the fact that the living resources of his life are derived from his earth-home and not from his mind-power. With one hand he harnesses great waters, with the other he dries up the water sources. He must change with changing conditions or perish. He *conquers* a continent and within a century lays much of it into barren waste. He must move to find a new and unspoiled land. He must, he must — but where? His numbers are increasing, starvation taunts him — even after his wars too many are left alive. He causes the life-giving soils for his crops to wash into the oceans. He falls back on palliatives and calls upon a host of chemists to invent substitutes for the organized processes of nature. Can they do this? Can his chemists dismiss nature and take over the operation of the earth? He hopes so. Hope turns to conviction — they *must*, or else he perishes. Is he not nature's "crowning glory"? Can he not turn away from his creator? Who has a better right? He has seemingly "discovered" the secrets of the universe. What need, then, to live by its principles!

One of the "palliatives" that the chemists had invented was particularly disturbing. "Most recently," he wrote, "a powerful chemical known as D.D.T. seems the cure-all." He knew what a deadly impact such poisons could have on the whole environment. "Will the day ever come," he wonders, "when this is generally realized?"

As the years passed, Osborn came to believe that control of the worldwide population explosion overshadowed all other issues. It was central to the whole conservation movement; if this problem could not be solved, the entire structure would collapse. I recall one occasion when he was scheduled to lecture on water resources, or something of the sort. When he stepped up to the podium he announced that he had abandoned his prepared speech; he was going to talk about the problem of too many people, which lay at the heart of our troubles. Unless we could do something about that, all other conservation efforts were bound to fail.

☙

No one agreed more completely with Osborn, or acted more effectively on his beliefs, than William Vogt, author of *Road to Survival*. Beginning life as an ornithologist, he would eventually become director of the Planned Parenthood Federation of America. It was the climax of a remarkable career. Vogt, like his friend (and occasional collaborator) Robert Cushman Murphy, spent his early childhood on Long Island. He was another of those valuable and all too rare members of society, a naturalist who knew how to write for the public. In his youth, language and literature were his major interests; in college he edited the literary magazine and won the poetry prize. Meanwhile he had become fascinated with birds, largely through the books of Ernest Thompson Seton. Soon he was busy editing *Bird-Lore*, managing a bird sanctuary, lecturing for the Audubon societies, writing for both the ornithological journals and the popular market. Enough, one might think, for one man. But the early forties found Vogt in South America, advising the guano industry in Peru, acting as consultant to the U.S. War Department, studying the whole complex problem of the relation of human populations to their environment — in short, becoming an ecologist. The South American continent, he discovered, far from being a storehouse of untapped resources as generally supposed, had already, through shortsighted exploitation, gone well down the road to destruction. Vogt's findings shocked his Spanish-American friends.* And he would shock millions of readers all

* It is tragic to realize that they have gone unheeded. As I write, vast areas

over the world when he broadened his survey to show that the peoples on every continent were following the same fatal road.

Ecology has been called "the subversive science."* Vogt's *Road to Survival* is subversive in the best sense of the word. It calls for nothing less than a radical change in our attitude toward the natural world. "If we are to make peace with the forces of the earth," he writes, "that peace must begin in our minds." In the United States, for example, "we have produced a waster's psychology that would have appalled our frugal forebears and that is regarded as lunacy — even criminal lunacy — by people in other parts of the world." Only a realization of the true relationship between man and his environment can assure our future: "We must understand this relationship, sense it so deeply that it colors our feeling about children, country, laws, survival, foreign relations, and nearly every other thought and emotion we have."

Vogt's early interest in natural history broadened to include economics, politics, and social behavior, but he remained a naturalist at heart. A consciousness of nature, he knew, had been a part of American culture from the beginning. "Today, as we are caught in the grinding mesh of a mechanized civilization and the monotony of unrewarding tasks, we need as never before to turn to the healing hills and forests, with their rich company of plants and animals." Like other naturalists before him, he considered destruction of the great works of nature even worse than vandalism of rare objects of man's art.

The condor that rides the winds over the California hills, the curlew

---

of the Brazilian rain forest, one of the planet's most fragile ecosystems, are being systematically destroyed to make way for ranches and mines and settlements. "The destruction gets cheaper and more efficient every year," writes a former United Nations ecologist. "If deforestation continues at its present rate, the Brazilians could very well end up creating another Sahara."

The Subversive Science: Essays toward an Ecology of Man. Edited by Paul Shephard and Daniel McKinley (1969).

that spanned two continents with its crying, were millions of years in the making. The very forces that shaped the earth molded their form, determined their destiny. Through thousands and tens of thousands of generations, the wind and the cold, the march of the seasons, the changes on the land, the failure and success of plants, and the craftiness of enemies hammered at the malleable substance of these creatures. Endless sorting, endless discarding, endless change brought them to ultimate perfection for the world in which they live. Can man, like some blundering sorcerer's apprentice, afford to smash the crucible in which they have been refined, reduce them to a mere memory, a bunch of stuffed feathers in a museum? Not, it seems to me, without pitifully impoverishing himself!

Bernard DeVoto, historian and authority on the literature of conservation, considered *Road to Survival* "by far the best book so far in this literature. It is more basic, more comprehensive, more thorough-going than any of its predecessors . . . and it is written with marked brilliance and drama."

❦

DeVoto himself, though he never claimed to be a naturalist, may well have been the most potent one-man force for the conservation of nature in the mid-twentieth century. He was a volcanic character, fired by outrage at the greed and stupidity that continued to waste away our natural heritage; and when he erupted, all hell broke loose. In March 1948, he wrote to a friend in magnificent mixed metaphor: "I don't know when I came to a boil or just why but I suddenly realized that it had happened. I've just been knocking up practice flies in this game so far. Now I'm coming up to bat. Give me some offstage noises for I'm in the saddle again, off the reservation, and out for blood. Somehow I seem to have got mad." Two months later he wrote to William Sloane, publisher of *Road to Survival*: "I have been in so many places and talked Vogt's book to so many people that you and I will have to do some bookkeeping. Vogt himself turned up at a cocktail party at Elmer Davis's.* Elmer was reading and being depressed by

* The well-known writer and radio news commentator.

Our Plundered Planet and I told him it was merely milk for babies . . . I enormously enjoyed meeting Vogt. His talk was fascinating and eased my own inquiries considerably."

When DeVoto came up to bat in defense of the public domain he brought to bear both his knowledge of history and his personal experience. He had been born and raised in Utah, and he understood the West as few writers have. To him, it was "the plundered province." As a historian, he knew that the assault by private interests on the public reserves had been going on ever since they were created in the eighteen-eighties. The three principal objects of his wrath were the miners, "whose right to exploit transcends all other rights whatsoever"; the loggers, whom Theodore Roosevelt and Gifford Pinchot strove mightily to keep under control; and above all the cattlemen and the sheepmen, whose depradations in the early days had so enraged John Muir.

Two facts about the cattle business have priority over all the rest. First, the Cattle Kingdom never did own more than a minute fraction of one per cent of the range it grazed: it was national domain, it belonged to the people of the United States. Cattlemen do not own the public range now: it belongs to you and me, and since the fees they pay for using public land are much smaller than those they pay for using private land, those fees are in effect one of a number of subsidies we pay them. But they always acted as if they owned the public range and act so now; they convinced themselves that it belonged to them and now believe it does; and they are trying to take title to it. Second, the cattle business does not have to be conducted as liquidation but throughout history its management has always tended to conduct it on that basis.

As Wallace Stegner has pointed out, DeVoto was a highly vocal champion of environmental conservation long before it became a mass movement. What led him to take up his cudgel was an extended trip through the West in the summer of 1946. "DeVoto went West," writes Stegner, "a historian and tourist. He came back an embattled conservationist, one whose activities would eventually entitle him to be ranked with George Perkins Marsh, Powell, Karl Schurz, Pinchot, and Roosevelt. Appropriately, his strength was the strength of words." His principal forum was his monthly essay in *Harper's* magazine, "The Easy Chair." "Without it, the effort to preserve in the public interest the grass, timber, and scenery of the West would have been very much weaker and less effective." DeVoto kept hammering away at the basic issues: the fact that the public lands belonged to all Americans, not to the states or to special groups; that the national parks were "not only set aside as scenic and recreation treasuries for the people of the United States as a whole, but also are the only possible laboratories for studies in ecology on which the future determination of much land-use policy must be based"; that all the fundamental watersheds of the West, on which its very life depends, are in public lands. These incontrovertible facts, which various pressure groups were seeking to ignore, came to the fore in one of the key battles in the annals of modern conservation — the defense of Dinosaur National Monument from invasion by the Bureau of Reclamation and the Army Engineers.

The monument, which straddles the Utah-Colorado border just south of Wyoming, includes some of the most magnificent scenery in the United States. At the heart of it, where the Green and Yampa rivers join, lies Echo Park. This was the site chosen for a dam which (with a second one downstream) would reduce these awesome canyons to a huge fluctuating lake. In the words of Richard M. Leonard of the Sierra Club, which led the fight against the project, such dams would "constitute the greatest threat to the National Park System since its creation in 1916." The struggle to save Dinosaur first came to public notice in the summer of 1950, when the *Saturday Evening Post* ran an article by DeVoto entitled, "Shall We Let Them Ruin Our National Parks?" It culminated five years later with a handsome volume, *This Is Dinosaur*, edited and partly written by Wallace Stegner and published by Alfred A. Knopf, himself a devoted conservationist and a member of the National Parks Advisory Board. As a result of all this activity, both dams were forced out of the project plan. The conservationists had won their first clear-cut victory. Congressman Aspinall of Colorado — who would later use every devious device to prevent a vote on the Wilderness Bill — was quite right when he declared: "If we let them [the conservationists] knock out Echo Park dam, we'll hand them a tool they'll use for the next hundred years." The "tool" was nothing less than public awareness that the national parks and monuments had been created for the use and enjoyment of all the people; and that invasion of them for other purposes would set a precedent which could eventually make havoc of the entire national park system.

DeVoto did not live quite long enough to witness the happy ending of the Dinosaur story. For over twenty years he had demonstrated what intelligent journalism can accomplish in the political arena. When he died in the autumn of 1955, it became clear that there was no one who could quite replace him. His voice had helped to carry his country and its natural treasures, without too much loss, through the bleak period of the late forties and early fifties — a period when the public domain was under attack, the national parks were being starved for funds, and the Secretary of the Interior — an Oregon automobile dealer named Douglas McKay — dismissed the conservationists as "long-haired punks." One wishes that DeVoto might have lived to see, under the Kennedy administration, a very different type of man occupying that powerful position. Stewart L. Udall had been in office only a few months when, with the aid of Wallace Stegner and others, he began work on *The Quiet Crisis*, a book that brought the history of conservation in America sharply into focus on the problems of his own time. Once more, as in the age of Theodore Roosevelt, and again of Franklin Roosevelt, the federal government was encouraging rather than obstructing those dedicated to saving our land.

CHAPTER XII

The Wilderness Ideal

"We need the tonic of wildness — to wade sometimes in marshes where the bittern and the meadow-hen lurk, and hear the booming of the snipe; to smell the whispering sedge where only some wilder and more solitary fowl builds her nest, and the mink crawls with its belly close to the ground."

— Henry David Thoreau, WALDEN

W HEN WE TALK ABOUT "wilderness," what exactly do we mean? Not, certainly, what our forebears meant. The history of words is the history of ideas, and the traditional idea of wilderness is a far cry from that of the Sierra Club or the Wilderness Society. The word itself derives from Old English "wildeor," wild beast. In ancient times it was a place hostile to man. The Bible equates it with "desert," the last refuge for outcasts, into which one drove the scapegoat laden with the sins of mankind. The Puritan settlers brought this concept with them across the Atlantic. To them, everything beyond the cleared area of the settlements was

> *A waste and howling wilderness*
> *Where none inhabited*
> *But hellish fiends, and brutish men*
> *That Devils worshipped.*

In Europe, as we have seen, this attitude took a sudden turn in the late eighteenth century, beginning with philosophers like Jean Jacques Rousseau and culminating in the Romantic Movement, with Wordsworth as its English prophet. The American pioneer, however, had no time for daffodils dancing in the breeze. Now at last limitless land was within his grasp. In taming the wilderness, in making it work for him, he was doing God's work as well. As Jehovah said unto Noah after the Flood:

"The fear of you and the dread of you shall be upon every beast of the earth and upon every bird of the air and upon everything that creeps on the ground and all the fish in the sea. Unto you they are delivered."

In this subjugation of the wilderness the heroes were the destroyers: the buffalo hunters and the Indian fighters, wielders of the long rifle and the ax. Towering above them stood the legendary lumberman Paul Bunyan, who laid low the forests from coast to coast.

Yet from the early nineteenth century onward the American wilderness had an increasing impact on our culture, both in literature and in art. James Fenimore Cooper found in it the inspiration for his romances.* Washington Irving, though still writing in the European tradition, waxed eloquent over the American scene: "her mighty lakes, like oceans of liquid silver; her mountains, with their bright aerial tints, her valleys, teeming with wild fertility . . . her trackless forests, where vegetation puts forth all its magnificence . . ." William Cullen Bryant, for all his worship of Wordsworth, preferred American scenery to anything he saw abroad. So with the artists: Thomas Cole and the Hudson River School; George Catlin, the first painter of the American West and one of the first to advocate national parks; Charles Bodmer, who traveled up the Yellowstone in 1833, one year after Catlin, in company with the German naturalist, Prince Maximilian; Alfred Miller, whose watercolors are our freshest on-the-spot record of the frontier; John James Audubon, whose work has become a part of our cultural tradition. Artists and writers together — Audubon was both — had by mid-century established a new attitude toward wild nature.

Before the end of the century the so-called frontier had reached the Pacific, and been officially proclaimed dead. On its westward sweep, however, the course of empire had left many unspoiled areas in its wake, saved by their inaccessibility, islands in the sea of Progress. They are no longer inaccessible. But fortunately our sense of values was changing while the conquest was going on, at first among the few and later — thanks to the growing literature of nature — among

---

* Cooper described the view across the Mohawk Valley as "completely an American scene, embracing all that admixture of civilization and of the forest, of the work of man and of the reign of nature." Today, unfortunately, we have two extreme and needlessly hostile groups: those who speak scornfully of the "wilderness cult" and consider wilderness values a witless return to primitivism, and those who talk about "escaping to the wilderness" as if all man-made landscapes were false and ugly. The world is full of examples of how man has improved his environment, esthetically as well as practically. The fact that we no longer consider wilderness ugly and hostile to man does not mean that we must therefore consider civilization ugly and hostile to nature.

the many. The idea of preservation, as in the national parks, and of conservation, as in the national forests, became generally accepted. Most of wild America was gone; what remained had a scarcity value. Yet the significance of true wilderness as we know it today was little understood, either in terms of its contribution to science or its spiritual value to man. It is indeed a subtle concept, intuitively known years ago to Thoreau and Muir and a few others, first given official standing in the saving of Yosemite Valley, latent in the philosophy behind the national parks movement, yet recognized as a vital aspect of conservation only in the nineteen-twenties. And not for another three decades would it become a major political issue, to be embodied at last in federal law.

A long process, in terms of a single lifetime, but in historical perspective a remarkably sudden turnabout. "Thinking as a biologist," writes A. Starker Leopold of the University of California (a son of Aldo Leopold), "I see this emergence of a new idea as comparable to a macromutation in organic evolution — one of those sweeping shifts of evolutionary direction that come suddenly, and without forewarning." In preserving an undisturbed natural area, Leopold points out, we are "showing a respect for nature as it existed in the first place. It is the emergence of this element of *respect* that deserves special attention, for it marks a turning point in man's view of the earth." (Clearly he was referring to *Western* man.) In short, it is a moral issue. Not, however, in the sense that Emerson proclaimed moral law to lie at the center of nature, which itself was meaningful only in its relation to man. Here was the other side of the coin: man's moral obligation to save natural areas for their own sake, to recognize their right to exist.

Henry Thoreau had recognized this right, long before the last of our wilderness was threatened. In *Walden* Thoreau had expressed for all time the need we feel for a world not of our own making. "At the same time that we are earnest to explore and learn all things, we require that all things be mysterious and unexplorable, that land and sea be infinitely wild, unsurveyed and unfathomed by us because unfathomable . . . We need to witness our own limits transgressed, and some life pasturing freely where we never wander."

A wilderness philosophy is thus nothing new, though hitherto confined to a few prophetic individuals like Thoreau and Muir. The concept of the "wilderness area," however, is comparatively modern.* Fortunately it is supported by practical arguments more easily grasped by government administrators than are Thoreau's mystical insights. Largely responsible for the idea and its realization are two outstanding writers, both of whom were members of the U.S. Forest Service: Aldo Leopold and Robert Marshall.

❦

Aldo Leopold will always be associated with two regions of America: the Southwest, where he began his career as a professional forester and game manager, and central Wisconsin, the scene of his classic *A Sand County Almanac*. Born in Burlington, Iowa, in 1886, a graduate of Yale's School of Forestry, he came on the stage at the end of the Roosevelt era. In 1909, the National Forests, administered by Gifford Pinchot, were only four years old, as was the National Association of Audubon Societies. William T. Hornaday, that fiery convert from hunter and collector to conservationist, was at work on his trumpet call to action, *Our Vanishing Wildlife*. Leopold's first assignment under the U.S. Forest Service, to the Arizona and New Mexico territories, was a revelation and a challenge. Though settlement had come late to this rugged mountain country, a decline in the numbers of big-game animals was already evident. To Leopold, a country without wildlife was a spiritual vacuum. In contrast to Hornaday, Leopold did not consider sport hunting to be incompatible with conservation. But the goals of the two men were the same. A visit from

---

* With certain exceptions. See passage from *Man and Nature* by George Perkins Marsh, p. 93.

Hornaday encouraged young Leopold in his campaign among local ranchers and businessmen to establish game refuges — a concept still alien to the frontier mentality. "While making good progress," he wrote for his Yale class record, "I think the job will last me the rest of my life." A prophetic remark, since Aldo Leopold was to become the principal founder of the science of game management.*

Like Hornaday and most of his contemporaries, Leopold at first saw all predators as varmints to be exterminated; the principal enemies of the "game" were the mountain lion and the wolf. In the light of his future philosophy, one reads with a sense of shock a statement that he made in 1920: "It is going to take patience and money to catch the last wolf or lion in New Mexico, but the last one must be caught before the job can be called fully successful." But Leopold was entering on his career at a time when the importance of the predator to the balance of nature was at last being recognized, and when the deeper meaning of wildness to civilized man was becoming generally accepted. Long before *A Sand County Almanac* was published, his views about wolves and other predators had swung around 180 degrees. Their importance in keeping the deer herds under control had been tragically demonstrated in the Kaibab National Forest on the north rim of the Grand Canyon (to take the most notorious example). To protect the native deer, and the sheep and cattle introduced into the Forest, all large predators — wolves, coyotes, mountain lions, bobcats, and golden eagles — had been systematically exterminated. Result: a population explosion of deer, destruction of the range from overgrazing, and finally death of

* The title of Aldo Leopold's classic textbook, *Game Management* (as contrasted with "wildlife management," the more familiar term today), is characteristic of a period when the principal purpose of saving wildlife was for sport. His early journals in particular emphasize his own delight in hunting. Later, in reference to the birdwatcher or plant collector, he remarks: "Because his kind of hunting seldom calls for theft or pillage, he disdains the killer. Yet, like as not, in his youth he was one." True. It is also true that one's sources of pleasure often change with maturity.

the deer themselves from starvation and disease.* Appalled by what he saw in the Kaibab and elsewhere, Leopold frankly acknowleged the error of his previous position. "A deer herd deprived of wolves and lions," he concluded, "is more dangerous to wilderness areas than the most practical senator or the go-gettingest Chamber of Commerce." And his change of heart went deeper than simple considerations of game management. By the time he began writing *A Sand County Almanac*, he realized that the wolf embodied the very essence of the wilderness. "A deep chesty bawl echoes from rimrock to rimrock, rolls down the mountain, and fades into the far blackness of the night . . . Those unable to decipher the hidden meaning know nevertheless that it is there, for it is felt in all wolf country and distinguishes that country from all other land. It tingles in the spine of all who hear wolves by night, or who scan their tracks by day. Even without sight or sound of wolf, it is implicit in a hundred small events: the midnight whinny of a pack horse, the rattle of rolling rocks, the bound of a fleeing deer, the way shadows lie under the spruces. Only the ineducable tyro can fail to sense the presence or absence of wolves . . ." Leopold had an almost mystical sense of the place of the wolf in the scheme of nature, which he dates from the time he shot a splendid old female, the leader of a pack of gamboling pups, and saw her die.

I was young then, and full of trigger-itch; I thought that because fewer wolves meant more deer, that no wolves would mean hunters' paradise.

Since then I have lived to see state after state extirpate its wolves. I have watched the face of many a newly wolfless mountain, and seen the south-facing slopes wrinkle with a maze of new deer trails . . . I have seen every edible tree defoliated to the height of a saddlehorn. Such a mountain looks as if someone had given God a new pruning shears, and forbidden Him all other exercise. In the end the starved bones of the hoped-for deer herd, dead of its own too-much,

---

* Modern ecologists have questioned whether this was the principal cause of the population explosion.

bleach with the bones of the dead sage, or molder under the high-lined junipers.

To the practical job of saving the native fauna of the Southwest from ultimate annihilation, Aldo Leopold brought both the skills of a professional forester and the insights of an ecologist. Obviously the first step in protecting any form of wildlife is to assure the integrity of its habitat. Thus it was that Leopold, a founder of New Mexico's game protective associations, conceived the idea of setting aside certain wild areas in the national forests which would be permanently off limits to logging and road building — an idea which had been implemented over thirty years earlier on the state level when New York established the Adirondack Forest Preserve.

Leopold was still thinking as a member of the Forest Service, which adhered to Gifford Pinchot's doctrine of "highest use." The process of development, he wrote in 1921, "must of course continue indefinitely." But at the same time he questioned "whether the principle of highest use does not itself demand that representative portions of some forests be preserved as wilderness." Two years before, he had met in Denver a fellow employee of the Forest Service who shared his conviction. Arthur Carhart was a landscape architect employed by the Service to develop homesites on a choice spot in the high Rockies; instead, he had persuaded his superiors to keep the area free of all roads and houses. Shortly thereafter, he had done the same thing in the unique canoe country of northern Minnesota, laying the groundwork for what would become our first official "Roadless Area." Although his contribution to wilderness preservation does not rank with Leopold's, the two men were seeking the same goal.

The area Leopold chose for his initial effort was the mountainous Gila Forest in the southwest corner of New Mexico, near the Arizona border: a country well known to local sportsmen, with which he himself had long been familiar. He visualized its future as "a continuous stretch of country preserved in its natural state, open to lawful hunting and fishing, big enough to absorb a two weeks' pack trip, and kept devoid of roads, artificial trails, cottages, or other works of man." This is a fair description of a "wilderness area" as defined by the Wilderness Act of 1964.

In 1924 over half a million acres of the Gila National Forest were officially designated as wilderness, thus setting the pattern for 167 such areas within the national parks, forests, wildlife refuges, and lands under the Bureau of Land Management. To achieve official protection under Act of Congress, however, would require forty years of intensive work, and the efforts of countless talented writers in awakening the public to what was at stake. For in the final showdown, it is the votes that count.

Shortly before the Gila Wilderness was established, Leopold was transferred by the Forest Service to Madison, Wisconsin. It was a promotion, but it meant leaving a land which he had grown to love. After a few more years with the Service, and private practice as a consulting forester, he was appointed the first professor of wildlife management at the University of Wisconsin — where, back in 1860, a farmer's son named John Muir first found support for ideas much like Leopold's about man's place in the universe. In 1933 Leopold published his classic *Game Management* — a work whose literary and philosophic overtones have extended its influence beyond the confines of the profession, while it remains a standard text to this day. Two years later he bought a derelict farm on the Wisconsin River, in the heart of cut-over land where Daniel Muir had all but worked his children to death; and where Frederick Jackson Turner, growing up in a newly "tamed" wilderness, conceived his famous frontier thesis. The only usable structure on Leopold's eighty acres of river bottom land was a cow barn which, remodeled as a hunting camp, came to be known as "the shack." "For Leopold and his family," writes Susan Flader in *The Sand Country of Aldo Leopold*,

the shack years were an experience in the slow sensitizing of people to land, the evolution of a sense of country. The shack originally acquired as a hunting camp soon became a "weekend refuge from too much modernity," a place to hike and swim and savor the outdoors, to build with their own hands, to split oak and make sourdoughs in the dutch oven at an open fire, to play guitars and sing and talk and laugh together. It was also a place where one could experience a feeling of isolation in nature . . . And it offered rich country for the growth of perception. The more woodcock nests they discovered, the more trees and shrubs, grasses and flowers they planted, the more chickadees and nuthatches they got to know — in short the more familiar they became with the place — the more they found to anticipate, to ponder, and to marvel at . . . *Sand County Almanac* is eloquent testimony to the meaning and value of the experience.

It is all of that, and more. Here it was that Leopold's rare talents as a writer and philosopher of wilderness came to fruition; here he developed a "land ethic" which has profound social — and even religious — implications for our time. Probably not since Thoreau and Muir has there been a more thoughtful, and more quotable, piece of writing on the meaning of nature to man. The first part of the book, the "almanac," is a month-by-month record of outdoor observations based on the author's journal; like Thoreau's journal, it continually breaks through the surface to speculate on deeper meanings, as much in the realm of poetry as of science. Sawing through a huge lightning-killed oak on a February morning, Leopold recreates history in reverse as the blade bites through one growth-ring after another, deeper and deeper into the past: back through the years when "the largest pine rafts in history shipped down the Wisconsin River in full view of my oak" to the day when the acorn sprouted "perhaps on the wheel tracks of the covered wagons that once rumbled through this valley with settlers for the Great Northwest . . . At last there is a tremor in the great trunk . . . my oak leans, groans, and crashes with earth-shaking thunder, to lie prostrate across the emigrant road that gave it birth."

At misty daybreak in September, Leopold listens for the brief hesitant bird calls, so different from the swelling chorus of early spring. The silence is suddenly broken by a covey of quail, hidden from sight. "There is a peculiar virtue," he writes, "in the music of elusive birds. Songsters that wing from top-most boughs are easily seen and as easily forgotten; they have the mediocrity of the obvious. What one remembers is the invisible hermit thrush pouring silver chords from impenetrable shadows; the soaring crane trumpeting from behind a cloud; the prairie chicken booming from the mists of nowhere; the quail's Ave Maria in the hush of dawn. No naturalist has even seen the choral act, for the covey is still on its invisible roost in the grass, and any attempt to approach automatically induces silence."

Leopold lived too late to know the huge flocks of passenger pigeons that were a treasured memory for Burroughs and Grinnell and scores of other naturalists of an earlier generation. Sadly he reflects on the irony of a monument erected in a Wisconsin state park "to commemorate the funeral of a species."

This monument, perched like a duckhawk on this cliff, will scan this wide valley, watching through the days and years. For many a March it will watch the geese go by, telling the river about clearer, colder, lonelier waters on the tundra. For many an April it will see the redbuds come and go, and for many a May the flush of oak-blooms on a thousand hills. Questing wood ducks will search these basswoods for hollow limbs; golden prothonotaries will shake golden pollen from the river willows. Egrets will pose on these sloughs in August; plovers will whistle from September skies. Hickory nuts will plop into October leaves, and hail will rattle in November woods. But no pigeons will pass, for there are no pigeons, save only this flightless one, graven in bronze on this rock. Tourists will read this inscription, but their thoughts will not take wing.

Leopold's concern was not only with wildlife but with the very land itself. "Conservation is getting nowhere," he complained in the introduction to the *Almanac*, "because it is incompatible with our Abrahamic concept of land. We abuse land because we regard it as a commodity belonging to us. When we see land as a community to which we belong, we may begin to use it with love and respect." For him, our relation to the land was as much a matter of ethics as is our relation to our fellow man.

In mid-April of 1948, Aldo Leopold received a telephone call from New York. At last, after years of being turned down, *A Sand County Almanac* had been accepted for publication. A week later, full of happiness at the prospect, he was at work at the shack when he spotted smoke drifting east across the marsh. Rushing to the scene, he joined a handful of neighbors fighting a fire that was already out of control. His heart could not stand the strain, and so he died. His book, it is safe to say, will outlive us all. In the words of Roderick Nash, an authority on the American wilderness, "it became, in many ways, the bible of the surging environmental movement of the 1960's and early 1970's." It remains so today. The reason is clear: Leopold had framed in eloquent terms "an entirely new way of defining conservation."*

ぐ

Long before Leopold died, this radically new definition had been officially recognized by the Forest Service. Within the decade following the establishment of the Gila Wilderness in New Mexico in 1924, two significant events had taken place. In 1929 the Chief of the Forest Service issued a regulation creating "a series of areas to be known as primitive areas, within which . . . will be maintained primitive conditions of environment . . ." And five years later, almost by accident, a group of dedicated outdoorsmen who shared Leopold's philosophy met in the heart of the Great Smoky Mountains and conceived the idea for a nationwide organization devoted solely to wilderness preservation. The initial spark had been struck by a brilliant article in *Scientific Monthly* entitled "The Problem of the Wilderness" from the pen of a young member of the U.S. Forest Service named Robert Marshall.

---

*A second volume, *Round River*, was later edited from Leopold's early journals and unfinished manuscripts, but it is for *A Sand County Almanac* that he will be chiefly remembered.

꙼

Though Bob Marshall was only thirty-three years old at the time of that historic meeting in the Great Smokies, he already had more wilderness experience behind him than most of us enjoy in a lifetime. Born in 1901 in a brownstone house in New York City, he was the second son of Louis Marshall, a wealthy lawyer, Jewish leader, humanitarian, and conservationist. Louis Marshall had been a delegate to the famous New York State constitutional convention of 1894 which provided that the Adirondack Forest Preserve be "kept forever as wild forest lands." While they were still in their teens and early twenties, Bob and his younger brother George — today one of America's leading conservationists — climbed every high peak in the Adirondacks. "When he was fifteen," writes George, "Bob decided to become a forester so that he might spend the greater part of his life in the woods he loved." So, after graduating from the New York State College of Forestry and earning an advanced degree at Harvard — and later at Johns Hopkins — he joined the Forest Service, and was soon on intimate terms with wilderness country from the Appalachians to the northern Rockies. But devoted though he was to the Service, it could not provide all the romance of his youthful dreams. When he chose this career, he later recalled, "I didn't have the remotest idea what forestry was, but had vague notions of thrilling adventures with bad men, of lassoing infuriated grizzlies, and of riding down unknown canyons in Alaska. When I actually became a forester, I found life much more filled with keeping the meat at the fire camp from becoming flyblown, discussing the merits of various volume tables, measuring to a tenth of an inch the diameter of pine trees . . ." By ordinary standards, his job with the Forest Service offered plenty of wilderness adventure, but he had his heart set on something beyond that, something rapidly disappearing from the face of the earth: wild country no man had ever seen. One huge area, he found, remained a vital blank on the map: the stretch of Arctic wilderness north of Alaska's Yukon River. Here he would go. During three prolonged leaves of absence from the Service, he made his dream come true.

Bob had too much sense of humor to pretend that his flings at real exploration had any particular scientific or social justification, such as more solemn explorers like to attribute to their expeditions. His justification, if one was needed, was "that most glorious of all pastimes, setting foot where no human being has ever trod before." In "The Problem of the Wilderness," written just before the first of these trips, he had remarked: "Adventure, whether physical or mental, implies breaking into unpenetrated ground, venturing beyond the boundary of normal aptitude, extending oneself to the limit of capacity, courageously facing peril. Life without the chance for such exertions would be for many persons a dreary game, scarcely bearable in its horrible banality."

His own successful escape from banality is embodied in two books: *Arctic Village*, published in 1933, and *Arctic Wilderness*, edited posthumously from his journals and letters by George Marshall in 1956.* Despite his disclaimer, there was a scientific purpose behind these explorations, notably the mapping of wholly unknown territory and the study of tree growth at northern timber line. But in his own words his "far most important though not advertised objective was gaining the absolutely unassessable thrill of just looking at superb natural beauty."

Bob's base of operations was the village of Wiseman on the Koyukuk River, a tributary of the Yukon flowing southward from its headwaters in the Brooks Range. The largest "town" in this whole vast wilderness, it consisted of one hundred and twenty-seven people, whites, Eskimos, and a few Indians. From here, accompanied by one or two companions — miners, fur trappers, sourdoughs of all sorts — he traveled on foot for weeks at a time into unmapped country. It was an explorer's heaven. "Often, as when visiting Yosemite or

* *Arctic Wilderness* was reissued in 1970 under the title *Alaska Wilderness: Exploring the Central Brooks Range.*

Glacier Park or the Grand Canyon or Avalanche Lake or some other natural scenery of surpassing beauty, I had wished selfishly enough that I might have had the joy of being the first person to discover it . . . And now I found myself here, at the very headwaters of one of the mightiest rivers of the north, with dozens of never-visited valleys and hundreds of unscaled summits still as virgin as during their Paleozoic creation."

In page after page of *Arctic Wilderness* one recognizes the same sense of exaltation that Muir and Clarence King felt in the High Sierra, Olmsted in Yosemite Valley, Powell and Dutton in the depths of the Grand Canyon. Here we feel the impact of wild scenery, heightened by a sense of isolation, sharpened by knowledge of ever-present danger:

I spent more than three bright hours up there on top of the continent, looking in every direction over miles of wilderness in which, aside from Lew and Al, I knew there was not another human being. This knowledge, this sense of independence which it gave, was second only to the sense of perfect beauty instilled by the scenery on all sides. My time on the summit was spent by first giving myself to an enjoyment such as another person might experience listening to Beethoven's Fifth Symphony played by some dreamed-of super-Philadelphia Orchestra; I then took pictures and made sketch maps of the topography in every direction. I had to be careful on top because though the side from which I had climbed Limestack was gentle enough, the opposite side fell off vertically for about 1,500 feet.

Despite such almost transcendental experiences, Bob Marshall never took either himself or his hair-raising adventures too seriously. A few days after this inspiring climb he was working his way precariously up a narrow valley beside a rushing torrent.

There was a stretch of about forty yards which totally absorbed my attention as to how to place my feet. When I looked up, my heart stood still, as the books say. About 150 feet ahead were three grizzlies. This may seem like a long distance to a catcher trying to throw a man out stealing second, but not to a man faced by three bears, eleven miles from the closest gun, hundred and six from the first potential stretcher bearer, and three hundred from the nearest hospital. As in Goldilocks, the first bear was small, probably a two-year-old, the second was of medium size, the third appeared like two elephants plus a rhinoceros. They reared up, one after the other, from little to gigantic, just like so many chorus girls going through some sprout in sequence. They stood for a moment and then got down on their four legs and disappeared into the willows.

I continued upstream.

Back in Wiseman between journeys, Bob found time to write letters home which were duplicated for a small circle of his friends. These included Supreme Court Justice Benjamin M. Cardozo, whose warm acknowledgment goes straight to the core of the nature writer's art:

I suspect that being close to nature, as you have been during these many years, has an influence, in the end, even on one's choice of words. One no longer has any patience for thoughts or for phrases that are not genuine and honest. And how deftly you blend the concrete and the abstract. "Every mountain was covered with snow, every peak showed a clear white edge set against a pure blue background. Almost everything in life seems to be at least somewhat blurred and misty around the edges and so little is ever absolute that there was a genuine satisfaction in seeing the flawless white of those summits and the flawless blue of the sky and the razor edge sharpness with which the two came together."

I call that fine.

Perhaps the most significant discovery that Bob Marshall made in northern Alaska was the relation of wilderness life to human happiness. He returned from his first trip with the impression that the few white and Eskimo people who were scattered through this remote region were the happiest folk he had ever encountered. He knew, however, how mistaken first impressions can be. "And so," he writes, "I decided to return for at least a year in order to make a detailed study of this civilization of the North." The result was a unique book, *Arctic Village*, published in 1933 and an immediate best seller. His account of the people of the Koyukuk should bury once for all the simplistic notion that to love nature more is to love people less. This is patently untrue of most of our best nature writers — never more so than in the case of Bob Marshall, whose love for the sourdoughs and Eskimos of Wiseman, with whom he lived so intimately through a long Arctic winter, is matched only by their evident love for him. Seldom has a sociological study — for *Arctic Village* is nothing less — been characterized by such warmth and *joie de vivre*. At the same time it is utterly frank, uninhibited, unsentimental. As Justice Cardozo perceived, "in the wilderness one no longer has patience for thoughts or for phrases that are not genuine and honest."

In the summer of 1934 — the year after publication of *Arctic Village* — Bob Marshall was back at work, this time as Director of Forestry for the Office of Indian Affairs. By happy coincidence, his official duties took him to the Great Smoky Mountains National Park at the precise moment when a group of conservationists who had read his article, "The Problem of the Wilderness," were seeking a way to save the Park from the encroachment of a federal highway. The group included Benton MacKaye, a Pinchot-trained forester and the father of the famous Appalachian Trail; Harvey Broome, a Tennessee lawyer and authority on the Great Smokies; and Harold C. Anderson of the Potomac Appalachian Trail Club. On a day-long trip with Bob through the Park, and later a hike to the summit of Clingman's Dome, they discussed not only the immediate threat but the broader and deeper principles involved. Here in these ancient mist-clad mountains, surrounded by the greatest hardwood forest left in North America, they conceived the idea for uniting (in Marshall's words) "all friends of the wilderness ideal." By October they had been joined by Aldo Leopold and a few other like minds, including Ernest C. Oberholtzer (the eminent defender of the Quetico-Superior canoe country) and a talented writer named Robert Sterling Yard, former editor of *Century* magazine — the same publication which, so many years before, had encouraged John Muir in his struggle to save Yosemite. So the Wilderness Society was born. "There is just one hope," wrote Bob Marshall, "of repulsing the tyrannical ambition of civilization to conquer every niche on the whole earth. That hope is the organization of spirited people who will fight for the freedom of the wilderness."

Marshall himself was a fighter, but a persuader rather than a preacher, whose personal magnetism was doubtless more effective than the messianic solemnity which marks some conservation leaders. In September 1939, he achieved his goal. A set of new regulations, drafted by Marshall, gave the Secretary of Agriculture power to set aside unbroken tracts of 100,000 acres or more as "wilderness areas," and smaller tracts of 5000 acres or more as "wild areas." Existing primitive areas, such as the Gila Wilderness conceived by Aldo Leopold fifteen years earlier, would be restudied and included in the overall plan. Such was the origin of a wilderness system which, still in process of expansion, now embraces more than twenty million acres. It was Bob Marshall's crowning achievement. Two months later he was dead, of a heart attack. The vast, rugged Bob Marshall Wilderness of Montana is named in his honor. But today one thinks of him first of all as the man who knew, as few white men have, the greatest wilderness of them all, northern Alaska.

Marshall lived just long enough to see his commitment to wilderness accepted as a national policy. Execution of this policy, however, was still a matter of administrative decision, always subject to change. Another quarter-century would pass before Congress could be persuaded to give wilderness areas permanent protection through federal law. During these years the conservationists' problem was primarily one of public education. Here the nature writers played a key role. Beginning in 1949, a series of biennial wilderness conferences sponsored by the Sierra Club and the Wilderness Society gave them a public forum. As Daniel B. Beard of the National Park Service said at one of these meetings, "a distinct wild land or wilderness literature is required to bring into positive focus the values of such areas and such conditions to modern society." By 1961 Sigurd F. Olson, famous for his books on the Quetico-Superior canoe country, was feeling optimistic: "It seems like a monumental task to try to get our story across to the people, but when you look at the books that have been written recently on wilderness, the articles that have been written ... the fact that Congress is piling up millions of words in testimony for and against wilderness — these things to me are encouraging. Ten years ago this would have been impossible."

More and more Americans were becoming sensitive to their natural surroundings as they took a fresh look at the world through the eyes of our literary naturalists. More and more of them visited the national parks; and thanks to the Park Service's interpretative nature programs, fewer of them inquired with disappointment, "but what do we *do* here?" With knowledge came greater enjoyment. The value of wilderness areas to science — their importance as "outdoor laboratories" — was now recognized. The principles of ecology (a word that has since been degraded by misuse) were generally understood for the first time, as plants and animals were seen not simply as individuals but as part of a balanced, interdependent community. Along with this went a growing appreciation of the esthetic and spiritual values to be found in wild nature unmanipulated by man.

This was all very well, but in practical terms the problem was to translate these broad principles into votes on Capitol Hill. In 1956, a wilderness bill was introduced in Congress, drafted by one of the country's most articulate, experienced, and effective conservationists, Howard Zahniser of the Wilderness Society. Year after year it bogged down in committee, as the opposition, spurred on by the logging, mining, oil, and grazing lobbies, used every parliamentary trick to keep it from coming to a vote. But the public pressure was too strong to be resisted forever. On September 3, 1964, the bill became law. As Michael Frome has written in *Battle for the Wilderness*, "Virtually every happening associated with wilderness, both before and after the passage of the [Wilderness] Act, demonstrates that only the enthusiasm of people can make it work. An enlightened and involved public stands as the hope between the remaining parcels of wilderness and oblivion."

CHAPTER XIII

A New Direction

*"Poetry is as necessary to comprehension as science.
It is as impossible to live without reverence as it is
without joy."*
—Henry Beston, THE OUTERMOST HOUSE

THE CONFLICT over the future of our land is commonly seen as a battle between the exploiters and preservationists. But one can also think of it in less personal terms, as a race between unbridled technology and public education. The race began with the onset of the industrial revolution; today we are entering the home stretch. In the words of Allen H. Morgan of the Massachusetts Audubon Society: "What we save now is all we will ever save." Fortunately — in great measure thanks to our nature writers — we are aware as never before of what is at stake, from our last wilderness frontier in Alaska to the Florida Everglades, from the salt marshes of the Atlantic shore to the coastal redwoods of California.

Whenever one becomes deeply involved in a conservation issue, one acquires a new respect (if that is the proper term) for the sheer technical power that can now be brought to bear in reshaping the landscape according to man's whim. Back in the nineteen-fifties, when the Atomic Energy Commission decided to experiment with the excavating abilities of atomic bombs under the guise of creating a harbor for northwest Alaska, Dr. Edward Teller, the famous nuclear physicist, boasted that he had the power literally to move mountains.*
During the following decade the Army Corps of Engineers, backed by Alaska's governor and local boosters, were determined to dam the mighty Yukon River, thereby creating the world's biggest artificial lake and incidentally drowning one of its most valuable wildlife areas. Over five thousand miles away, in southern Florida, huge bulldozers began cutting a swathe through the Everglades in anticipation (happily unwarranted) of a super jetport and a new city to be built in the middle of a swamp, bringing slow death to the adjacent national park. Countless similar examples of brute force versus nature come to mind. Must Florida's uniquely beautiful Okla-

---

* The Fairbanks *News-Miner* saw Project Chariot (as it was called) as a sort of Fourth-of-July celebration: "We think that the holding of a huge nuclear blast in Alaska would be a fitting overture to the new era which is opening for our state."

hawa River, for example, be destroyed to make way for a needless "barge canal" simply because this is technically possible? Yes, said the Secretary of State for Florida: "Both intelligence and, for those of you who wish, the Bible dictate that man is to have dominion of all the resources of the earth. Since most of us either believe in our own intelligence and/or in the Bible, let us be about the task of exerting our dominion over these resources."

This definition of man's purpose on earth has fortunately become somewhat out of date. All the monstrous projects mentioned above — and scores of others — have been stopped in their tracks by the pressure of organized public opinion. The organizing has been done largely by conservation groups: national, regional, and local. Thanks to our nature writers, such groups can count on having their message put before the public, and ultimately translated into political action.

In this confrontation between blind "progress" and respect for the land, these writers have played two rôles, which in practice frequently overlap. One is essentially tactical: the creation of an informed public to confront a clear and present danger (as Rachel Carson did with *Silent Spring*) or, more frequently, to save some specific area from destruction. In so doing they are challenging what might be called the myth of the expert: the assumption that technical scientific matters, whether they involve private enterprise or government, lie beyond the grasp of ordinary citizens and had better be left to the professionals. The other rôle may be seen as strategic, in the broadest sense of that term. Our greatest nature writers have not necessarily been consciously promulgating any special doctrine or arguing on behalf of any specific cause. But in expressing their profound joy in nature — their observations, their experiences, their insights — they have sharpened our perception of what is at stake and strengthened our resolve to fight for its survival.

The recent practitioners in this field, like their predecessors, are a varied lot. Some are professional scientists with a gift for writing. Others are professional writers who have found natural science to be their principal source of inspiration. Still others, occupied with full-time careers, have turned to nature writing in their leisure moments. The sheer volume of their output is a tribute to earlier authors who have created an audience for it. In 1926 their field of literature received a sort of official recognition when the American Museum of Natural History joined with the John Burroughs Memorial Association to establish an annual award for distinguished nature writing. Looking back over the list of winners of the John Burroughs Medal, one gets a sense of the variety and the quality of this literature of nature over the last half-century. Most of the fifty-odd authors are familiar to American readers; some have been read all over the world. Many are still writing today. Their names conjure up a crowd of memories and pictures in the mind's eye. To take but a few of the most familiar: William Beebe, Ernest Thompson Seton, Frank M. Chapman, Robert Cushman Murphy, Edwin Way Teale, Roger Tory Peterson, Rachel Carson, Joseph Wood Krutch, Archie Carr, John Kieran, Loren Eiseley, Charlton Ogburn, John Hay. Some works of the past fifty years are already on their way to becoming classics. There is Henry Beston's *The Outermost House*, which inevitably recalls the writings of Thoreau. There are Roger Tory Peterson's *Field Guides* which, by simplifying identification of birds and other creatures in the wild, have introduced countless thousands to the joys of nature study and hence to the cause of conservation. There are Edwin Way Teale's travels through the four seasons, a landmark in the literature of nature.

Merely to list a few of these authors and their books suggests the richness of the field. Add to them the scores of others whose reputations are secure, still others whose work is not yet complete, and one realizes the impossibility of doing justice, in a single volume, to all the individual writers of today and of the immediate past. The stage is too crowded and we are too close to the actors to see the whole play in perspective. Rather let us consider briefly the career of one writer whose gift for words, scientific integrity, and social conscience symbolize the achievement of the nature writer in our time: Rachel Carson. Eight years after her death in 1964, a newspaper editorial concluded: "A few thousand words from her, and the world took a new direction."

The fame of *Silent Spring*, and its key role in launching the environmental movement, has tended to obscure the fact that Rachel Carson was at heart a writer, not a crusader. Many readers today appear to know her through that book alone. Yet by the time it was published in 1962 she was already the author of three unique works on natural history including — in *The Sea Around Us* — one of the top best-sellers of the twentieth century.

Born in 1907 in the town of Springdale in Pennsylvania's Allegheny Valley, Rachel assumed from early childhood that she was going to be a writer. "I have no idea why," she once remarked. "There were no writers in the family." Nor were there any naturalists. But almost from infancy her mother both encouraged her reading and fostered her curiosity about the natural world on their doorstep. "I can remember no time when I wasn't interested in the out-of-doors and the whole world of nature . . . I was a rather solitary child and spent a great deal of time in woods and beside streams, learning the birds and the insects and flowers." Her writing, however, came first. By the age of eleven she had sold a story to *St. Nicholas* magazine. In high school she continued to write, and at Pennsylvania College for Women (now Chatham College) she majored in English, on the dubious assumption that this was the gateway to the writing profession. A classmate remembered her as "quiet and self-effacing," an earnest scholar, not socially popular. Then in her junior year she made a sudden decision that was to be a turning point in her life. A compulsory course in biology fascinated her to the point where she impulsively decided to become a scientist rather than a writer, and switched her major to zoology. "I thought I had to be one or the other; it never occurred to me, or apparently anyone else, that I could combine the two careers." In fact, she had discovered what she wanted to write about. It was the merging of these two powerful currents — the imagination and insight of the creative writer with the scientist's passion for fact — the blend of beauty with authority — that would make her books so memorable.

Rachel Carson was a grown woman before she ever saw the sea, yet it had cast a strange spell on her as far back as she could remember. Here, she felt, lay her destiny. So she now turned to marine biology as her special field of study. It was not an easy road; in the nineteen-twenties there still existed a strong prejudice against women in science. The college authorities, she remarked, "would be just as happy if there were no science majors." Fortunately her zoology professor was able to get her a scholarship to Johns Hopkins University where she took her M.A. (The title of her thesis, "The Development of the Pronephros During the Embryonic and Early Larval Life of the Catfish," fails to suggest the best-sellers to come.) Most important for her career were her summers at the Woods Hole Marine Biological Laboratory in Massachusetts. Her romantic passion for the sea now became a practical part of her life. When her father died and she had to be the main support of her family, she managed to get a job with the Bureau of Fisheries in Washington — outstripping all the male applicants on her examination, and becoming one of the first two women to be hired in other than a clerical capacity. Not, one would think, a spawning ground for future writers. But here she began publishing feature newspaper ar-

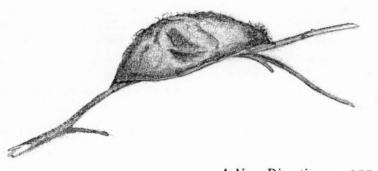

ticles on marine life. And here, of all places, she got the break she was waiting for. A writing assignment from the Bureau turned out to be too "literary" for their purposes; her boss suggested that she send it to the *Atlantic Monthly*. Entitled "Undersea," it appeared in 1937. From this short essay, she recalled, "everything else followed" — notably her first and least-known book, *Under the Sea-Wind*, and, ten years later, *The Sea Around Us*.

There is a sentence in "Undersea" that may at first glance seem obvious, but which suggests a principal reason for Rachel Carson's success as a nature writer. It also suggests the pitfalls in this field of literature that await a less skillful practitioner than she. "To sense this world of waters known to the creatures of the sea," she writes, "we must shed our human perceptions of length and breadth and time and place, and enter vicariously into a universe of all-pervading water." Like Henry Thoreau, whose *Journal* she kept by her bedside, she felt a sense of identification with the creatures about whom she wrote — as did also her other favorite writer, Henry Williamson, author of *Salar the Salmon* and *Tarka the Otter*. But she was well aware of the dangers of anthropomorphism: "To get the feeling of what it is like to be a creature of the sea requires the active exercise of the imagination and the temporary abandonment of many human concepts and human yardsticks . . . On the other hand," she continues, "we must not depart too far from the analogy with human conduct if a fish, shrimp, comb jelly, or bird is to seem real to us — as real a living creature as he actually is." She deliberately uses terms that are taboo in scientific writing and, like Williamson, she gives names to the creatures of *Under the Sea-Wind;* but she never succumbs to the pathetic fallacy which, for example, makes certain of Ernest Thompson Seton's otherwise accurate stories border on the ludicrous.

Published in the fall of 1941, a few weeks before Pearl Harbor, *Under the Sea-Wind* was a commercial failure.* But Ra-

* Reissued a decade later, after the great success of *The Sea Around Us*, it immediately became a best-seller.

chel always recalled it with particular affection. And for good reason. Few writers can recapture the freshness of their first book. "I came nearest to achieving that complete losing of myself in writing the *Sea-Wind*." One can sense this in every page of the book. Here is how she concludes her account of the mysterious migration of the Atlantic eels — a phenomenon which to William Beebe was an "almost unbelievable aspect of natural history."

Now they waited in the gray March sea, creatures of the deep sea, ready to invade the land. They waited off the sloughs and bayous and the wild-rice fields of the Gulf Coast, off the South Atlantic inlets, ready to run into the sounds and the green marshes that edged the river estuaries. They waited off the ice-choked northern rivers that came down with a surge and a rush of spring floods and thrust long arms of fresh water into the sea, so that the eels tasted the strange water taste and moved in excitement toward it. By the hundreds of thousands they waited off the mouth of the bay from which, little more than a year before, Anguilla and her companions had set out for the deep sea, blindly obeying a racial purpose which was now fulfilled in the return of the young . . .

As the moon waned and the surge of the tides grew less, the elvers pressed forward toward the mouth of the bay. Soon a night would come, after most of the snow had melted and run as water to the sea, when the moon's light and the tide's press would be feeble and a warm rain would fall, mist-laden and bittersweet with the scent of opening buds. Then the elvers would pour into the bay and, traveling up its shores, would find its rivers.

Some would linger in the river estuaries, brackish with the taste of the sea. These were the young male eels, who were repelled by the strangeness of fresh water. But the females would press on, swimming up against the currents of the rivers. They would move swiftly and by night as their mothers had come down the rivers. Their columns, miles in length, would wind up along the shallows of river and stream, each elver pressing close to the tail of the next before it, the whole like a serpent of monstrous length. No hardship and no obstacle would deter them. They would be preyed upon by hungry fishes — trout, bass, pickerel, and even by older eels; by rats hunting the edge of the water; and by gulls, herons, kingfishers, crows, grebes, and loons. They would swarm up waterfalls and clamber over moss-grown rocks, wet with spray; they would squirm up the spillways of dams. Some would go on for hundreds of miles — creatures of the deep sea spreading over all the land where the sea itself had lain many times before.

And as the eels lay offshore in the March sea, waiting for the time when they should enter the waters of the land, the sea, too, lay restless, awaiting the time when once more it should encroach upon the coastal plain, and creep up the sides of the foothills, and lap at the bases of the mountain ranges. As the waiting of the eels off the mouth of the bay was only an interlude in a long life filled with constant change, so the relation of sea and coast and mountain ranges was that of a moment in geologic time. For once more the mountains would be worn away by the endless erosion of water and carried in silt to the sea, and once more all the coast would be water again, and the places of its cities and towns would belong to the sea.

❧

Though the lack of sales of her first book was disappointing, Rachel took heart from the enthusiastic response of the scientific community, which generally has little patience with "popularizations" of science. She herself rejected the idea of "writing down" to reach the reader's supposed level of comprehension, be he child or adult. "I feel that if the author has something to say, and says it clearly, an intelligent reader of almost any age will understand him." She avoided technical jargon. "My relation to technical scientific writing," she stated on receiving a literary award, "has been that of one who understands the language but does not use it." Writing never came easily to her. Like John Muir, she had no trouble with personal correspondence, but when she undertook "something that is going to be bound between the covers of a book," she suffered real anguish. "I am a slow writer," she admitted, "enjoying the stimulating pursuit of research far more than the turning out of manuscript."

During World War II, Rachel Carson wrote conservation bulletins for the government, and took over the management of the publications program of what had become the United States Fish and Wildlife Service. Her colleague and close friend, Shirley Briggs, recalled that "her qualities of zest and humor made even the dull stretches of bureaucratic procedure a matter for quiet fun, and she could instill a sense of adventure into the editorial routine of a government department." Every spare moment she spent outdoors, birding or pursuing other nature studies. After the war, she had an opportunity to engage in the sort of field work she most enjoyed, writing (or editing) a series of twelve illustrated booklets on the national wildlife refuges, which set a new literary standard for government publications.

During these years, Rachel Carson was in the classic position of the would-be writer who cannot afford the time for creative work. Her job allowed her little literary outlet. Her salary was modest, and she had a mother and two orphaned nieces to support. "If I could choose what seems to me the ideal existence," she wrote to a friend, "it would be just to live by writing. But I have done far too little to dare risk it." She did manage to supplement her income by writing magazine articles on natural history subjects. Meanwhile she had for years been quietly working on a book that would make her famous.

As a writer she may have been slow, but she was also bold. For her next book she had chosen no less a subject than the sea itself. It was an overwhelming job. "More than once," she later recalled, "I asked myself why I should have ever undertaken such a task . . . The backbone of the work was just plain hard slogging." She knew that she could not cope alone with so vast, complex, and mysterious a theme, but she also knew where to find assistance. "A difficult task was transformed into a richly rewarding experience by the generous help and encouragement of leading oceanographers everywhere." Among them were Henry B. Bigelow of Harvard, and her old friends William Beebe and Edwin Way Teale.

The Sea Around Us was ten years in the making, but in a sense Rachel had been working on it all her life. Published in 1951, it became an immediate best-seller, and remained so for a year and a half. Reviews were ecstatic. "Rarely," wrote a critic for the *New York Times*, "does the world get a physical scientist with literary genius." Literary awards followed, translations were made into thirty-eight languages. Yet this was not the first good book about the sea to be written for the general reader. Wherein lay the magic? In her character-istically factual, understated way, Rachel Carson herself gives a clue:

When I planned my book, I knew only that a fascination for the sea and a compelling sense of its mystery had been part of my own life from earliest childhood. So I wrote what I knew about it, and also what I thought and felt about it.

Many people have commented with surprise on the fact that a work of science should have a large popular sale. But this notion, that "science" is something that belongs in a separate compartment of its own, apart from everyday life, is one that I should challenge. We live in a scientific age; yet we assume that knowledge of science is the prerogative of only a small number of human beings, isolated and priestlike in their laboratories. This is not true. The materials of science are the materials of life itself. Science is part of the reality of

living; it is the what, the how, and the why of everything in our experience. It is impossible to understand man without understanding his environment and the forces that have molded him physically and mentally . . .

My own guiding purpose was to portray the subject of my sea profile with fidelity and understanding. All else was secondary. I did not stop to consider whether I was doing it scientifically or poetically; I was writing as the subject demanded.

The winds, the sea, and the moving tides are what they are. If there is wonder and beauty and majesty in them, science will discover these qualities. If they are not there, science cannot create them. If there is poetry in my book about the sea, it is not because I deliberately put it there, but because no one could write truthfully about the sea and leave out the poetry.

Rachel Carson was not one to rest on her laurels. "I am always more interested in what I am about to do," she remarked, "than in what I have already done." Months before publication of *The Sea Around Us* she was already wading in the tide pools and combing the sand beaches in preparation for a complementary volume, *The Edge of the Sea*. The new book would deal not with the physical forces of the ocean depths but with the teeming life of the seashore. Her aim was "to take the seashore out of the category of scenery and make it come alive . . . An ecological concept will dominate the book." Once more she was grappling, slowly and painfully, with a huge and complex subject. This time, however, the research was sheer joy. "For the first time, I'm writing about something that is right under my nose, and it gives me a very different feeling about it . . ."

As any writer knows, there is nothing more difficult than the book which follows a sensational success. Yet Rachel managed to bring it off. When serialization of *The Edge of the Sea* began in *The New Yorker*, she received a letter from Teale: "You have done it again! The wonderful part of it is that in spite of the strain and struggle and frustration that I know went into shaping the book in its final form there is no hint of 'tired writing' in any of the portion I have read. It is serene and fresh and strong with no residue of fatigue or stress in it — and that, in truth, is a very great accomplishment." *The Edge of the Sea* would bring her new honors, including the citation from the National Council of Women of the United States for "the outstanding book of the year."

Rachel Carson's last, great book, *Silent Spring*, was inspired not by joy but by fury — fury at the way one species of life on earth, man, was blindly altering the very character of the planet. Ever since the days of John Muir and George Perkins Marsh, our nature writers have fought against the heedless destruction of the landscape: the drowning of river valleys with needless dams, the clear-cutting of forests and consequent erosion of watersheds, the overgrazing of the western range, the marginal agriculture that creates dustbowls and deserts. Most of these brutal uses of our power over nature are all too visible. Not so with the newly developed chemicals that, following World War II, began subtly to contaminate the entire environment. The insecticide known as DDT was discovered during research into chemical warfare. "The discovery," writes Rachel Carson, "did not come by chance; insects were widely used to test chemicals as agents of death for man." When these new chemicals first came into agricultural and other civilian use, she and other scientists were well aware of the dangers inherent in such synthetic, nonselective, and persistent poisons. She tried to place a magazine article on the subject, but in vain. Finally, in 1958, she felt that she had to speak out: "There would be no peace for me if I kept silent." Other projects were abandoned, and the pleasurable research that had gone into her books on the sea was replaced by an almost religious dedication as she gathered her evidence from scientists throughout America and Europe. What was to have been an article grew into a book which dealt not only with the dangers of DDT but with other and still more toxic chemicals with which modern man was poisoning earth, air, and water on a worldwide scale.

The success of this difficult enterprise, which with hindsight may seem obvious, was by no means assured. Could any writer, even one of Rachel Carson's skill and reputation, make a readable book of so grim a subject? Some of her friends doubted it; and so at times did she. But once started, she never wavered. Immediately on publication *Silent Spring* was violently attacked — as the author knew it would be — by the agricultural chemical industry and others who felt their interests threatened. Treating the matter as a public relations problem, the industry spent enormous sums to ridicule both the book and its author. However, these attempts to discredit her facts were not successful. A direct result of the revelations in *Silent Spring* was the formation, at the direction of President John F. Kennedy, of a special panel of the President's Science Advisory Committee to study the effects of pesticides on the environment. Its report amounted to an official endorsement of Rachel Carson's position.

The storm aroused in certain quarters by the publication of *Silent Spring*, the attempts to brand the author as a "hysterical woman," cannot be explained simply by the concern of special interest groups for their power or profits. The reasons lie deeper than that. Rachel Carson's detractors were well aware of the real danger to themselves in the stance she had taken. She was not only questioning the indiscriminate use of poisons but declaring the basic responsibility of an industrialized, technological society toward the natural world. This was her heresy. In eloquent and specific terms she set forth the philosophy of life that has given rise to today's environmental movement.

Rachel Carson died in 1964 at the age of fifty-six, having lived just long enough to witness the initial impact of her solitary crusade. The final phase of her life was at once the saddest and the most splendid. The product of immense labor and talent, *Silent Spring* also represents an act of great moral courage. She had abandoned other plans to tackle this repugnant subject, aware that she would be personally vilified. And though only her closest friends knew it at the time, she was suffering from what she later referred to as a "whole catalogue of illnesses." She was convinced of the importance of what she was doing, and somewhere she found the strength for this final effort. Not only that, but she managed to make this book about death a celebration of life.

As she neared completion of the manuscript of *Silent Spring*, Rachel Carson wrote to a close friend: "No, I myself never thought the ugly facts would dominate, and I hope they don't. The beauty of the living world I was trying to save has always been uppermost in my mind — that, and anger at the senseless brutish things that were being done. I have felt bound by a solemn obligation to do what I could — if I didn't at least try I could never again be happy in nature. But now I can believe I have at least helped a little. It would be unrealistic to believe one book could bring a complete change."

It may have been unrealistic, but history has proved it true.

Further Reading

Index

FURTHER READING

The following list of titles, arranged by chapters, is not a formal bibliography. It is a personal selection of characteristic books by each of the authors mentioned here. Standard biographies — where they exist — are also included. Since this book concludes with the publication of *Silent Spring*, I have chosen 1962 (except for biographies) as a cut-off date.

Introduction

RALPH WALDO EMERSON (1803–1882)
  Nature, 1836
HENRY DAVID THOREAU (1817–1862)
  Walden, 1854
  Journal
  Essays
Walter Harding: *The Days of Henry Thoreau*, 1965

Chapter I

JOHN BURROUGHS (1837–1921)
  Wake-Robin, 1871
  Winter Sunshine, 1875
  Locusts and Wild Honey, 1879
Clara Barrus: *The Life and Letters of John Burroughs*, 1925
Farida A. Wiley (editor): *John Burroughs' America*, 1951
JOHN MUIR (1838–1914)
  My First Summer in the Sierra, 1911
  The Story of My Boyhood and Youth, 1913
  Travels in Alaska, 1915
  A Thousand-Mile Walk to the Gulf, 1916
William Frederic Bade: *The Life and Letters of John Muir*, 1923–1924
Edwin Way Teale: *The Wilderness World of John Muir*, 1954

Chapter II

[THOMAS] STARR KING (1824–1864)
The White Hills, 1860
A Vacation Among the Sierras: Yosemite in 1860
(Edited by John A. Hussey), 1962
Charles W. Wendte: *Thomas Starr King, Patriot and Preacher*, 1921
CLARENCE KING (1842–1901)
Mountaineering in the Sierra Nevada, 1872
FREDERICK LAW OLMSTED (1822–1903)
Walks and Talks of an American Farmer in England, 1852
"Yosemite Valley and the Mariposa Big Trees"
(*Landscape Architecture*, XLIII, 1952)
Florence Wood Roper: *FLO: A Biography of Frederick Law Olmsted*,
1973

Chapter III

WILSON FLAGG (1805–1884)
Studies in the Field and Forest, 1857
The Birds and Seasons of New England, 1875
THOMAS WENTWORTH HIGGINSON (1823–1911)
Outdoor Papers, 1863
Army Life in a Black Regiment, 1870
Anna Mary Wells: *Dear Preceptor: The Life and Times of Thomas
Wentworth Higginson*, 1963
SIDNEY LANIER (1842–1881)
The Marshes of Glynn (Poems, 1877)
Florida: Its Scenery, Climate and History, 1875
Edwin Mims: *Sidney Lanier*, 1905

Chapter IV

GEORGE PERKINS MARSH (1801–1882)
Man and Nature, 1864
(New edition, with introduction by David Lowenthal, 1964)
JOHN WESLEY POWELL (1834–1902)
Report on the Exploration of the Colorado River of the West, 1875
Wallace Stegner: *Beyond the Hundredth Meridian*, 1954
CLARENCE EDWARD DUTTON (1841–1912)
The Physical Geography of the Grand Canyon District
(U.S. Geological Survey Annual Report), 1881
Stegner: See above
LOUIS AGASSIZ (1807–1873)
Contributions to the Natural History of the United States of America, 1857–1863

Elizabeth Cary Agassiz: *Louis Agassiz, His Life and Correspondence,* 1886

Edward Lurie: *Louis Agassiz: A Life in Science,* 1960

Chapter V

THEODORE ROOSEVELT (1858–1919)
  Hunting Trips of a Ranchman, 1885
  Ranch Life and the Hunting Trail, 1888

Paul Russell Cutright: *Theodore Roosevelt the Naturalist,* 1956

Farida A. Wiley (editor): *Theodore Roosevelt's America,* 1955

GEORGE BIRD GRINNELL (1849–1938)
  American Big Game and Its Haunts (*Boone and Crockett Club*), 1904 (Grinnell was both editor and a contributor)

WILLIAM TEMPLE HORNADAY (1854–1937)
  Our Vanishing Wildlife, 1913

HENRY FAIRFIELD OSBORN (1852–1935)
  "Preserving Our Wild Animals," in *American Big Game and Its Haunts,* 1904
  Impressions of Great Naturalists, 1928

Chapter VI

ELLIOT COUES (1842–1899)
  Key to North American Birds, 1872
  Birds of the Colorado Valley, 1878

BRADFORD TORREY (1843–1912)
  Birds in the Bush, 1885
  A Rambler's Lease, 1889

WILLIAM BREWSTER (1851–1919)
  October Farm, 1936
  Concord River, 1937

Henry W. Henshaw: "Memorial," in *The Auk,* January 1920

FRANK BOLLES (1856–1894)
  Land of the Lingering Snow, 1891
  At the North of Bearcamp Water, 1893

William R. Thayer: "Frank Bolles," *Harvard Graduates Magazine,* March 1894

EDWARD HOWE FORBUSH (1858–*1929*)
  Birds of Massachusetts and Other New England States, 3 Vols., 1925–1929

John Bichard May: "Edward Howe Forbush, Friend of the Birds," in Vol. III of above

FRANK M. CHAPMAN (1864–1945)
  My Tropical Air Castle, 1929
  Autobiography of a Bird-Lover, 1933

Robert Cushman Murphy: "Frank Michler Chapman, 1864–1945," in
The Auk, July 1950

Chapter VII

OLIVE THORNE MILLER (1831–1918)
With the Birds in Maine, 1904
MABEL OSGOOD WRIGHT (1859–1934)
The Friendship of Nature, 1894
Birdcraft, 1895
FLORENCE A. MERRIAM (1863–1948)
A-Birding on a Bronco, 1896
Birds of Village and Field, 1898
Paul H. Oehser: "In Memoriam, Florence Merriam Bailey," in *The
Auk*, January 1952
NELTJE BLANCHAN (Mrs. Frank Nelson Doubleday) 1865–1918
Birds That Hunt and Are Hunted, 1898
GENE STRATTON-PORTER (1863–1924)
The Song of the Cardinal, 1903

Chapter VIII

MARY AUSTIN (1868–1934)
The Land of Little Rain, 1903
Earth Horizon, 1932
JOSEPH WOOD KRUTCH (1893–1970)
The Desert Year, 1952
The Voice of the Desert, 1954

Chapter IX

ERNEST THOMPSON SETON (1860–1946)
Wild Animals I Have Known, 1898
Lives of the Hunted, 1901
Trail of an Artist-Naturalist, 1940
ENOS MILLS (1870–1922)
In Beaver World, 1913
The Story of a Thousand-Year Pine, 1914
Hildegarde Hawthorne and Esther S. Mills: *Enos Mills of the Rock-
ies*, 1935
DALLAS LORE SHARP (1870–1929)
The Face of the Fields, 1911
THORNTON W. BURGESS (1874–1965)
Old Mother West Wind Stories

Chapter X

THOMAS BARBOUR (1888–1946)
Naturalist at Large, 1943
DAVID FAIRCHILD (1869–1954)
The World Was My Garden, 1941
DONALD CULROSS PEATTIE (1898–1964)
An Almanac for Moderns, 1935
Flowering Earth, 1939
WILLIAM BEEBE (1877–1962)
Jungle Peace, 1918
Galapagos: World's End, 1924
Half Mile Down, 1934
ROBERT CUSHMAN MURPHY (1887–1973)
Bird Islands of Peru, 1925
Oceanic Birds of South America, 1936
Logbook for Grace, 1947

Chapter XI

RUSSELL LORD (1895–)
Behold Our Land, 1938
PAUL B. SEARS (1891–)
Deserts on the March, 1935
STUART CHASE (1902–1968)
Rich Land Poor Land, 1936
FAIRFIELD OSBORN (1887–1969)
Our Plundered Planet, 1948
WILLIAM VOGT (1902–1968)
Road to Survival, 1948
BERNARD DeVOTO (1897–1955)
The Easy Chair, 1955
Wallace Stegner: *The Uneasy Chair: A Biography of Bernard DeVoto*, 1974

Chapter XII

ALDO LEOPOLD (1887–1948)
A Sand County Almanac, 1949
ROBERT MARSHALL (1901–1939)
Arctic Village, 1933
Alaska Wilderness, 1970

Chapter XIII

HENRY BESTON (1888–1968)
The Outermost House, 1928
LOUIS J. HALLE (1910–)
Spring in Washington, 1947

Roger Tory Peterson (1908–   )
   A Field Guide to the Birds, 1934
   Birds over America, 1949
   Wild America (with James Fisher), 1955
Edwin Way Teale (1899–   )
   The American Seasons (Beginning with *North with the Spring*, 1951)
Archie Carr (1909–   )
   The Windward Road, 1956
Loren Eiseley (1907–1977)
   The Immense Journey, 1957
John Kieran (1892–   )
   A Natural History of New York City, 1959
John Hay (1915–   )
   The Run, 1959
Charlton Ogburn (1911–   )
   The Winter Beach, 1966
Rachel Carson (1907–1964)
   Under the Sea-Wind, 1941
   The Sea Around Us, 1951
   The Edge of the Sea, 1955
   Silent Spring, 1962
Paul Brooks: *The House of Life: Rachel Carson at Work*, 1972

INDEX

A-Birding on a Bronco (Merriam),
174
Academy of Natural Sciences
(Philadelphia), 106
Accepting the Universe (Burroughs),
31
Adams, Ansel, 53n
Adams, Henry, 42, 48n, 49, 84; De-
Voto quoted on, 99
Adirondack Forest Preserve, 201,
259, 264
Agassiz, Louis, 83–88; variety of
interests, 221; mentioned, 17, 20,
43, 67, 76, 90, 106, 108, 128, 165, 222
Agassiz Museum, see Museum of
Comparative Zoology
Agee, James, 240
Alaska Wilderness (Marshall), 265n
Alcott, Bronson, 14, 37
Alcott, Louisa May, 4
Alden, Betty, 115
Aldrich, Thomas Bailey, 62
Allen, Francis H., 140, 141n
Allen, Joel A., 158
Amadon, Dean, 230, 231
American Ethnology, Bureau of, 99
American Museum of Natural
History, 23, 84, 127, 152, 157, 158,
229; annual report (1872), 105;
educational program, 215; Bur-
roughs Medal established by, 275
American Natural History (Hor-
naday), 125
American Ornithologists' Union,
118, 137, 143, 157, 158, 166, 169
"American Scholar, The" (Emer-
son), xiv
American Society for Psychical
Research, 137

America's Natural Wealth (Lieber),
241
Among Birds in the Grand Canyon
National Park (Merriam), 175
Analysis of Female Beauty (Flagg),
62
Anderson, Harold C., 268
Appalachian Trail, 268
"April Days" (Higginson), 67
Arctic Village (Marshall), 265, 267–68
Arctic Wilderness (Marshall), 265,
266
Army Corps of Engineers, U.S., 273
Army Life in a Black Regiment
(Higginson), 71
Arrow Maker, The (Austin), 192n
Atlantic Monthly, mentioned, 4, 6, 9,
20, 24–25, 28, 52n, 61, 62, 66, 67, 71,
85, 86, 140, 165, 184, 210, 278
Atomic Energy Commission, 273
At the North of Bearcamp Water
(Bolles), 148
Audubon, John James, 6, 107, 115,
123, 143, 154, 158, 232, 254
Audubon, Lucy, 115, 118
Audubon (magazine), 118, 135, 158,
159–60, 172
Audubon societies, xvi, 106, 118, 143,
153, 158–59, 165, 169, 172, 212n,
216, 256; founding of, 172
Austin, Mary, 183–92, 194, 195

Bade, W. E., 172n
Bailey, Florence Merriam, see Mer-
riam, Florence A.
Bailey, Vernon, 174, 175
Baja California, 196–97
Barbour, Thomas, 88, 146, 222
Barrus, Clara, 5, 14, 27, 31

trips, 126n; death, 132; Frank Chapman and, 157; journal quoted, 171; Smith College girls and, 172; on Neltje Blanchan, 175–76; criticism of nature fakers, 210–16; mentioned, 48, 61, 64, 73, 100, 115, 122, 128, 130, 136, 139, 165, 166, 167, 169, 205, 221

Burroughs, Mrs. John (Ursula North), 7, 15, 31

Burroughs, Julian (son), 14

Burroughs Medal, 175n, 195, 210, 223, 275

Burroughs Memorial Association, John, 275

Butler, James Davie, 18

Cable, George W., 80
Cady, Harrison, 216
Cannon, Joseph, 203
Cardozo, Benjamin M., 267, 268
Carhart, Arthur, 259
Carr, Archie, 275
Carr, Ezra, 84, 87
Carr, Mrs. Jeanne C., 19–20, 74
Carson, Rachel, 275–86; Burroughs Medal winner, 275; mentioned, xiii, xvi, xvii, 3, 160, 223, 228, 230, 274
Cather, Willa, 192
Catlin, George, 4n, 254
Cattle business, Bernard DeVoto on the, 248
Central Park (New York City), 49, 51, 52
Century Club, 49
Channing, Ellery, 66
Channing, Mary, see Higginson, Mrs. Thomas Wentworth
Chapman, Frank, 157–62; on books by Mabel O. Wright, 168; lecture on "Woman as a Bird Enemy," 174; commissions Seton to illustrate his books, 208; on nature fakers, 212; Burroughs Medal winner, 275; mentioned, 105, 136, 137, 147–48, 174, 201, 229, 232
Chase, Stuart, 240–41
Check List of North American Birds (Coues), 137
Children's Book of Birds, The (Miller), 166
Chocorua, Mt., 148, 150, 167

"Christmas Census," annual, 161
Citizen Bird (Wright and Coues), 168
Civilian Conservation Corps, 236
Clark, Irving, 242n
Clark, William, 138
Cleveland, Grover, 14
Colby, William E., 57
Cole, Thomas, 254
Coleridge, Samuel Taylor, 135
Colorado River, 94–99, 100, 184, 191
"Colors and Fragrance of Flowers, The" (Flagg), 65
Compleat Angler (Walton), 114
Concord River (Brewster), 146
Concord River Valley, 141–42, 146
Conrad, Joseph, 191
Conservation movement, xv, xvi, 3, 4n, 11, 235–50; Burroughs and the, 31–32; Marsh and the, 93; Powell and the, 93; Boone and Crockett Club and the, 121; Forbush and the, 153; New England naturalists and the, 156–57; women and the, 165, 169; Bernard DeVoto and the, 247–48; Aldo Leopold and the, 263
Cooper, James Fenimore, 4n, 254
"Corn" (Lanier), 73, 75
Cotton Kingdom, The (Olmstead), 51
Coues, Elliott, 135–39, 168
Cousteau, Jacques, 224
Cram, William Everett, 201
Crow, Forbush quoted on the, 154–55
"Crown of the Continent, The" (Grinnell), 121
Cushman, Charlotte, 73
Custer, George H., 116
Cutright, Paul R., 107
Cuvier, Baron, 86

Dana, James Dwight, 43
Darwin, Charles, 55–56, 76, 86, 127–28
Davis, Elmer, 247
DDT, 244, 284
Death Valley, 202
Deming, Harold S., 213
Desert country, 183–98
Deserts on the March (Sears), 238–40
Desert Year, The (Krutch), 194–95
DeVoto, Bernard, 247–50
Dickinson, Emily, 66, 67, 71

Dinosaur National Monument, 249–50
Doubleday, Frank N., 175, 177
Downing, Andrew Jackson, 51, 55
Dutton, Clarence Edward, 100–102, 202

Earth as Modified by Human Action, The (Marsh), 92n
Earth Horizon (Austin), 190
Echo Park, 249–50
Ecology, xvi, 55, 65, 91, 122, 162, 246, 283
Edge of the Sea, The (Carson), 283–84
Edison, Thomas A., 30
Eels, Atlantic, Rachel Carson on, 279–80
Eiseley, Loren, 275
Elliott, D. G., 137
Ellis, Havelock, 36
Emerson, Edward, 84
Emerson, Ralph Waldo: literary works, xiv, 36, 83; influence on Thoreau, xv, 6, 105; influence on Burroughs, 6–7; Muir's letters sent to, 20; on Wordsworth, 38–39; on Agassiz, 83; Agassiz and, 84; influence on Mary Austin, 186; mentioned, 37, 38, 72, 74, 195, 255
Evans, Walker, 240
Everglades, 273
Extinction of species, 116, 135, 156

Fairchild, David, 222
Farquhar, Francis P., 46n
Fein, Albert, 55
Field and Study (Burroughs), 31
Fields, James T., 38, 44
"Fifty Common Birds and How to Know Them" (Merriam), 172
Firestone, Harvey, 30
First Book of Birds, The (Miller), 166
Fisher, Clyde, 218
Fish-shape Paumanok (Murphy), 232
Flader, Susan, 260
Flagg, Wilson, 61–65, 68, 140, 141; on nature study for women, 165
Florida (Lanier), 77–79
Folk Tales (Grinnell), 122
Forbush, Edward Howe, 145n, 151–56, 167, 168, 169

Ford, Henry, 30–31
Forest Reserve Act, 201
Forest Reserve system, 121
Forests, national, xvi, 201, 255, 256, 259
Forgotten Peninsula, The (Krutch), 197
Fortieth Parallel Survey, 49n, 144n
Freckles (Stratton-Porter), 178, 179, 180
French, Daniel Chester, 41, 143, 145, 148; Brewster Medal designed by, 148n
Friendship of Nature, The (Wright), 168
Frome, Michael, 270
Frontier, 3, 254, 260
Fuertes, Louis Agassiz, 160, 168, 174, 217
Fuller, Margaret, 35
Future, the, 273–86

Galapagos: World's End (Beebe), 224
Game Management (Leopold), 257n, 260
Game refuges, 257
Garland, Hamlin, 213
General Grant National Park, 57
Geology of the High Plains of Utah (Dutton), 100
Gila Wilderness, 259–60, 263, 269
Gilder, Richard Watson, 11
Girl of the Limberlost, A (Stratton-Porter), 179
Glacier National Park, 121, 202
Governmental Preservation of Natural Scenery (Olmsted), 56
Grand Canyon, 95–97, 100–102, 196, 202
Grapes of Wrath (Steinbeck), 240
Gray, Asa, 51, 86, 108
Great American Desert, 48
Great Smoky Mountains National Park, 268
Greeley, Horace, 35, 40, 51
Grey, Viscount, 113
Grinnell, George Bird, 115–23; *Forest and Stream* and, 117, 153, 171–72; Harriman Expedition and, 122; *Audubon Magazine* launched by, 135; Audubon Society founded by, 171–72, 216–17;

mentioned, 105, 114, 124, 127, 129, 139, 143, 158, 159, 202

Half Mile Down (Beebe), 224
Halle, Louis J., 11n
Handbook of Birds of Eastern North America (Chapman), 158, 208
Handbook of Birds of the Western United States (Merriam), 175
Hanley, Wayne, 139, 208n
Harding, Walter, 85n
Harriman, E. H., 28n, 58
Harriman Alaska Expedition, 14, 26–27, 58, 122, 144n
Harte, Bret, 20, 31, 45
Hawthorne, Nathaniel, 78, 142, 146
Hay, John, 275
Hayden Surveys, 137
Hellman, Geoffrey, 158
Henshaw, Henry, 143
Hetch Hetchy, 29, 130, 204
Higginson, Thomas Wentworth, 38, 61, 62, 66–71, 72, 78, 108, 140, 165
Higginson, Mrs. Thomas Wentworth (Mary Channing), 66, 67
History of British Birds (Bewick), 154
Hofstadter, Beatrice K., 178
Holland, W. J., 223
Holmes, Oliver Wendell, 41, 118
Homer, 36
Hooker, J. D., 24
Horace, 36
Hornaday, William T., 123–27; Aldo Leopold and, 257; mentioned, 105, 139, 156, 215, 217, 256
Horsfall, R. Bruce, 160
Hosmer, James Kendall, 85n
Howells, William Dean, 9, 13, 45, 90, 213
Hudson, W. H., 183
Hunting Trips of a Ranchman (Roosevelt), 109, 111, 114
Hussey, John A., 38n, 42
Hutchings, James Mason, 40
Huxley, Aldous, 193
Huxley, T. H., 76, 127

Illinois Society of Natural History, 94
Indians, 122, 189
Ingersoll, Ernest, 106, 201

"In Warbler Time" (Burroughs), 159
Irving, Washington, 4n, 51, 254

Jaques, Francis Lee, 230
Jessup, Morris K., 107
Jewett, Sarah Orne, 31
Johnson, Robert Underwood, 22–24, 57, 58, 122n, 202
Johnson, Thomas H., 67n
Jones, Holway R., 122n
Jungle Peace (Beebe), 223

Kaibab National Forest, 257–58
Katahdin, Mount, 67
Kennedy, John F., 285
Key to North American Birds (Coues), 136–37
Kieran, John, 275
King, Clarence, 42–49; compared to Clarence Dutton, 100; mentioned, 52, 53, 89, 94, 98, 99, 102, 105, 135, 150, 157
King, Thomas Starr, 37–42; statue of, 143; mentioned, 51, 52n, 89, 94, 97, 202
King's Canyon National Park, 42
King's River, 42
Knopf, Alfred A., 249
Krutch, Joseph Wood, 192–98; Burroughs Medal winner, 275; mentioned, 183, 201, 221

Lacey Bill, 201
LaFarge, John, 43
Land of Journey's Ending, The (Austin), 192
Land of the Lingering Snow (Bolles), 148
Land of Little Rain, The (Austin), 184, 185, 187, 190, 191, 192, 194
Lands of the Arid Region, The (Powell), 98
Lanier, Sidney, 61, 71–80, 84, 135, 152, 165, 236n
Lassen's Peak, 44
Leatherstocking Tales (Cooper), 4n
Leaves of Grass (Whitman), 8, 9
LeConte, Joseph, 88
Leonard, Richard M., 249
Leopold, A. Starker, 255
Leopold, Aldo, 255, 256–62, 268, 269

(Harvard), 84, 86, 106, 144, 157, 158, 222
"My Out-Door Study" (Higginson), 67
My Tropical Air Castle (Chapman), 160

Nash, Roderick, 263
National Council of Women, Rachel Carson cited by, for outstanding book of the year, 284
National Museum, U.S., 124
National Park Service, 205, 242, 249
Natural History in America (Hanley), 139, 208n
Natural History of the Ducks, A (Phillips), 222
Natural History of Selborne (White), 10, 141
Naturalist at Large (Barbour), 222
Nature (Emerson), xiv, 36
Nature fakers, 210–15
"New England May Day, A" (Wright), 168, 170
New York Zoological Society, 125, 127
Niagara Falls, 56, 57
Noble, John W., 121
Norris, Frank, 72
Norton, Charles Eliot, 51
Notes on Walt Whitman (Burroughs), 8, 9
Nuttall, Thomas, 143
Nuttall Ornithological Club, 108, 118, 143

Oberholtzer, Ernest C., 268
October Farm (Brewster), 146
Oehser, Paul H., 174
Ogburn, Charlton, 275
Oklawaha River, 78–79, 152–53, 273–74
Old Mother West Wind (Burgess), 216
Olmsted, Frederick Law, 49–57, 88, 89, 98, 100
Olney, Warren, 23
Olson, Sigurd F., 269
Olympic National Park, 242
Oregon Trail (Parkman), 35, 114
Origin of Species, The (Darwin), 56, 76, 86
Ornithological Biography (Audubon), 154

Ornithology, established as a science, 135
Osborn, Fairfield, 243–45
Osborn, Henry Fairfield, 23, 24, 31, 105, 124, 127–32, 243
Osgood, Samuel, 168
Our Friend John Burroughs (Barrus), 31
"Our Last Buffalo Hunt" (Hornaday), 124
Our National Parks (Muir), 25, 57
Our Plundered Planet (Osborn), 243, 248
Our Vanishing Wild Life (Hornaday), 124, 127, 256
Outdoor Papers (Higginson), 71
Outermost House, The (Beston), 275
Overland Journey, An (Greeley), 40
Owens Valley (California), 186, 191

Page, Walter Hines, 25, 26, 27
Parakeet, Carolina, 135
Parkman, Francis, 35, 114
Park Protection Act, 121
Parks, national, xiii, xv, 3, 4n, 22–23, 24, 42, 55, 57, 161, 249–50, 255, 270
Partridge, Forbush quoted on, 156
Pawnee Hero Stories (Grinnell), 122
Peacock, Gibson, 73
Pearson, T. Gilbert, 152
Peattie, Donald Culross, 222
Penguins, Robert Murphy on, 230–31
Perry, Bliss, 10, 202, 211
Pesticides, 285
Peterson, Roger Tory, 159, 162, 207, 221; Burroughs Medal winner, 275
Pheasants of the World (Beebe), 223
Phillips, John C., 222
Physical Geography of the Grand Cañon District (Dutton), 100
Pigeon, passenger, 115–16, 135, 262
Pinchot, Gifford, 23, 90, 235, 248, 256, 259
Plateau Province, 94–99, 100
Population explosion, 244–45
Porcellian Club, 108
Powell, John Wesley, 93–100, 102, 202, 248
Powell Survey, 98
President's Science Advisory Committee, 285

Snow, C. P., 238
Society of Natural History (Boston), 106
Soil Conservation Service, 236–39, 242
Solar heat, 92
Song of the Cardinal, The (Stratton-Porter), 178
Spencer, Herbert, 56
Spring in Washington (Halle), 11n
Stegner, Wallace, 45, 93, 98, 100, 248, 249, 250
Steinbeck, John, 240
Stone, Witmer, 106, 201
"Story of a Thousand-Year Pine, The" (Mills), 203
Story of My Boyhood and Youth, The (Muir), 16, 28n
Stratton-Porter, Gene, 177–80
Studies in Field and Forest (Flagg), 63
Sullivan, Mark, 214
Summit of the Years, The (Burroughs), 31
Sutton, George Miksch, 160
Systematic Geology (King), 48

Tarka the Otter (Williamson), 278
Taylor, Bayard, 51, 73, 74
Teal, John and Mildred, 77n
Teale, Edwin Way, xiv, 221, 228, 281, 283; Burroughs Medal winner, 275
Teller, Edward, 273
Thalatta (anthology), 38
Thaxter, Celia, 118, 159, 166
Thayer, William, 150
Theosophical Society, 137–38
There's Always Adventure (Murphy), 230
Thoreau, Henry David: hundredth anniversary of death of, xiii, 223; Emerson's influence on, xv, 6, 105; journal of, xv, 5, 18, 35, 71, 140, 141, 146, 278; death, 3, 4; obituaries, 4; literary works, 4, 19, 61; impact on young readers, 5; Burroughs' writing compared with that of, 11–13, 32; Burroughs visits grave of, 14; Muir compared with, 19; quoted on the west, 35; Lowell's denigration of work of, 62n; on Wilson Flagg, 63;

opinion of Thomas Higginson, 66; fondness for the flute, 75; on science, 83; Agassiz and, 84; establishment of wilderness areas recommended by, 92–93; T. Roosevelt compared with, 114; on extinction of species, 116; Concord River and, 141, 142; compared with William Brewster, 146; Mary Austin compared with, 187, 189, 192; Krutch's biography of, 194, 195; Barbour's dislike of, 222n; mentioned, 13, 38, 43, 61, 64, 66, 74, 78, 83, 91, 92, 135, 140, 141, 143, 145, 146, 152, 155, 160, 165, 183, 193, 221, 255, 256
Thousand Mile Walk to the Gulf, A (Muir), 17
Through the Brazilian Wilderness (Roosevelt), 131
Thrush, hermit, Mabel Wright quoted on, 169–71
Time and Change (Burroughs), 31
Tom, Mt., 72
Torrey, Bradford, 140–41, 156, 159, 165
Transcendentalists, xiv, 38
Travels in Alaska (Muir), 29
Tryon Mountain, 76
Turner, Frederick Jackson, 3, 260
Twain, Mark, 45, 213
Tweed, Boss, 107
Twelve Seasons, The (Krutch), 194
Tyndall, John, 43, 47
Tyndall, Mount, 46–47

Udall, Stewart L., xiii, 250
Under the Apple Tree (Burroughs), 31
Under the Maples (Burroughs), 31
"Undersea" (Carson), 278
Under the Sea Wind (Carson), 228, 278–79
United States Northern Boundary Commission, 137
Useful Birds and Their Protection (Forbush), 153

Van Doren, Mark, 195
Vogt, William, 243, 245–46, 247–48
"Voyage to Heard's Island, A" (Bolles), 49